Wolfram von Eschenbach

PARZIVAL

The German Library: Volume 2
Volkmar Sander, General Editor

Wolfram von Eschenbach

PARZIVAL

Edited by André Lefevere

CONTINUUM · NEW YORK

PT
1682
.P8
E 54
1991
1 54738
Feb. 1992

1991
The Continuum Publishing Company
370 Lexington Avenue, New York, NY 10017

The German Library
is published in cooperation with Deutsches Haus,
New York University.
This volume has been supported by a grant from
Robert Bosch Jubiläumsstiftung.

Printed in the United States of America

Library of Congress Cataloging-in-Publication Data

Wolfram, von Eschenbach, 12th cent.
   [Parzival. English]
   Parzival / Wolfram von Eschenbach ; edited [and translated] by
André Lefevere.
      p.   cm. — (The German library ; v. 2)
   Includes bibliographical references.
   ISBN 0-8264-0345-X — ISBN 0-8264-0346-8 (pbk.)
   1. Perceval (Legendary character)—Romances. I. Lefevere, André.
II. Title. III. Series.
PT1682.P8E54   1991
831'.21—dc20
                                                      90–26191
                                                      CIP

Contents

Introduction

Very little is known about Wolfram von Eschenbach, and very little knowledge can be obtained about him through speculation. The information that can be "distilled" from his work is scanty at best: he obviously spent some time at the court of Hermann of Thuringia, and maybe the patron for whom *Parzival* was written was a noble lady, with whom Wolfram may have been romantically linked, but then again maybe not. Periodically, new candidates appear with a claim to be "the" Eschenbach Wolfram should "really" be linked to. In truth, the only fact about Wolfram von Eschenbach we can assume with some certainty, precisely *because* we know so little, is that he must not have been a member of the higher nobility. If he had been, chances are we would have known more about him, the way we know more about the majority of lyrical poets of the time who happened to belong to the higher nobility.

Wolfram von Eschenbach was a knight, as he reminds his audience occasionally in *Parzival*, and proud to be one in a time when the ideals of knighthood had lost much of their appeal. He was probably born in 1170, and he must have died relatively soon after 1217. He was not a rich and powerful knight, but one of the poorer knights, or *ministeriales*. His family, in other words, had not been lucky: it had not acquired the land that could have made it rich and powerful, as other families had, who by Wolfram's time proudly produced dukes, counts, and bishops. As a result Wolfram, like so many other *ministeriales*, saw himself forced to work for dukes, counts, bishops, or even the emperor of all Germany in various ways.

Like all writers, Wolfram found his language, his world, and his art prescribed for him; and like all writers he tried to inscribe himself in that language, that world, and that art. He did not like the world he had been born into all that much, also because it made life relatively difficult for people of his social status. For two centuries, the emperors of the Holy Roman Empire of the German Nation, as Germany was to be officially known until the beginning of the nineteenth century, had been trying to keep and increase their own power by trying to play off potential rival groups against each other. Basically, the empire consisted of the four "constituent" duchies of Bavaria, Franconia, Saxony, and Swabia. The leaders of those duchies, or dukes, represented the real—because hereditary—power in the land. The fact that one or the other of them was elected emperor once in a while did not markedly change the equation, since the election itself did not provide the emperor with a larger power base. Since the monarchy was officially elective, not hereditary, the dukes, the counts, and some archbishops—in short, the princes of the realm whose duty it was to elect the emperor—could never really be relied on to provide dynastic stability. They had to be placated, cajoled, fought.

But then again, maybe dynastic stability was not the ideal if the man on the throne proved to be incapable of ruling well, or turned out to be a tyrant. However that may have been, the emperors began to rely more and more on the church to offset the power of the princes: bishops and clerics became the mainstay of the imperial administration. A not negligible advantage of entrusting the administration to clerics was, of course, that these clerics were unable to—at least officially—build up a dynastic base of their own because they were bound by a vow of celibacy. The whole arrangement went relatively well until a reform movement in the church redefined the bishops' and clerics' loyalty as primarily to the pope, not the emperor. Small wonder that the emperors tried to reassert their authority over "their" bishops. The result was chronic war. War between the emperor and the pope broke out before Wolfram's birth, and it was to break out again in his lifetime. The first great confrontation took place from 1077 to 1099. Since the emperor's attention was engaged elsewhere, the princes saw their chance to reassert and increase their power.

Another factor had entered the equation, and it would be increasingly instrumental in the construction of a new social order: the city. The city did not really fit in well with feudal society as the latter had slowly evolved since the fall of the Roman Empire. The first relatively powerful cities, therefore, arose in those regions of Europe in which dynastic power was relatively weak: in Northern Italy and in Flanders. Because they had no natural protectors, the cities banded together in leagues to protect themselves. They soon became a power to be reckoned with. When Wolfram von Eschenbach was six years old, the League of Lombard cities defeated Emperor Frederick Barbarossa and drove him out of Italy.

Caught up in their conflict with the popes, the emperors began to rely more and more on the social group to which Wolfram von Eschenbach himself belonged: the *ministeriales*. They used them in their own administration, and they tried to use them as a private army, one emperors could rely on absolutely, unlike the troops put at their disposal by the princes of the realm. The *ministeriales* reaffirmed the old bond of loyalty that had always linked all knights to their overlord until some of the knights had become too rich and powerful themselves to pay more than lip service to that loyalty. The *ministeriales* looked on themselves more and more as the "real" knights, true to the old ideal of loyalty, or *triuwe*, in Wolfram von Eschenbach's Middle High German, as opposed to the princes who had betrayed and kept betraying that loyalty.

The *ministeriales* were also at odds with the church. After 1050, the reformed papacy upgraded the role played by clerics in the church to the detriment of the laymen. Whereas the "old" church had been—at least in theory—a congregation of lay people guided by clerics, the popes now tried to build up a rigid hierarchy of archbishops, bishops, and priests, defining it as the "real" church, and to relegate the laymen to a status perilously approaching that of outsiders. The *ministeriales* were less than pleased with this kind of demotion, the more so because they were, after all, competing with clerics for positions in the imperial (and local) administrations. They most likely saw it as a ploy to keep them out of the purviews of learning. The clerics were trained in Latin, of course, as the *ministeriales* were not.

In Wolfram's time, then, the options open to the *ministeriales* were relatively limited. They could enter the administration, but with relatively little chance of rising very high in it, since they did not, or at least not always, possess the requisite learning, their main qualification being loyalty. If they did not become administrators, they could use the main skill they had been trained in almost from birth: fighting. They would then become mercenaries or, more likely, leaders of bands of mercenaries, ready to fight for any of the parties mentioned above.

Wolfram himself chose a third possibility, open to relatively few *ministeriales;* he became a writer or, rather, a composer of poems and, especially, stories. This naturally required a certain talent, but not necessarily the high degree of literacy that is matter of factly associated with writing today. In fact, Wolfram himself goes out of his way to say that he cannot write, which definitely put him among the majority of the people of his time, but which need not have been a handicap preventing him from composing long tales in verse, which could be written down by others. Since modern readers have no experience at all of the workings of any oral civilization, they will find it relatively hard to relate to this aspect of Wolfram's work.

Whatever Wolfram may have "really" meant by boasting about his illiteracy, it seems fair to assume that he did not know Latin, the "official" language of the European Middle Ages. That does most emphatically not mean that he was "illiterate" in his own language as well, or that he did not possess any real learning. Quite the contrary, *Parzival* and his other works prove beyond a doubt that Wolfram's learning was vast, if not always deep, and certainly not systematic. Wolfram's works also show quite conclusively that he was familiar with the unofficial "lingua franca" of the European Middle Ages: French. Again, it is doubtful whether he "really" knew it well, but he certainly was conversant with it. He probably picked up what French he knew during visits he made to France as part of the household of Hermann of Thuringia or another patron.

The routing of Emperor Frederick Barbarossa by the Lombard League was the beginning of a long process of dissolution, which lasted all through Wolfram's lifetime, even though Barbarossa's son and grandson managed to halt it occasionally, or slow it down. In fact, Frederick II, Barbarossa's grandson, may well have provided the model for Wolfram's ideal ruler, just as Frederick's kingdom of Sicily, which he ruled separately from the German empire, and which was not a prey to the machinations of either the local princes or the local church, may well have provided the model for Wolfram's ideal state. The so-called constituent duchies of the empire referred to above (Bavaria, Franconia, Saxony, and Swabia) began to break up. All kinds of people, knights and clerics, saw their chance and tried to grab some power, based on some land. Once it started, the process of decomposition proved irreversible. In fact, the "Germany" that was the outcome of it, hopelessly divided into a myriad of states and statelets, was to last until Napoleon reorganized it. Everybody was more or less fighting everybody; law and order broke down; and the future most definitely did not look bright.

Faced with the dissolution of his world, Wolfram constructed an alternative world in his works, especially *Parzival*, and one that looked almost improbably bright. It would not be unfair to say that like most knights of his time, Wolfram was not exactly interested in or knowledgeable about the economic underpinnings of what was happening. In fact, he had little sympathy for merchants, as is obvious from book 7, in which Gawan goes to great lengths not to be mistaken for a merchant. He also has little understanding of cities, nor does he have much sympathy for them, except where cities, as in the same book 7, are utterly and totally loyal to their prince, as they most definitely were not in the reality from which *Parzival* arose. Wolfram also had little or no sympathy for the "official" church of clerics and bishops. He mentions them only once in *Parzival*, in passing, and probably to put them on the same level as women.

With hindsight it is easy for the modern reader to say that Wolfram did not see where the future lay; it is also possible that he did see it and that he disliked it so much that he decided to go back to the past. Wolfram's prescription for the ills of his time is a conservative one indeed. He simply, quixotically and earnestly, calls for a return to the "true" ideals of "real" knighthood.

The kingpin of Wolfram's conservative worldview is *triuwe*, loyalty, which is, or rather should be, the true foundation for all three of man's fundamental relationships: the relationship with his peers and superiors, the relationship with God, and the relationship with women. As is obvious from the end of book 16, in which all adventures narrated in the sixteen books of *Parzival* are traced back to one family, "kin" is the primary expression of *triuwe*. The family (extended or not) is the nucleus in which its members are initiated to relationships of loyalty. It is also significant that Parzival is more often than not helped, advised, and admonished by people of his own kin: Herzeloyde, although reluctantly; Sigune, even though she does so in anger at first; and Trevrizent.

A knight is supposed to be loyal to those of his kin first and foremost, as Feirefiz, Parzival's half brother, is to Parzival, or as Trevrizent, Parzival's uncle, is to Parzival. Parzival's "sin" in not asking the question that could have cured Anfortas, the keeper of the grail, is compounded by the fact that Anfortas was his uncle, even though Parzival did not know that at the time. "Kin" is demarcated primarily by blood. When Gahmuret, Parzival's father, leaves his heathen wife Belakane, just as Feirefiz, Parzival's half brother, leaves his heathen wife Secundille, the offense is not considered of major consequence by the Christian audience, ostensibly because marriages between Christians and heathens have no validity in the Christian world, but also—perhaps even mainly so—because the offense is not really directed at "kin." This probably goes a fair way to explaining the rather perfunctory manner in which women are treated in *Parzival:* they are seen much more as potential contributors to the further propagation of kin than as kin themselves. As long as they are mothers and wives, their reproductive capacities securely anchored in one kin group, little attention is paid to them. They enjoy a brief moment of power only before they are married or when they are widows, but they can keep that power only if they share it with a man who is willing to defend it for them, as Belakane does with Gahmuret, and Condwiramurs with Parzival.

Herzeloyde is a widow too, but her attempt at creating a world of her own crumbles when Parzival, the center of that world, which is the world of nature and innocence, decides to leave it in search of knighthood and experience. Parzival is made into a knight by Gurnemanz, but he soon realizes that Gurnemanz does not have all the answers and that Gurnemanz's knowledge cannot deal with the world of the grail.

The kinship that holds the family together is metaphorically projected on power relationships: the king is the head of the kin group, and the members of the group are linked to him by a loyalty that is to be mutual if it is to be effective, as Kingrimursel reminds his king and kinsman Vergulath in book 8. The king is responsible for the well-being of his subjects. One of the reasons why Sigune inveighs against Parzival is that he, who is by right her slain lover's king, has done nothing to come to that lover's aid. The fact that the young Parzival, who had grown up in the forest, did not know that he was a king does not really change anything: he will have to live up to the role prescribed for him by society if that society is to continue in existence.

Furthermore, the king has to abide by the code that is the objectification of the various power relationships: when Anfortas, the grail king, who is supposed to live in chaste wedlock only, is led astray by what Wolfram would call "uncontrolled" love, he himself and his people suffer until he is replaced by another king: Parzival. Since kin in the real world does not always do as kin should, Wolfram builds a corrective into his utopian blueprint for a just society: kings who do not live up to their calling can be replaced by means other than death, whether natural or self-inflicted.

What Wolfram designed as a utopian blueprint became, against the background of the reality of his time, more like an elegiac farewell to a crumbling social order that was unable to regenerate itself on the basis of Wolfram's call for a return to the old and trusted virtues. All the more amazing, therefore, that Wolfram was not to be thrown off course. Patient and unperturbed he went on building his ideal world. The family and society are to be complemented and lifted on a higher level altogether by the addition of a third type of relationship based on loyalty toward God. That loyalty has little or nothing to do with the church, a rival kin group Wolfram—and other knights—increasingly came to regard as a faithless usurper of what was not meant to belong to it: power. That is why, as stated above, the "official" church is distinctly underrepresented in *Parzival*.

At the time when the papacy was actively trying to marginalize laymen, Wolfram was actively giving them a very important role in his new society: loyal knights belong to the kinship of the grail; they are the true guardians of law and order, peace and justice; and they even rule the world. When a nation that has lost its ruler approaches the grail king with the request for a just ruler, a knight is sent to them. Wolfram even goes out of his way, in a "coda" appended to book 16, to tell the story of Parzival's son Loherangrin, who is sent to rule Brabant in this manner. The ideals of the grail kingdom sound remarkably like those propagated by Frederick Barbarossa's grandson, Frederick II, who believed in a strong central power that would derive its legitimacy from the fact that it was able to ensure law and order, peace and justice. The grail kingdom can therefore be seen as a solitary dreamer's attempt at a religious legitimation of a vanishing society.

Those same ideals allow laymen, knights, *ministeriales*, to act in a meaningful way in the world of the grail. They become—and Wolfram advisedly uses the name in his work—a variant of the historical Knights Templar, who dedicate themselves to the defense of the "faith," the Christian faith to be sure, but over and above that the "central" faith that is the foundation of all meaningful relationships. They become the guarantors of a new and better order, and Wolfram tries to demonstrate again and again that they, the knights, are the only ones who can really guarantee that order. When Herzeloyde tries to construct a world without knights around the young Parzival, that world turns out to be both relatively uncouth and relatively short-lived. Fishermen, ferrymen, and merchants are all shown in the final analysis to depend on the social framework kept in existence by the knights, even if they profit from it in ways no knight would ever stoop to. No other alternative societies are described in *Parzival*.

Except one, of course: that of the heathens, the Orient. Wolfram's Orient is an amalgam of India and the Middle East. Like his patron Hermann of Thuringia, Wolfram was fascinated by the Orient. Wolfram may well have incorporated so much "Oriental" material into his work precisely because his patron liked it. Relatively unhampered by any real knowledge of the Orient, Wolfram felt free to project his ideal society into it. All "heathens" in *Parzival* behave like perfect knights and ladies as prescribed by Wolfram's social model. It is also relatively strongly suggested that Islamic society is technologically farther advanced and, on the whole, more civilized, than its European counterpart, even though the eventual moral superiority of that counterpart is never in doubt. It would have been most impolitic even to suggest that it might be: people were burnt at the stake as heretics for much less. In the meantime, though, Islam's superiority in many fields might well be ascribed in no small measure to the fact that the heathens seem to cultivate Wolfram's brand of loyalty among each other to an admirable extent.

The final apotheosis of Wolfram's social utopia is to be found in the union of East and West: Parzival becomes king of the grail, and his half-brother Feirefiz becomes the most powerful ruler in the Orient. He even goes as far as to introduce Christianity in India after his own conversion and subsequent marriage to Anfortas's sister. As always, though, in Wolfram, lofty ideals go hand in hand with pragmatic considerations, which is one of the reasons why *Parzival* is a potentially inexhaustible text. As we learn from the Gahmuret episode in books 1 and 2, the Orient did indeed offer chances of tangible social advancement to younger sons of noble families in Europe. It is also obvious that Gahmuret needs this kind of social advancement, whereas the other main heroes Parzival and Gawan do not: money is no object in the Arthurian world.

No wonder Wolfram's villains are guided by the antithesis to loyalty or, rather, by a perversion of loyalty limited to mere loyalty to the self. True loyalty preserves and enhances; false loyalty—loyalty to the self only—destroys. Parzival, too, is the victim of his own self-centeredness, even though he does not seem to be guilty of it in any personal sense: it is his mother's fault, not his. But one of the religious insights Wolfram wants to share with his audience by victimizing the ostensibly guiltless Parzival is precisely that man is entangled in sin because he is man (the Christian idea of original sin); only when he submits to God, more or less as a vassal submits to his lord, can he hope to enter the world of salvation. The concept of original sin is reinforced by that of *felix culpa*, or "fortunate sin": only because Parzival did sin, even if he did not really know he did, can he be saved and exalted.

False loyalty brings shame on King Vergulath, as does the false loyalty masquerading as arrogance that brings shame on king Gramoflanz. There is a very thin line indeed between "high spirits"—the feeling that accompanies true loyalty and the ensuing confidence in one's own right, one's own power, and one's own cause—and mere arrogance. Among other characters Orgeluse remains an insufferable woman as long as she is driven only by revenge; she becomes a good woman as soon as she is joined to Gawan in true loyalty. Woman's betrayal of loyalty is all the more detrimental because the family relationship is the central relationship that should be relied on to inculcate a sense of loyalty in the next generation. In practice, this task falls to the wife (Condwiramurs, for instance), since the husband (Parzival) is more often than not away for long periods of time.

Self-love leads to pride, which, in turn, leads to rage and all kinds of uncontrolled passions, not least among them sexual passion, which is potentially the most destructive to the social fabric. The concept of love as uncontrolled passion, or "Ovidian love," was introduced in the German Middle Ages by Henric van Veldeke, the Dutch-German poet, in his 1180 verse epic *Eneide*, based on Virgil's *Aeneid*. This earns him a few sweet and sour remarks in Wolfram's *Parzival*. The potential danger inherent in uncontrolled passion also explains why Wolfram tends to look on the ideal of courtly love, so strongly propagated in his time, with a rather jaundiced eye within the confines of *Parzival*. Love as passion uncontrolled, which sweeps people off their feet, cannot be conducive to loyalty. Even love as passion controlled, unconsummated, but directed at a woman whose loyalty is already given elsewhere, as in courtly love, remains morally ambiguous in Wolfram's eyes, and he does ridicule it more than occasionally in *Parzival*.

It should be clear that the social utopia Wolfram constructs in *Parzival* went more or less totally against the grain of his own time. He was probably able to ignore most of his own reality, simply because he regarded it as the wrong image of utopia. If reality does not correspond to utopia, then reality has to be abandoned, not utopia. But the writer Wolfram von Eschenbach was a keen observer of his own reality. In fact, most of the "tension" and "distance" that is often ascribed to his style results from the clash between the utopia that is asserted in the broad outlines of the backcloth, and the myriad stitches of myriad threads taken from lived and living reality that fill in that backcloth. Broadly outlined utopian ideals do not have to conflict with an ironic, at times satirical observation of current reality. On the contrary, the ironic description of existing reality can be used cumulatively to suggest that it should be replaced by something better. Wolfram has most fun when he can use this tension to debunk the kind of ideal he cannot really bring himself to believe in, such as the ideal of courtly love—as in the comparison of a lovely lady to a rabbit on a skewer—but he also debunks excesses of loyalty, such as Sigune's necrophiliac attachment to her slain love. A love stronger than death does not necessarily seem to imply for Wolfram that a lady should travel through forests with the embalmed corpse of her slain beloved, which she occasionally (in book

5, for instance) has to lean against a tree when she wants to sit and rest for a while.

Wolfram the social engineer could point to the Orient as the place where his utopia was approximating reality. He could do so with relative impunity because his own ignorance corresponded to that of his readers. Wolfram the writer/composer of tales could not avail himself of a similar ignorance on his audience's part. There was another kind of "backcloth" he had to work with or, rather, against. Literature that was centered on the legendary King Arthur and his knights of the Round Table had been produced at least since Wace's *Roman de Brut* (1155) had made Geoffrey of Monmouth's *Historia regum Britanniae* (1137) available in a language other than Latin. The "Matter of Arthur" became well-known, so well-known in fact that audiences approached any new variation on the theme with a rather set "horizon of expectation." Any writer/composer of a new version of one of the "adventures" associated with Arthur and/or the Round Table could not do what he wanted to. It would simply be unacceptable, for instance, to have Gawain kill Arthur and Lancelot elope with Guinevere.

Moreover, medieval writers/composers were by no means free to compose what they wanted; nor could they compose in any way they wanted. In these, as in most other matters, they had to defer to the wishes of the patron or patrons who guaranteed their livelihood. "Acceptable" (and accepted) German Arthurian literature owed much to Hartmann von Aue, whose *Erec* (1190) had introduced the Arthurian adventures to Germany. Hartmann had translated/adapted Chrestien de Troyes' tale of the same title and set a trend by doing so. As a result, Wolfram von Eschenbach was given Chrestien's *Li contes del graal* as the source of his *Parzival* on the assumption that he would faithfully follow his original.

Unfortunately, Wolfram had some problems with his original, just as he had some problems with his audience's Arthurian horizon of expectation. His predecessors seemed to him to have preempted both the plots (adventures) and the symbols he wanted to make use of to narrate his social blueprint to the only audience that mattered to him, because it was the only one that had the power actually to do something about it, if it was so inclined. Since he was supposed to follow a source anyway, Wolfram followed Chrestien rather closely, but made up another, additional source of his own, a Provençal writer, called "Kyot," who supposedly found the original manuscript of a Parzival adventure in the city of Toledo in Moorish Spain and who could therefore be seen as the "real" source of it all, his work having been "altered" by Chrestien in unwarranted ways. By deviating from Chrestien, in his turn, Wolfram was therefore not tampering with his source, but rather restoring the rightful authority of the original source. That this original source did not exist in any semblance of reality served Wolfram rather well, especially since Arthurian adventures as such did not serve him as well.

Fortunately, Wolfram was asked to "work from" Chrestien's last tale, which itself already represents a departure from the strict Arthurian adventure in that it introduces a religious dimension in the person of Parzival. Wolfram seized on this new dimension, most likely introduced by Chrestien in response to the wishes of his then patron, Philip of Alsace, count of Flanders. It gave him the opportunity to separate decisively the Arthurian world from the world of the grail, which was the important world to him. Gurnemanz's teachings had turned Parzival into a knight capable of functioning in the Arthurian world. But only Trevrizent's teachings give Parzival the opportunity really to convert to an unconditional acceptance of the divine plan, which alone will lead him to salvation. Gawan, whom Wolfram "inherited" from Chrestien, is presented as Parzival's "foil" in the Arthurian world. Gawan is very close to the perfect knight in Arthurian terms, but he lacks the extra dimension Parzival has. Gawan more or less merrily goes from adventure to adventure, saving women and righting wrongs, but he cannot actually project any vision for a future world as Parzival can. It is also significant that Wolfram "drops" Gawan as soon as he gets to the end of Chrestien's *Contes*. His real interest in retelling Chrestien lies elsewhere.

In the course of its transplantation from France to Germany, though, Arthurian adventure acquired an additional function; rather, one of its original functions was more strongly emphasized. Hartmann von Aue played up to the curiosity of the German nobility for things French, which were considered more refined and therefore worthy of emulation. His tales therefore seemed to acquire an "obvious" didactic function: descriptions of banquets, fashions, and jousts were meant to serve as a how-to guide and were avidly listened to by the audience for that reason. It seems fair to assume that Wolfram grew a little impatient with this "elementary" didacticism, not in the least because it could obscure or weaken his own, more fundamental didactic purpose. It should be noted in passing that the term *didactic* as applied to literature did not carry any negative connotation in the Middle Ages; on the contrary, the audience was supposed to learn from literature while being entertained by it. Wolfram's impatience shows most clearly in books 14 to 16, which are totally his own. Chrestien's tale ended with what corresponds to Wolfram's book 13, for the simple and final reason that Chrestien died when he had reached that point. It was not considered exceptionable for one poet to finish another's work, and that is what Wolfram did, judiciously eschewing overlong descriptions of castles, banquets, and jousts as he did so.

It would be fair to say that Wolfram used the Arthurian adventures as a vehicle for his own moral tale and that he did not always feel at ease with the material at his disposal. In fact, he frequently seems to make fun of the fairy tale elements that had been subsumed into Arthurian adventure. He may have considered these elements somewhat too close to the grotesque or the ridiculous for the comfort of his message. To prevent the "medium" from obstructing the "message," Wolfram can be said to have had recourse to other means as well. He consciously wrote against the existing "acceptable" Arthurian literature in German as propagated by Hartmann von Aue. At one point in his own work, he actually throws down the gauntlet for Hartmann to pick up, warning him to be "nice" to his own characters, or else he, Wolfram, will subject Hartmann's characters to ridicule in *Parzival*. At another point, he taunts the audience with the matter-of-fact announcement that his Arthur is not connected with the month of May, as the "backcloth" Arthur is. His defense of Keie, the boorish knight of the Round Table in the "backcloth," should also be seen as part of the same tactic.

For a tactic it is and not a fairly gratuitous exercise in annoying the audience for no obvious purpose: by keeping a distance between himself, his audience, and the story, Wolfram tries to point that audience's attention also beyond or behind the story, to what we are still most comfortable with calling "the message." Another tactic Wolfram uses is that of consciously not writing in the elegant and polished imitation French style propagated by Hartmann von Aue and imitated by later writers, but in the style of the older, more authentically German tales, which is less elevated, more down to earth, and therefore allows for more freedom of expression where that is needed.

Small wonder that Wolfram was both praised and condemned by his contemporaries. Gottfried von Strassburg, a follower of Hartmann von Aue and the author of another major Middle High German epic tale—his *Tristan* centers on adultery, which may have given Wolfram some grim satisfaction—attacked Wolfram for the obscurity of his style and for his use of bad language. To this day, Wolfram's style is not infrequently referred to as "gnomic," and/or "sententious," even where the connection with the older Germanic epic is not overtly made. Once he consciously opts for a certain style, though, Wolfram should be allowed to follow it and to produce gnomic and sententious lines of his own. That style can also be said to have been closer to the kind of language actually spoken by the less sophisticated, less French-oriented (because poorer?) *ministeriales*. In style, too, Wolfram can be said to advocate some kind of a return to a simpler, less courtly (and by implication more truly loyal?) past.

It would be preposterous to suggest that Wolfram merely writes in a certain style. His style is his own, particularly where the choice of words is unusual, and where the irony shows through most clearly. In addition to this, his style also strikes the modern reader as unusual because it is geared to, if not necessarily oral composition, at least definitely oral recitation. That recitation could be done from memory, by the poet/composer himself or by a professional reciter; or else the poet/composer or a reciter might read aloud from a manuscript. In this kind of situation, the reciter had much more direct contact with the audience, and he could supplement his reading with gestures to clarify matters or, even, with short impersonations of whatever character happens to be speaking. As a result, the syntax of literature composed to be recited in this manner can be much freer than the syntax of literature composed to be read by one individual. In fact, the older form of receiving the work not infrequently asserts itself over the modern one: it is often not just useful, but imperative to read certain passages aloud in the original Middle High German if you want to decipher their meaning. Once you hear the text spoken, as it was meant to be, the meaning becomes more immediately obvious.

Composition for oral recitation obviously had to observe other conventions as well. One of those conventions is rhyme, used mainly for mnemonic reasons: to help the reciter remember the text. As with all conventions, this one may well have outlived its usefulness for a number of decades: even when the possibility to have written texts available had established itself as more or less normal and acceptable, poets/composers would still use rhyme in their compositions. In its turn the use of rhyme had an inevitable impact on the syntax of the composition. Not only did it lead to inversion and the kind of use of the passive voice modern readers would be quick to call "unjustified," but also to the—what modern readers would again be relatively quick to call exaggerated—use of circumlocutions, which had the additional advantage of relieving incipient boredom and keeping the audience interested. Finally, oral composition or composition for oral recitation may well have been responsible for the format in which *Parzival* has actually come down to us: in units of thirty lines each, perhaps because that is a relatively convenient number to keep in memory. (The division into sixteen books, on the other hand, goes back to the first editor of *Parzival*, Karl Lachmann.)

In summing up, we might say that Wolfram needed to reinterpret certain aspects of the Arthurian adventures for his own purposes and that he invented Kyot as his very own carte blanche that would allow him to do so. It is not inconceivable that in doing so he was mildly attempting to ridicule the belief held by at least part of his audience that tales without a source were suspect. Wolfram may well have done so with all the more relish because he must have already written the first two books, Gahmuret's adventures, which deal most decidedly with the Orient and have nothing at all to do with Chrestien, before he was given Chrestien's *Li contes del graal* to work with. It is eminently possible that the Gahmuret books, whose hero is loosely modeled on Richard the Lion-Hearted, might have grown into a tale without a source. As it was, Wolfram had to devise a way to merge them with Chrestien's material. The solution he found was not universally acclaimed. It is generally believed that he provisionally "finished" his work at the end of book 6 and that books 1–6 circulated as a relatively "finished" work for a while, drawing both praise and criticism. Wolfram then reacted to that criticism both in the later books, and in interpolations added to books 1–6 after a few years.

Previous translators of Wolfram's *Parzival* often cite the obscurity of his style as the main stumbling block they have encountered. I would agree with them, but I would also insist on going one step beyond, that is, to examine the degree to which that style is tied to a mode of literary production contemporary readers are no longer familiar with: production for oral recitation. Obviously, part of Wolfram's obscurity is and will always remain Wolfram's alone. Yet the translator cannot help but think that Wolfram's syntax, for instance, might not have been quite so confusing in places if he actually had composed with an audience of readers only in mind. It is hard to translate *Parzival*, not only because Wolfram's Middle High German is not always easy to understand and because his style is not always the model of polished elegance and clarity he abhorred in Hartmann von Aue and Gottfried von Strassburg, but also because he expected his work to be "received" in a way that has become alien to the contemporary reader.

I have tried to translate *Parzival* in such a way that the result reads well as a contemporary English language narrative text and that it can also be used by those of its readers who are wrestling with the Middle High German original to try to decipher that original. I have therefore tried to stay as close to the syntax of the original as I thought compatible with the demands of elegance and readability. In short, I have tried to achieve the impossible: a hybrid growth struggling to survive somewhere between the literal—even, inter-linear—and the freely creative translation.

Since language can be said to reflect most closely the world-view of a civilization, I have tried to stay as close as possible to those Middle High German words or expressions that represent key concepts of Wolfram's world view and the world view of his time. That is why the phrase that is most commonly translated by means of the simple noun *knighthood* in most existing translations is rendered by means of the phrase: "the calling of the shield" in mine.

Metaphors probably represent the crystallization of the central concepts operational in a culture. I have therefore tried to translate them as literally as possible. I realize that many of these metaphors may already have degenerated to "dead" metaphors in Wolfram's own time. The phrase "the calling of the shield," for instance, may not have struck many of Wolfram's listeners with anything remotely resembling the shock that accompanies sudden exposure to what is new and unknown. However, in this respect time is on the translator's side for once: its passage has invested many of these dead metaphors with an aura of the poetic, and resuscitated the cliché as poetry for better or for worse. I do not judge whether time has served the contemporary reader well or badly in this. I merely observe that it has had this effect, and I have decided to exploit this effect to give the contemporary reader the kind of access to a vanished civilization that is perhaps the most immediate and enlightening of all.

It seemed to be more worthwhile to introduce the contemporary reader to a lost civilization in this manner rather than by means of elaborate (and elaborately footnoted) descriptions of objects used by those who participated in that civilization. To make the introduction even more immediate, I have used English cognates to the Middle High German words or phrases expressing these metaphors wherever possible, even at the risk of having them sound slightly off at first reading. In many cases this kind of adverse effect can be remedied by a second reading—aloud.

Since Wolfram's work was composed primarily for oral recitation, the text that has come down to us can be extremely confusing at times. Since the reciter has the possibility of impersonating a character at his disposal, the author rarely bothers to mention explicitly who is speaking. He blithely skips from "he" to "he," and then again "he," changing characters up to three times within the same speech or description without informing the reader of this. The listener/viewer would not have had any trouble understanding that same text provided it was brought to him or her by a competent reciter. Needless to say, I have had to step in and "forcibly" identify the speakers and those spoken about to make matters clear for readers who are no longer part of an oral culture.

I have also "regularized" Wolfram's syntax to no small extent where it seemed to me to be constructed primarily in response to the demands of meter and rhyme. Many of Wolfram's passives and elaborate circumlocutions have found their way into the eventual text because of the need to rhyme, rather than as the expression of any original verbal artistry. Since my translation no longer uses rhyme as a mnemonic device, I did not see any reason to keep close to Wolfram's passives and circumlocutions. In most if not all cases I have silently regularized them in the interest of readability.

For the same reason, I have silently dropped the innumerable *then*'s and *there*'s, or even *over there's* that appear all the time in Wolfram's work to satisfy the demands of meter. I felt all the more justified in doing so since my translation is written in prose and therefore does not rely on meter at all.

Wolfram also uses personal names in a somewhat creative manner, often adding or subtracting a *sjwa* to meet the requirements of meter. Condwiramurs, for instance, is queen of either Pelrapeir, or Pelrapeir*e*, and not many people seem to have taken exception to this. I have therefore left Wolfram's variations in place, and I have also not tried to "regularize" the names he uses to bring them more in line with the generally accepted Arthurian "backcloth." Wolfram's "Artus"—the name he got from Chrestien—therefore remains "Artus" in this translation. He does not become "Arthur," just as Wolfram's "Gawan" does not become "Gawain."

For reasons of space, the text had to be abbreviated to some extent. I have cut mainly what I have referred to in the notes as the "*Ladies Home Journal*-equivalent" passages, that is, the didactic passages in the form of long descriptions of jousts, banquets, or dresses, which take up a fair number of lines in Wolfram's *Parzival* in response to the audience's demand. I have done so because the objects referred to in many of these passages are now totally unknown to the contemporary reader, and the fact that they have become alien to contemporary readers might well contribute to alienating those readers altogether. I believe this kind of alienation cannot be remedied by descriptions—no matter how elaborate—of said objects in the notes.

I have also left out a fair number of repetitions because those can also be said to have been caused by the conventions of oral recitation. Since the complete text of *Parzival* is so long, it cannot possibly be recited in a single sitting. In fact, it is extremely unlikely that many people alive in Wolfram's time and the century immediately following would ever have heard the complete text of *Parzival*. For this reason Wolfram often has one character inform another of past events. Readers who have the complete text at their disposal and can go back to it whenever they please can do without these conventions characteristic of another mode of literary production.

It is my hope that the present translation will not alienate the contemporary reader in any way, but that it will help him to come to terms with Wolfram's text, whether in combination with the original, or as a text that can stand for that original in another culture. In either case, I hope the translated text will also succeed in giving the contemporary reader some of the pleasure Wolfram's text gave its original audience. I have no doubt at all that it will succeed in irritating its contemporary audience at least to the same degree Wolfram's text succeeded in irritating the audience that was first exposed to it.

A. L.

Parzival

Book One

Doubt's nearness to the heart must become bitter to the soul. Shame and honor are together where a man's undaunted courage is chequered with its opposite, as is the color of a magpie.[1] He may still become happy, since both heaven and hell have a share in him. The companion of disloyalty, on the other hand, has black for his color and takes on the shade of darkness. A man with steadfast thoughts clings to white. This flying example is much too swift for the stupid; they cannot figure out what it means, because it will run clear away from them like a rabbit scared by sound.[2] They are like tin on the other side of glass[3] and like a blind man's dream: they give an image of the face. But the glow of that darkly light cannot be steadfast: it brings short joy indeed. Who pulls my hair where no hair grows, in the palm of my hand? He has learned how to grab me very close.[4] If I scream "ouch!" for fear of him, that does not conflict with common sense.[5] Do I want to find loyalty where it can disappear, like fire in a spring, and dew before the sun?[6] I have never yet met a man so wise he would not want to know what deeds might match these words and what good learning they provide. Wise men never tire of this: they flee from it and hunt for it, they turn back and they turn away, they give honor and dishonor. Wisdom has given its due to men who can live with these changes, who do not sit too long, or go too far, and stand on their intelligence in all things.[7] The ways of a faithless companion are fit for the fires of hell and they beat high honor down like hail.[8] His loyalty has such a short tail that it can hardly hit back after the third bite when it is pursued by gadflies in the forest.[9]

These many different ways of life are not just for men. I also set this goal for women.[10] Whoever wants to heed my advice must know where she aims her honor and her praise and, consequently, to whom she is prepared to give her love and her respect, so that she will not regret her chastity and her fidelity. Before God I pray that good breeding may be a companion to good women. Modesty is the lock on all virtue: I do not need to pray for any greater happiness for them. The false earn false praise. How steadfast is thin ice that gets the heat of the August sun?[11] Their fame vanishes very quickly too. Many a woman's beauty is widely praised, but if her heart is counterfeit I shall praise it as I would a piece of saffron-colored glass set in gold. I do not consider it a small matter when somebody sets a noble ruby and all the good things it may bring in worthless brass.[12] To the ruby I compare a good woman's behavior: if she is true to her womanhood I shall not inspect the color of her skin, nor her head, the roof of her heart we can see with our eyes. If she is loyal within her breast noble praise will not be given there in vain.

If I were to examine men and women rightly, as I can, that would spawn a long tale. Listen to the nature of this adventure. It will let you know both love and sorrow: joy and care walk along with it. If there were three of me, and each one on his own were able to do something that would match my art, it would take wild inventiveness on their part to tell you what I shall tell you all by myself. It would require a lot of work. I want to tell you, retell[13] you a story that speaks of great loyalty, of good behavior on the part of women, and of a man's behavior so steadfast it never bowed before any hardship. His heart did not lie to him in that respect. He was like steel: where he came to battle his victorious hand took many a prize highly praised. Bold he was, and slowly wise, the hero I greet in this manner. He made women's sweet eyes ill, and their hearts as well. In truth he fled from all injustice. The man I have chosen for this, the man spoken of in this adventure, is as yet unborn in my story, and many wondrous things happen in it.

It is still done as before where French law was laid down and is still—and also on German soil here and there, as you have heard without me[14]—that whoever ruled the land could order without shame (in truth, beyond all doubt)[15] that the oldest brother should have his father's whole inheritance. The younger ones suffered the misfortune that death took away the endowment their father's life had given to them. Before his death all brothers held that endowment in common; after his death it all belongs to the oldest alone. A wise man ordained that age should have possessions. Youth has many virtues; age has sighs and suffering. Never was anything as unhappy as age and poverty combined. It is a strange custom that kings, counts, dukes (this I tell you, and I do not lie), should be disinherited of their goods except for the oldest child. The good and bold Gahmuret, the hero, lost his castles and his land where his father had already carried the scepter and the crown with great kingly power until he lay dead in knightly combat.

They mourned him much. He had brought great loyalty and honor with him until his death. His eldest son called on the rulers of the realm. They came as knights do when they were to receive great fiefs from him by rights, without a doubt. When they had come to the court, and when their claims had been heard so that they all received their fiefs, listen what they began to do. Guided by their loyalty the whole group, rich and poor, made a meek, earnest plea for the king to increase his brotherly affection for Gahmuret and to honor himself by not casting his brother out completely. Rather he should leave his brother some land in freehold so that people could see he was able to claim his freedom and his name based on that estate. That was no displeasure to the king. He said: "Your plea is fitting, I shall grant you this and more. Why do you not call my brother Gahmuret Anschevin? Anschouwe[16] is my country, let us both be called after it."

The high-placed king spoke: "My brother may expect more loyal help from me than I can mention just now. He shall belong to my household. Indeed, I shall show you clearly that one mother bore both of us. He has little and I have much; therefore my hand shall share with him in such a way that my salvation shall not be lost before Him who gives and takes away as is right and fitting to Him." It was a good day indeed when the noble rulers heard all together that their lord upheld loyalty. They all bowed before him, each of them on his own. Gahmuret was no longer silent at their assent; he spoke kindly to the king as his heart told him: "My Lord and My Brother, if I wanted to belong to your household, or that of any other man, I would have arranged things to please myself. Now test my fame, for you are loyal and wise, give me fitting advice and support me in a helpful manner. I have nothing but this suit of armor. If I had done more in it, that would have brought me widespread praise: I would be remembered in many places."

Gahmuret said again: "I want to go into the world. I have already traveled here and there. If luck will keep me I shall obtain a good woman's greeting.[17] If I have to serve her after that and if I am worthy of it, my best sense advises me to do so with true loyalty. May God show me the ways of happiness. We used to ride together when our father Gandin still had your kingdom, and many a heartsick pain we both endured for love. You were a knight and a thief,[18] you could serve for love and hide it. If only I, too, could steal love now! Alas, if only I had your skill and a woman's true favor too."

The king sighed and said: "Alas that I ever set eyes on you: you have cut up my whole heart with your joking words, and you are cutting it up still, since we must part. My father has left many possessions to both of us. I shall stake out an equal claim for you. I love you with all my heart. Sparkling stones, red gold, servants, weapons, horses, clothes, take as many of them freely from my hand as will allow you to travel as you like and be true to your generosity. Even if you had been born in strange lands, or if you had come to me from there, I would always want to have you here because I love you very much. You are my brother beyond all doubt." "My lord, you praise me of necessity since your breeding commands it. Show me your help accordingly. If you and my mother are willing to share your movable property with me I shall go up and never down. But my heart strives after higher things. I do not know why it beats so hard that my left breast is swelling so. Alas, where does my desire drive me? I shall discover it if I can. Now the day of my departure is near." *The king gives Gahmuret gold and jewels for his journey.*

When he went to his mother and she clasped him tightly to her, sorrow could not be avoided. "Son of King Gandin, do you no longer want to be with me?" said the great lady. "Alas, my body has carried you; you are Gandin's child too. Is God blind when He gives help? Or has He gone deaf, maybe, that He does not notice me? Must I have new sorrow now? I have buried the strength of my heart, the sweetness of my eyes. Does He now want to rob me of more? And yet is He not the Highest Judge? Then the story they tell about His helping people is a lie since He lets me down like this."

Gahmuret's mother also gives him gifts for the journey. He takes his leave, not without thanking all those he is beholden to in any way.

Gahmuret's deeds found their counterpart in right measure only, not in anything decreed by chance. His boasting was small, he submitted patiently to great honor, dishonorable ways stayed far from him. Yet the well-educated man thought nobody bore a crown: king, emperor, empress, to whose household he wanted to belong, except for him who held the highest power on earth over all countries. That desire lay in his heart. He was told that there was a man in Baldac[19] so powerful that two-thirds of the world or more were subject to him. His name was so exalted in the heathen language that they called him the "Baruc," the Blessed One.[20] The sweep of his power was so wide that many kings were his vassals, subject to him with their crowned persons. The office of the Baruc still exists today. You see, just as the Christian faith has its center in Rome—as Christianity tells us—so the pagan order is established there. They take their papal right from Baldac, and they think this is entirely proper. When they have sinned the Baruc gives them proof of their conversion. *Gahmuret enters the service of the Baruc. He adopts a new coat of arms: an anchor cut from white ermine.*

From Baldac he went to the kingdom of Zazamanc. There they all mourned Isenhart, who had lost his life in the service of a woman. Belakane, the woman without falsehood, had forced him to do this. Because she never gave him her love he lay dead for love of her. His kinsmen avenged him in combat on the open field and in ambushes, besieging the lady with an army. She resisted them heroically when Gahmuret came into her country that had been burnt by the Scotsman Vridebrant with his army before he sailed away on his ships. Now listen what happened to our hero. The sea cast him down in a storm so that he hardly got away with his life. He came sailing into the harbor, close to the queen's high hall, from where he was observed by many people. Then he looked out over the field. Many a tent had been pitched there, all around the city, but none close to the sea. There two powerful armies lay. Then he had inquiries made about the situation: whose castle it was, since neither he nor any of the men with him on the ship had ever obtained any news about it. The inhabitants graciously told his messengers the city was Paetelamunt. They implored him by their gods that he should help them: their distress was great, they were fighting a struggle of life and death.

The young man from Anschouwe heard their pain and sorrow; he offered his services for remuneration, as a knight does many a time,[21] or else they should tell him for what reason he should incur the hatred of their enemies. Then the sick and the well said from one mouth that their gold and their jewels would all be his; he would be lord of all and he could live his life among them. Yet he did not need much payment since he had brought many an ingot of Arabian gold. All those of Zazamanc were people dark as the night and the time seemed long to him among them. Yet he commanded that lodgings be taken. It pleased them very much to give him the best. The women leaned out of the windows and looked down. They observed his pages and his armor very well, how it was adorned. The generous hero bore I do not know how many sable pelts on an ermine shield. The queen's marshal took them for a big anchor and he was by no means sad to see it. His eyes had to tell him that he had seen this knight or his counterpart before. It must have been in Alexandria when the Baruc was besieging it. Nobody equaled his fame there. *Gahmuret and his retinue enter the city. They are much admired. The marshal bids them welcome and goes to the queen. He tells her about Gahmuret. The queen decides to invite Gahmuret to the high hall. He comes.*

The queen's eyes caused her pain when she saw the man from Anschouwe. He looked so much the part of love that he opened her heart, the whole heart her womanhood had kept locked until then, for love or sorrow. She walked a little ways toward him then and asked her guest to kiss her. She herself took him by the hand and along the wall that faced the enemy they sat in the wide window on a cushion upholstered with samite under which a soft mattress lay. If there is anything lighter than the day, the queen did not resemble it. She had the nature of a woman, but otherwise she behaved like a knight, and unlike roses covered by the dew. Her appearance was black in color, her crown a shining ruby, and her head could be seen through it. The hostess told her guest that she enjoyed his coming. "My Lord, I have heard much of your knightly valor. Do not take offense in your courtly way if I bemoan for you the sorrow I carry close to my heart."

"My help shall not fail you, My Lady. My hand shall turn away whatever was or is an obstacle to you. Let it be marked for your service. I am just one man, on my own, but I hold my shield against whoever does or has done anything against you, even if the enemy will not think too much of this." *One of the Princes of Zazamanc now describes the military situation to Gahmuret.*

The guest spoke to the hostess as a knight should: "Tell me if you will why people seek you out in such anger, with an army. You have so many a bold knight. It hurts me to see them so oppressed by the hatred of their enemies, to their detriment." "That I shall tell you, My Lord, since you want me to. Once a knight of great valor served me. His body was a branch that bore many virtues. The hero was bold and wise, a fruit that had taken root in loyalty. He was a true knight beyond all true knights. He was even more chaste than a woman and his body showed courage and bravery. A knight with a hand so generous never prospered before him in any land (I do not know what may happen after us; let other people talk about that): he was ignorant of false behavior, and black of color as I am, a Moor. His father was called Tankanis, a King; he had great fame as well. My friend's name was Isenhart. My womanhood was imprudent when I accepted his service in love since it did not lead to joy for him. That is why I have to bear sorrow always. They think I caused him to be slain but I am little skilled in treachery, even though his vassals accuse me of it. He was dearer to me than to them. I am not without witnesses in this, and with their help I shall prove this true. My gods know the real truth, and so do his. He gave me much pain. Now my coy womanhood has made him wait longer for his reward and my sorrow. My virginity earned the hero much praise among true knights. I tested him then, to see if he could be a friend. That became very obvious. For me he gave away his armor. But when the hero was without armor his body was little spared. After that he sickened at life and sought many an adventure without armor. When things stood like this a prince (he was called Prothizilas) of my household, free of cowardice, rode out to adventure where great harm did not avoid him. In the forest of Azagouc a duel did not cheat him of death; he fought it with a brave man who also met his end there. That was my friend Isenhart. Each of them felt a spear pierce his shield and his body. And that I, wretched woman, still lament: both their deaths cause me pain always. Sorrow flowers on my loyalty. I never became the wife of any man." Gahmuret thought at once that even though she was a heathen, greater loyalty and better womanly behavior never stole into any woman's heart. Her flawless nature was a pure baptism, as was the rain that fell on her, the water that flowed from her eyes down to her furs and on her bosom. The art of mourning and the knowledge of true sorrow were her joy. She told Gahmuret more after this: "Then the King of the Scots and his army came for me from across the sea. My friend was his uncle's son. They could not do me more harm than what had befallen me on account of Isenhart, that I must say." The lady sighed often. Through her tears she coyly observed Gahmuret with many a look. Her eyes soon told her heart that he was well shaped. She knew how to look at men of light color because she had seen many a fair-skinned heathen before. There was a very loyal desire between them then: she looked there and he looked here. She soon ordered the wine poured; if she had dared she would have let it be.[22] It hurt her that the pouring of the wine could not be delayed since it always drove knights away who liked to talk to a lady. Yet her body was now his body, and he had also given her the feeling that his life was now the lady's life. Then he stood up and said: "My Lady, I am causing you discomfort. I have been known to sit for too long. I do not always keep my wits about me. It gives me much pain, as it should a vassal, that your sorrow is so vast. My Lady, command me: where you choose, there is my vengeance. I shall serve you in every way I should." "My Lord, I certainly believe you will." *The marshal invites Gahmuret to ride with him and shows him the battlefield. He tells him about an enemy knight who challenges the inhabitants of the city to a joust every day. He has killed many of them. Gahmuret and the marshal go back to the latter's castle, where the queen joins them somewhat unexpectedly for supper. Gahmuret and the queen continue their conversation.*

Shyly he looked at the lady and said self-consciously: "Never in my life, My Lady, have I been used to such honor as you now give me. If I could teach you anything it would be that I would soon desire of you the kind of treatment I deserve. Then you would not have ridden down here. If I dare ask this of you, My Lady, let me live according to good breeding. You have given me too much honor."

She did not want to put an end to this now, but went to where his squires sat and invited them to eat well. This she did to honor her guest. These young noblemen were very fond of the queen. After this the lady did not forget another thing: she also walked to where the host sat with his wife, the lady of the castle. The queen raised her cup and said: "Let our guest be commended to you: the honor is yours. That is why I enjoin this upon you both." She said farewell. Then she went away, but turned again to her guest. His heart carried the burden of her love, and the same happened to her on his account. Her heart and her eyes spoke of it: they had to take part in it together with her. With good breeding the lady said: "Command me, my lord, I shall do whatever you desire because you are worthy of it. And let me now have leave of you. If good comfort comes to you here we shall all be overjoyed." Her torch-holders were made of gold, and four torches were carried before her on them. She rode away to her high hall, where she found a plenitude of torches.[23]

The rest of the company did not eat any longer there either. Lord Gahmuret was sad and full of joy. He was overjoyed that they gave him great honor, but a heartache of another kind also weighed on him. That was imperious love that bends high minds. The marshal's wife went to her room. Hardly had this happened when the hero had his bed made, and it was done with care. The host spoke to the guest: "Now you must sleep soundly and rest tonight: you will need it." The host ordered his men to go away from there. The guest's squires, whose beds lay all around his, had their heads close to his, since that was his custom.[24] Candles stood there, very big, and burned with light. It pained the hero that the night was so long. The black Moor, the queen of the land, often brought him to help-lessness. He turned often, like twigs twisted into a trap, so that his limbs cracked. Combat and love were his desire: pray now that he may obtain them. His heart made a noise as it was beating, because it swelled for deeds of knightly valor. Then the hero's chest began to stretch as the crossbow stretches its strings. His desire was too intense.

The lord lay without any sleep and he saw the gray day even though it did not yet give bright light. Then his chaplain had to be ready for mass. He soon sang it for God and for his master. They carried Gahmuret's armor to him then and he rode where he found the jousting. *Gahmuret's armor is described at great length, as are his jousts against various knights. Gahmuret overcomes all his* opponents, captures the four leaders of the enemy armies, and sends them to the city. Finally the queen's marshal brings the jousting to an end. He leads Gahmuret into the town.

The queen rode up to him. She took his bridle in her hand and undid the binding of his visor. The host had to leave it to her. The squires did not forget: they quickly ran up to their lord. You could see the wise queen leading her guest, who had won the prize, through the city. She dismounted when she thought the time had come. "Oh, how loyal you squires are! Do you think you will lose this man?[25] He will be taken care of without you. Take his horse and lead it away. I am his companion here." Many ladies he found up there, but he was disarmed by the queen with her black hands. More honor was done to him in secret, in a bed well made with sable covers. Nobody else was there: the young ladies went out and closed the door behind them. Then the queen devoted herself to sweet and noble love and Gahmuret was the lover of her heart, even though their skins were not alike. *Gahmuret, the queen, and the four captive enemy commanders begin peace negotiations.* Then came the rulers from everywhere in the queen's land of Zazamanc. They thanked Gahmuret for the price he had paid there. In fair jousting he had brought down twenty-four knights and brought their horses back for the most part. Three princes had been captured. Many a knight who was with them rode to the court in front of the high hall. The highest guest had slept and broken his fast and he was dressed splendidly in well-tailored robes. She who was called a virgin before was now a wife, and led him forth by her hand. She said: "My body and my land are subject to this man if my enemies will leave them to him." *Negotiations are successfully concluded. As the new ruler of Zazamanc Gahmuret has to invest his new vassals with fiefs and to present them with gifts. He proceeds to do so.*

Even though his land was laid waste Gahmuret's hand was able to bestow such endowments as if all the trees had been bearing gold. He divided great gifts. His vassals, his kinsmen accepted the hero's goods from him; such was the queen's wish. The wedding feast was preceded by many a great joust. They were all reconciled in this way. I did not think this up myself. They told me that Isenhart was given a royal funeral. Those who had known him well did so. They spent the taxes levied in his lands on his funeral, as much as might account for a year. They did so of their own free will. Gahmuret ordered

Isenbrant's people to make use of their king's great wealth, each as they pleased. In the morning the guests left the walls of the city behind. Those who were there parted and took many stretchers with them. The field stood all bare of encampment, except for one tent, and that one was very large. King Gahmuret ordered it to be taken to the ship; then he began to tell the people he wanted to take it to Azagouc. With these words he deceived them.[26]

There he was, the proud brave man and soon he began to feel grief because he did not find deeds of knighthood to engage in; therefore his joy was the pawn of care. Yet the black woman was dearer to him than his own body. There was never a woman more graced with all things. The lady's heart never forgot to guide along a worthy retinue of true flawless womanly nature. In the city of Seville was born the man Gahmuret asked to guide him away from there, a little while later. He had guided him many a mile before; he had brought him there. He was not colored like a Moor. The wise mariner said: "You shall keep this quiet from those who show black skin. My ships are so fast they cannot come near us; we shall go away from here." Gahmuret ordered his gold carried to the ship. Now I must tell you of parting. That night the noble man went; it was done in stealth. When he ran away from the woman she had in her body a child alive for twelve weeks. Quickly the wind then guided him away.[27]

The lady found in her purse a letter that her man's hand had written in French, a language she knew. The writing began to tell her: "Here love sends love to another love.[28] I am a thief in these travels: I have to steal away from you to spare you grief. My Lady, I cannot conceal from you that if your religion were mine I would always yearn for you.[29] Even now I suffer pain for you always. If our child should look like a man, he shall truly be rich in courage. He is born from Anschouwe. Love shall be his lady, but in combat he shall be like a storm of hail, a harsh neighbor to his enemies. My son should know his grandfather was called Gandin. He died in deeds of knighthood. *Gahmuret further pursues his genealogy and concludes:* from them is my line descended that will forever give brilliant light. Each one of them has worn a crown since then, and they have proved of greatest valor. Lady, if you want to be baptized you may still win me." She did not want to change his wish.[30] "Alas, how soon this happens! If only he would turn back I would get it done quickly. For whom has his manly valor left the fruit of his love here? Alas, lovely companionship, now sorrow must rule my body always with its power! To honor his God," the lady said, "I would gladly be baptized and live the way he wants." Grief fought with her heart. Her joy sought the withered branch as does the turtledove whose mood is always the same: when its love is broken its loyalty chooses the withered branch.

At the right time the lady gave birth to a son who was of two colors. God had decided to work a miracle in him: he shone with colors white and black. The queen kissed him without hesitation over and over again on his white flecks. The mother called her child Feirefiz[31] Anschevin. He became a waster of forests: the jousts of his hands splintered many a spear and riddled shields with holes. His hair was colored like a magpie and so was his skin, all over. Now it was beyond the time of a year that Gahmuret had been highly praised in Zazamanc. His hand had won victories there. He was still with his ship on the sea. The quick winds were giving him grief. He saw a silken sail, red. A ship carried it, and also the messengers Vridebant of the Scots had sent to the lady Belakane. Vridebant asked her to forgive him for having raised an army against her, even though he had lost his kinsman through her. They also carried the diamond helmet, a sword, a breastplate and two leg guards. Here you must listen carefully to a great marvel, namely that the ship met Gahmuret, as the adventure assured me. They gave the armor to Gahmuret. He promised that his mouth would be the bearer of the message when he came to her.[32] The ships parted. They told me that the sea carried Gahmuret into a harbor. He turned away from the sea in Seville. Gahmuret the brave soon rewarded the mariner very well for his work, with gold. They, too, parted. The mariner felt sorrow in his heart.

Book Two

Gahmuret rides on with his retinue until he reaches the site where a great tournament is prepared. He orders one of his squires to gather information about it. The queen of Waleis had ordered a tournament organized in Kanvoleis, the kind of tournament that still scares many a coward when he sees anybody organize anything like it: nothing is done there by his hand.[1] She was a virgin, not a wife, and she offered two countries and her body to whoever won the prize there.[2] This news felled many on the field, throwing them off their horses. Those who took such a fall were said to have lost their chance. There brave heroes engaged in noble pursuits and they made true knighthood shine. Many a horse was there brought to jump, charging at the gallop, and many a sword made to sound.

From the field a drawbridge, guarded by a gate, went across the current of a stream. The squire, undaunted, opened the gate as he had intended to. Above it was built the high hall and in it sat the queen by the windows with many worthy ladies. They began to observe what the squires were doing. They had consulted each other and pitched a tent. That tent was without a king for the sake of unrequited love: Belakane had made it that way.[3] With hard work was raised what thirty pack horses had to carry: a tent that displayed wealth. The plain was so wide that the tent's ropes were stretched taut across it. Gahmuret the worthy man breakfasted outside. Afterwards he eagerly prepared himself to ride forth in a courtly manner. There was no more waiting there. His pages immediately tied his spears together. Each one carried five lashed together and a sixth one, with a banner, in his hand.[4] So came the proud one riding.

It was rumored in the queen's presence that a guest no one there knew had arrived from a far country. "The members of his retinue, both heathen and French, display courtly manners. Judging from their speech some of them may well be Anschevin. Their bearing is proud, their clothes are magnificent, cut to perfection, to speak the truth. I was among his squires: they are free of wrongdoing. They say that if anyone wants possessions, he should seek out their lord, and he will keep hardship away from him. I asked for news about him. They said without hesitation that he was the King of Zazamanc." A squire told her that story. "Look there, what a pavilion! Your crown and your country would not be half a pledge[5] for it." "You don't have to praise it to me so; my mouth replies to you that it has to belong to a worthy man who has no knowledge of poverty." So spoke the queen. "Well, when is he going to arrive in it himself?" She asked the squire to find that out.

Gahmuret and his retinue are described in some detail. When they came close to the bridge, people belonging to another household and also to his were struck by the bright radiance that shone forth from the queen. Then his leg jerked back[6] to his side; the worthy hero raised himself up like a hunting bird that wants to fall on its prey. The hospitality seemed good to him. Such was the hero's mood; she also was moved, the hostess, the queen of Waleis.

Gahmuret meets again with the four knights he overcame in Zazamanc. They tell him what other heroes are present at the tournament. It was then the middle of the day. The lord lay in his tent. Then the king of Zazamanc observed that knights were charging on horseback along the length and width of the field as true knights should. He too went in that direction with many a banner light in color. He did not turn to swift action at once: he wanted to see at his ease how things were done on both sides. They laid his carpet on the field where the charges whirled around and the horses grunted when they were pricked by the spurs. There was a ring of squires around him and beyond it the clink and clank of swords. How they fought for the prize, the men whose blades rang like this! There was great breaking there of spears. Gahmuret did not need to ask anyone where. The charges were his walls, built by the hands of the knights. The throng of knights was so near that the ladies could closely observe the work of the heroes from the high hall. But it pained the queen that the king of Zazamanc was not in the fray with the others. She said: "Alas, why did he come, that man, and I have heard so many tales of wonder about him."

Now the king of France was dead, whose wife had often brought Gahmuret in great distress with her love.[7] The worthy queen of France had sent for news of Gahmuret, to inquire whether he had come back into the country from heathen lands. The power of great love forced her to do so.[8] Much excellent fighting was done there by many a brave poor knight who did not desire the highest, the goal the queen of Waleis had promised: her body and her land. They wanted other pledges.[9]

Gahmuret now puts on his armor. Its splendor is described. He enters the fray. Gahmuret unhorsed Pytewin de Prienlascors and many another worthy man of whom he gained assurance.[10] Whatever crossed knights there rode, they enjoyed the hero's labor: he gave them the horses he had won—he was the source of all their gain. *The description of the tournament continues. Gahmuret rides away from it to rest.* There is a lady I have named before;[11] her chaplain and three young pages came by there. Strong squires rode with them, two packhorses were led by their hand. Queen Anpflise had sent the messengers there. Her chaplain was wise. Very quickly he recognized Gahmuret and soon he greeted him in French: "Welcome, Noble Lord, to my lady and to me. She is queen of France and the lance of your love strikes her." He delivered a letter into Gahmuret's hand. In the letter the hero found greetings and a small ring. That was supposed to be a keepsake, for his lady had received it once from the man of Anschouwe himself.[12] He bowed when he saw the writing. Do you want to hear what it said?

"To you I offer love and greetings. I have never been without sorrow since I felt love for you. Your love is the lock and bond of my heart and its joy. Your love makes me waste away. Love will do me harm if your love should stay far from me. Come back and take from my hand crown, scepter, and country. They came to me after my father's death. Your love has obtained them for you. Take also these rich presents in the four chests on the horses as your reward. You shall also be my knight in the country of Waleis before the capital city of Kanvoleis. I do not care if the queen sees it: not much harm can come to me of it. I am more beautiful and richer and I can also receive and give love more lovingly. If you want to live according to worthy love, take my crown as love's reward."

Gahmuret did not find more in this letter. A squire's hand pulled his coif of mail over his head again. Gahmuret fled from sadness. They tied the diamond helmet on him; it was thick and hard.[13] He wanted to fight in combat. He ordered that the messengers should be taken under his pavilion to rest. Where knights were entangled in fighting he made room. One lost, another won. There a man might make good on deeds he had left undone: there was enough opportunity there. They could ride jousts or charge in formation. They dispensed with the tricks people call friendly taps, and closely knit groups were torn apart with the force of anger. There crooked behavior rarely becomes straight. Knightly justice was little done: whoever won something kept it and did not care if that gained him another's hatred.[14] They came from many lands, who followed the calling of the shield there with their hands. Anpflise's request was granted by Gahmuret: that he should be her knight. A letter told him that news. Oh, how he let himself go. Did love and true knighthood admonish him to do so? Great love and strong loyalty made his strength all new in him.[15] *The tournament goes on. A squire brings Gahmuret the news that his brother has died. Gahmuret withdraws from combat and sends the queen of Waleis his surcoat. She declares that he has won the prize. The tournament comes to an end.*

They forgot the darkness where my lord Gahmuret was sitting as if it were day. It was not, but there were untold numbers of lights there and many bundles of small candles tied together. On olive tree branches was laid many a richly wrought cushion, and many a wide carpet stretched carefully in front of them. The queen rode up to the tent ropes with many worthy ladies: she dearly wanted to see the worthy king of Zazamanc. Many tired knights pressed behind her. The tablecloths had all been removed before she had come inside the pavilion. The host jumped up very quickly, together with four captured kings, and with them was many a prince. Then he received her with good breeding. He pleased her well when she saw him. The lady of Waleis spoke with joy: "You are the host here where I found you, but I am the hostess in the whole country. If, therefore, you want me to give the kiss of welcome to you, that would be well to my liking." "Your kiss shall be mine if you will kiss these lords too. If any king or prince should be deprived of it, I dare not desire it from you either." "That is true and it shall be done. I had not seen any of them before." She kissed those there who were worthy of it, obeying Gahmuret's wish.

He asked the queen to sit. My lord Brandelidelin sat by the lady, with good breeding. Green rushes, wet with dew, were lightly strewn on the carpet. Thereon sat he who gave joy to the worthy lady of Waleis. His love forced her hand: as he was sitting down close to her she took hold of him and pulled him so that he was close to her on the other side. She was a virgin and not a wife, who made him sit so close. Do you now want to hear what she was called? The queen was called Herzeloyde,[16] and her cousin Ritschoyde; King Kaylet, whose aunt's son was Gahmuret, had her cousin for a wife. The lady Herzeloyde radiated so much light that there would still have been enough coming from her if all of Gahmuret's candles had gone out. If great sorrow from afar had not cut down the height of his joy, his love would have been ready to receive her well. They exchanged greetings as is the custom of good breeding. *The knights acknowledge Gahmuret as the winner of the tournament. They wonder why he looks sad.* From her heart the queen asked a sweet request of Gahmuret. "Whatever right I may have to you, do not begrudge it to me. Beyond that, my affection desires mercy. If I am to be deprived of both here in case you think granting them would weaken your fame, let me go away."

The chaplain of Queen Anpflise, the chaste and wise, soon jumped up. He said: "No. By right My Lady should have him, who sent me into this land for his love. She lives for him in pining of love. Her love has possession of him. She should obtain him because she loves him before all other women. Here are her messengers, three princes, young men free of wrongdoing." All three ran up to him. They said: "My Lord, the queen of France gives you a chance of worthy love, if you want it. You may play without a pledge: your joy is freed from care at once."[17] *The queen of Waleis withdraws. Gahmuret promises to settle matters according to law. The vanquished knights negotiate their freedom from Gahmuret. They again notice he looks sad.*

Their host's loyalty goaded him to sad longing once more, for sorrow is a sharp sting. It entered each man's mind that he was wrestling with sorrow and all his joy was too weak. Then his aunt's son became angry; he said: "You know how to be impolite." "No, I have to be with sorrow: I am longing for the queen.[18] I left in Patelamunt a sweet wife of pure disposition and that grieves my heart. Her flawless honor makes my body grieve for her love. She gave me her people and her land. The Lady Belakane deprives me of a man's joys; but it is fitting for a man to be ashamed of wavering in love. The lady's care for me tied me down so that I could not do a true knight's deeds. Then I thought that true knight's deeds would deliver me from the power of sad longing. I have done my fair share of them. Now many an unknowing man thinks that her blackness chased me away from there; I looked on it as the sun. Her womanly fame gives me pain: she is an embossment on the shield of worthiness. This I must lament, and more besides: I saw my brother's shield carried with the point upside down."[19] Alas for those words! The story was sad then. The worthy Spaniard's[20] eyes grew rich with water. "Alas, foolish queen, for your love Galoes gave his life, whom all women should loyally lament with all their heart if they want their behavior to bring praise where it is remembered. Queen of Averre, how little it pained you that through you I lost my kinsman, who chose an end fitting for a knight in a joust that felled him, and who was wearing your token. Princes, his companions, show their heartfelt sorrow. They have turned the broad side of their shield towards the earth, as is sorrow's rule: great mourning teaches them so. In this way they show they are true knights. They are weighed down with the power of sorrow since Galoes, my aunt's son, shall no longer be in the service of love."

When Gahmuret heard of his brother's death, that was the other sorrow of his heart. With lamentation he spoke these words: "How has my anchor's tooth[21] sunk into the harbor of land in sorrow!" He divested himself of his weapons then. His sorrow spoke in the grief of his heart. The hero spoke with true loyalty: "Galoes of Anschouwe! From now on nobody is allowed to ask this question: never was a man born better groomed for manhood. The fruit of true generosity blossomed from your heart. I mourn your goodness." Then spoke King Hardiz: "Now turn your spirit to what befits a man. If you can bear being a man you shall lament your sorrow with good breeding." Gahmuret's sorrow was too great, unfortunately: water gushed out of his eyes. He saw to the comfort of the knights and then went into his own chamber, a small tent of samite. That night he suffered the time of sorrow.

The next morning the queen herself rode out to the worthy men in the field and brought them with her into the town. The best men there she asked to ride to the lion's field. Her request was not denied. They came where they were singing mass for the sad king of Zazamanc. When the benediction was spoken the Lady Herzeloyde arrived. She bespoke Gahmuret's person: she wanted what the verdict[22] had promised her. Then he said: "My Lady, I have a wife; she is dearer to me than my body, and if she were no longer alive I would still know a story that would help me escape from you if somebody were to care for my rights."

"You shall give up the Moorish woman for my love. The blessing of baptism has greater power. Rid yourself of heathen things and love me according to our religion since I have a longing for your love in me.[23] Or shall harm come to me because of the queen of France? Her messengers spoke sweet words, they played out their story to the hilt." "Yes, she is my real lady. I took her advice and my good education to Anschouwe. Her help lives with me even today because that lady, who always fled from women's wrongdoing, educated me. We were both children then, and yet happy to see each other. The queen Anpflise lives close to woman's fame. The fair one gave me the best taxes of her land. (I was poorer then than I am now.) I took them willingly. Count me still among the poor: I should make you take pity on me, My Lady, since my worthy brother is dead. Leave me without hardship by your wisdom. Turn love to where joy may be, since nothing but sorrow lives with me." "Let me not waste my person any longer: tell me, with what will you defend yourself?" "I shall tell you as your question desires. A tournament was announced here; it did not take place. There is many a witness thereof for me." "The evening games have lamed it. The bold ones have been so tamed that the tournament came to nothing because of them." "I took on the defense of your city with those who have done well here. You must absolve me from further forced speech. Many a knight did better here. Your right is weak against me; I am only obligated to you for the greetings you have given to all, if I may have them from you."

As the adventure tells me the knight and the young lady took counsel from a judge because of the lady's complaint. It came closer to the middle of the day. A verdict was given on the spot: "Any knight who has tied on his helmet here, who has come to this place as a true knight should, if he has taken the prize here—the queen should have him."[24] Then the verdict was ratified. The queen of Waleis said: "My Lord, now you are mine. I shall serve you to gain your devotion and I shall provide you with such a share of joy that you will become happy after your sorrow." Yet he had grief of his sorrow. Then was the light of April gone. After it had come small, short, green grass. The field had grown all green. That makes fearful hearts bold and gives them high spirits. Many trees stood in bloom with the sweet air of May. Gahmuret's elfin nature had to love or desire love, and his lover was willing to allow him that. Then he looked at the lady Herzeloyde and his sweet mouth spoke with good breeding: "My Lady, if I shall live with you, let me not be kept. If the power of sorrow ever leaves me I would like to be a knight again. If you do not let me go to tournaments I still know the old trick: I ran away from my wife whom I also won with deeds of knighthood. When she tied me down to keep me from combat I left her, her people, and her land." She said: "My Lord, set yourself a goal: I leave you to do your will in many things." "I want to help break many spears yet: one tournament a month. You will have to allow me to seek them out, My Lady." This she promised, I was told; he received the land and also the virgin.

The three pages of Anpflise the queen had stood there, as had her chaplain, when justice was done and the verdict rendered where he could hear and see it. In secret he said to Gahmuret: "They told my lady you obtained the highest prize before Patelamunt and you wore two crowns there. She also has land and a mind to give you her body and her goods." "Since she gave me knighthood I must abide by it undaunted as the power of the order demands, as the calling of the shield tells me. If I had not obtained my shield from her, other things, too, would not have happened. Whether it makes me sad or happy, knightly justice holds me here. Go back, tell her I am at her service: I shall be her knight after all. Even if all crowns were prepared for me, my highest longing would still be for her."[25] He offered them his great wealth; they declined his gift. The messengers went to their country without any shame to their lady.[26] They did not ask for leave, as still happens in anger now. The queen's young princes were almost blind with much weeping.

Those who had carried their shields upside down had a friend in the field. He began to say to them: "The lady Herzeloyde, the queen, has won the Anschevin." "Who was there from Anschouwe? Our lord is elsewhere, unfortunately, to obtain a knight's praise among the Saracens. That is now our highest pain." "One man who has won the prize here, who unhorsed so many a knight, who thrust and hit like this, and who bore the precious anchor on his bright bejeweled helmet, that is the man you mean. King Kaylet told me the Anschevin was Gahmuret. Success has come to him here indeed." They jumped to the horses then. Their clothes were wet from the tears in their eyes when they came where their lord sat. They welcomed him, he welcomed them too. Joy and sorrow both were here. Then he kissed the faithful men and said: "My brother should not bring you mourning beyond measure: I may well replace him for you. Turn the shield as it should be and keep yourselves steady in the course of joy. I shall wear my father's coat of arms: my anchor has hit its land. The anchor is the sign of a wandering knight; let whoever wants to take it and wear it. I must now act according to my station in life: I am rich. Shall I be the ruler of people? My sorrow would hurt them. My Lady Herzeloyde help me, that we may ask, you and I, of the kings and princes who are here that they should remain with us for my service's sake until you grant me the love fulfilled by love desired." Both their mouths spoke that request. The worthy ones promised at once. Everyone went to his chamber. The queen said to her lover: "Now keep yourself in my care." She showed him hidden ways. Care was well taken of his guests wherever their host might have gone. The two groups of servants were united, yet he went all alone, except for two pages. Young maidens and the queen led him to where he found joy and all his mourning disappeared altogether. His sorrow was vanquished in triumph and his high spirits all new: that must have been because of love. The lady Herzeloyde, the queen, was left without her virginity there. Their mouths were not spared: they began to wear them out with kisses and to keep sorrow away from joy.

Gahmuret sets his captives free and gives generous gifts to all and sundry. When he hears that the Baruc has come under attack, he goes back to Baghdad to help him. What happened there, how things went, how it stood with winning and losing the lady Herzeloyde did not know. She was bright as the sun and had a body made for love. Riches and youth together did the woman cultivate, and joys more than too many: she was altogether beyond the highest pale of wishing. She turned her heart to good knowledge. That is why the world's favor pursued her. The lady Herzeloyde's—the queen's—behavior earned gain of fame, her flawless nature was recognized for praise. Queen over three countries, she was the lady of Waleis and Anschouwe and she also wore the crown of Norgals in the capital city of Kingrivals. Her husband was so dear to her that if ever another woman won such a worthy lover—what was it to her? She could let it happen without envy. When Gahmuret stayed away for half a year she waited for his coming in true faith: that was the sustenance of her body. Then the blade of her joy broke in two at the hilt. Alas and alack that goodness should come to such grief and loyalty always awaken such sorrow! So it goes with mankind: love today, sorrow tomorrow.

On a midday the lady slept a fearful sleep. A terrible fright came to her. She thought that the light of a star was carrying her against the heavens where many a fiery thunderbolt touched her with great power. Then her long braid crackled and hissed with sparks. The thunder sounded its claps; burning tears were its flush. After this she found her body again; then a griffin tore something from her right hand. With this all things were upside down for her. She thought of wondrous things, how she was a serpent's wet nurse, that afterwards ripped open her womb and sucked her breasts like a dragon, and that it fled away from her so fast she never saw it again. It broke her heart out of her body, but her eyes had to see the horror. Rarely has grief like this come to a woman in her sleep. Before that she was a knight's true lady; alas, that had changed utterly. She now becomes of sorrow's color, her misery becomes long and wide, future sorrow of the heart is coming closer to her. Then the lady began what she could not do before: to writhe and to moan, and to shout in her sleep. Many young ladies sat there; they jumped up and woke her.

There rode up Tampanis, her husband's wise chief squire, and many young pages. Then things went beyond the border of joy. They announced and lamented the death of their lord. The lady Herzeloyde came into her need: she fell down senseless. The knights said: "How was my lord overcome in his armor, as well armed as he was?" Even though sorrow pursued the squire, he told the heroes: "Length of life fled from my master. He took off his coif of mail: the strong heat forced him to do so. Shameful heathen artifice has stolen the good hero from us. A knight had taken goat's blood in a tall glass. He poured it on the diamond helmet. Then it became softer than a sponge. May He whom they paint in the shape of a lamb with a cross put between its hooves have mercy on what was done there. *Gahmuret is killed before Baghdad. He is buried there.*

This, then, was the squire's tale. You could see many Waleisians weeping as it was their duty to do. The lady had carried a child that moved in her body, and they left it lying there without help. For eighteen weeks[27] it had lived, whose mother fought with death, the lady Herzeloyde, the queen. The others were weak in their mind not to help the woman, since she bore in her body who was to become the flower of all knights, if death misses him here. Then came a wise old man to be with the lady in her time of lament, when she was struggling with death. He forced her teeth apart, they poured water into her mouth, and she came back to her senses. She said: "Alas, where has my beloved gone?" The lady lamented him very loudly. "Gahmuret's honor was my heart's wide joy. His bold desire took him from me. I was much younger than he, and I am his mother and his wife, since I carry his body here and the seed of his bravery that our love gave and took. If God is of loyal mind let him come to fruition in me. I have already endured too much harm on account of my proud, worthy husband. What has death done to me! He never received a share of woman's love without being happy in all her joys and he cared much about woman's sorrow. His loyalty as a good man told him so, for he was devoid of falsehood." Now listen to another story the lady began there. She grasped her child and her belly in her arms and in her hands. She said: "May God send me the worthy fruit of Gahmuret. That is my heart's request. May God turn more senseless grief away from me, for it would be Gahmuret's second death if I should kill myself while I carried in me what I have received from the love of him who showed a man's loyalty to me."

The lady did not care who saw this: she tore the dress from her bosom. She turned her attention to her little breasts, soft and white; she pressed them to her red mouth. She displayed a woman's nature. The wise one said: "You are the vessel of a child's food: it has sent you here ahead of itself ever since I found it alive inside my body." The lady saw her wish fulfilled in that the food was the roof of her heart, the milk in her little bosom. The queen pressed it out. She said: "You have come from loyalty. If I had not taken baptism, you would be the instrument of my baptism. I shall besprinkle myself often with you and with my eyes, in public and in private, for I want to lament Gahmuret." The lady ordered a shirt brought closer, the color of blood, in which Gahmuret had lost his life among the Baruc's men. He chose a fighting end with a man's true desire. The lady also asked for the spear that gave Gahmuret his death. Ipomidon of Ninive gave him true reward in this, the proud fighting Babylonian. The shirt was all torn with blows. The lady wanted to put it on her as she had done before when her husband returned from knightly feats. They took it out of her hand. The best in the whole country buried the spear and also the blood in the minster, as is done with the dead. They knew sorrow then in Gahmuret's land.

After this, on the fourteenth day, the lady gave birth to a child, a son, who had such big limbs that she hardly recovered at all. Here the first throw of the adventure is done and its beginning established: he has just now been born, for whom this story has been chosen. You have heard a fair share of his father's joy and need, his life and death. Now know from where he has come to you, the mover of this story, and how they cared for him. They hid him from knighthood until he came into the power of his intelligence. When the queen came back to her senses and recovered her child, she and the other ladies began to look all over his little penis between his legs. He had to be much fondled since he had a man's member. Since then he became a smith with swords, so much fire did he beat out of helmets, and his heart showed a man's courage. The queen found her joy in that she kissed him very often. She spoke to him with great devotion: "My good son, my dear son, my beautiful son."

Then, without hesitation, the queen took the red, somewhat discolored spots, I mean the nipples of her bosom. These she pushed into his little mouth. She herself was his nurse, who had carried him in her womb. To her breasts she pulled him, the lady who fled from woman's wrongdoing. She thought she had enticed Gahmuret back to her arm again. She did not turn to levity; humility stood prepared for her. The lady Herzeloyde spoke with good sense: "The highest queen offered Jesus her breasts, who afterwards, in human shape, suffered a very bitter death on the cross for us, and showed us his loyalty. Whoever counts his anger for little, his soul will not find peace without great difficulty, no matter how flawless he be and has been. That I know for a true story." The lady of the land besprinkled herself with the dew of her heart's sorrow. Her eyes rained down on the child. She knew how to keep a woman's loyalty. Her mouth could utter both sighs and laughter very well. She found joy in the birth of her son; her delight drowned in the ford of sorrow.

Whoever speaks better of women, in truth I let him do so without jealousy. I would gladly hear their great joy. But I am not prepared to do loyal service for one of them. My anger is always new against her since I have seen her wavering. I am Wolfram von Eschenbach, I know a little about singing,[28] and I am a tenacious pair of tongs in my anger against a woman who has done such an evil deed to me that I know not what to do with my hatred.[29] Because of this I have incurred the hatred of others. Alas, why do they do this? Although their hatred hurts me, it is their womanhood that causes it since I have spoken amiss and done myself harm. That will probably never happen again, yet they should not be too hasty to come up to my bastion with instruments of siege. They will find a stiff fight there. I have not forgotten, I can judge full well both their behavior and their nature. I want to be the champion of the honor of whatever woman follows the flawless mean; their pain is heartfelt sorrow to me.

His praise limps at the knee, who pronounces all women checkmate compared to his lady alone.[30] Whoever wants to see my right, see it and hear it, her I shall not fool. I am born to the calling of the shield. Whoever slights my courage, whoever loves me for my song I consider weak in intelligence. If I desire the love of a good woman and I cannot earn the reward of her love with my shield and spear, she should treat me accordingly, since a man who aims at love with deeds of knighthood plays a very risky game of dice. If women would not take it for flattery I would offer you more unknown words in this story, I would recite the adventure further for you. Whoever wants me to do so, let him not seek it among any books.[31] I do not know a single letter.[32] Enough others find the beginnings of their stories among them, but this adventure sails without the steering of books. Rather than have people take it for a book I would prefer to be naked without a towel as I would be in the bath if I did not forget to bring my brush of twigs.[33]

Book Three

It makes me sad that so many are called woman. Their voices are all just as clear, but many of them are inclined to falsehood while many are devoid of it. Things are divided in this way. My heart is filled with shame because they are called the same. Womanhood, your true nature always walks and walked with loyalty. Enough people say that poverty is good for nothing, but the fires of hell will spare the soul of those who endure it for loyalty's sake. A woman endured it for loyalty's sake; therefore her gift became new in heaven with endless giving. I think there are very few alive now who left the riches of the earth behind in their youth, all for the glory of heaven. I do not know of any of them. Men and women are all the same to me, they avoid it all alike. The Lady Herzeloyde, the rich one, became a stranger to her three countries. She bore the burden of lack of joy. Falsehood had completely disappeared from her, eyes nor ears ever found it there. The sun was a mist for her: she fled the comfort of the world. Night and day were alike to her: her heart was engaged with nothing but sorrow.

Persevering in her sorrow the lady withdrew from her land into a forest, to the wasteland in Soltane, and not because of flowers on the meadow.[1] Her heart's sorrow was so total that she did not want any garland, be it red or faded. There she brought the child of worthy Gahmuret for security. People who are there with them must work the land and clear it.[2] She was well able to love her son. Before he reached the age of sense she had all her people come before her, man or woman. She ordered them all upon their life that they would never utter a sound about knights. "If the love of my heart were to know what the life of a knight is, that would be great hardship to me. Now keep your wits about you and avoid all mention of knighthood."

These orders set a fearful course. And so the boy was raised hidden in the wasteland of Soltane, cheated of his royal destiny, except for one custom: bow and arrows. Those he cut with his own hand and shot many a bird he found. When he shot a bird down whose singing sound had been so beautiful before, he wept and tore his hair, and took revenge on it. His body was fair and proud. He washed himself every morning on the meadow by the river.[3] He did not know how to worry, except when the singing of the birds, sweet, moved into his heart: that made his little chest swell. Weeping he ran to the queen. She said: "Who has done anything to you? You were outside in the meadow." He could not tell her, as may well happen to children still. She kept track of it in her mind for a long time. One day she saw him gaping at the trees, at the song of the birds. It entered her mind that her child's chest swelled up with the voices. His nature and his enjoyment made it so. Lady Herzeloyde turned her hatred against the birds, she did not know why: she wanted to destroy their sound. She ordered her men who worked the soil and tended the cattle to catch the birds quickly and strangle them. The birds were faster: many a death was avoided. Part of them stayed alive, who since became happy with their song.

The boy said to the queen: "What do they have against the birds?" He desired peace for them at once. His mother kissed him on the mouth. She said: "Why should I turn away the command, of Him Who is the highest God after all? Shall birds take leave of their joy because of me?" The boy quickly said to his mother: "Alas, mother, what is God?" "Son, I tell you without jest: He is brighter still than the day, Who took on features modeled after the features of man. Son, mark this: it is good to know Him and to implore Him in your need: His loyalty has always offered help to the world. There is another one who is called the host of hell: he is black, falsehood does not avoid him. Turn your thoughts away from him, and also from the wavering of doubt." His mother made the distinction for him between light and dark. After that he jumped far away with his usual speed and practiced throwing the javelin. With it he brought down many a stag, which his mother and her people enjoyed. His throws would pierce the game where there was snow on the ground or where the sun had melted it. Now listen to a strange story, when he laid low a heavy one that would have been enough to load down a mule, and carried it home in one piece.

One day he went down a hunting path on a slope, and a long path it was. He broke off a branch to make animal sounds by whistling on a leaf.[4] Close by him there ran a path. Then he heard the sound of hoofbeats. He began to weigh his javelin in his hand. Then he said: "What have I heard? What if the devil were to come now in an angry rage! I would certainly stand up to him. My mother says horrible things about him, but I think her courage is a bit daunted." And so he stood in the desire of combat. *Parzival meets four knights, riding in hot pursuit of two other knights who have abducted a young lady. Parzival thinks the leader of the knights must be God, because of his shining armor. The leader tells him about knighthood. The knights leave Parzival and ask the lady Herzeloyde's people for information about the fugitives. The people realize Parzival must know about knights by now, and they are afraid of the lady Herzeloyde's reaction.*

The boy also did not care any more who killed the stags there, small or big. He went back to his mother and told her his story. She fell down: she was startled so much by his words that she lay senseless before him. When the queen came back to her senses—and not before, when she was unable to—she said: "Son, who told you about the order of knights? Where have you heard it?" "Mother, I have seen four men more radiant than God himself. They told me about knighthood. Artus's royal power should guide me toward the calling of the shield as a true knight's honor demands."[5] A new lament ascended here. The lady did not know well how to invent a ruse to turn him away from his purpose.

Simpleminded and worthy, the boy often demanded a horse of his mother. She began to lament in her heart. She thought: "I do not want to deny it to him, but it must be a very bad one." Then the queen thought again: "Many people are inclined to ridicule. My son should wear strange clothes on his radiant body. If he is beaten and has his hair torn out he may well come back to me here." Alas, the sorrow and the suffering! The lady took sackcloth: she cut him a shirt and a pair of pants that appeared to be of one piece and reached down until the middle of his white leg. That was recognized as a buffoon's dress. A hood was found on top of it. From the rough hide of a calf two shoes were cut for his legs. But great sorrow was not avoided there. The queen had thought it out: she asked him to stay that night. "You should not go away from here. I want to teach you knowledge first. On untrodden paths you must leave dark fords alone; shallow fords and clear ones, those you can boldly ride into. You must observe politeness and give greetings to the world. If a gray wise man wants to teach you good behavior, as he is well able to, you must follow him gladly and not be angry with him. Son, let this be recommended to you: where you can obtain a good woman's ring and her greeting, accept them; they will free you from care. You should hasten to her kiss and embrace her body firmly: that brings happiness and high spirits when she is chaste and good. You should also know, my son, that the proud brave Lehelin has taken two countries away from your vassals, who should have served your hand: Waleis and Norgals. One of your vassals, Turkentals, received death from his hands; he conquered your people and made it captive." "That I shall avenge, mother, if God wills it: my javelin will wound him yet."

The next morning, when the day appeared, the boy soon decided for himself on swift progress toward Arthur. The lady Herzeloyde kissed him and ran after him. The greatest sorrow in the world came to be there. When she no longer saw her son (he rode away: to whose betterment?), the lady free from falsehood fell on the earth, where sorrow cut her so that she did not avoid death. May her most loyal dying keep hell's torment away from women. Hail her that she ever became a mother! So she went on the journey that brings reward, a root of goodness and a trunk of humility. Alas, that we do not have her offspring to the eleventh generation with us now! As it is, many a person is exposed to falsehood. But now loyal women should wish this boy well, who has taken himself away from her here. *Parzival rides on until he finds a tent.*

Under it he found the wife of Duke Orilus de Lalander.[6] She lay there lovely, the rich duchess, like a knight's beloved. She was called Jeschute. The lady had fallen asleep. She was wearing love's coat of arms: a mouth that shone bright red, and that is the mark of a knight's desiring heart. While the lady was sleeping her lips moved away from each other, carrying the fire of love's heat. So lay the fulfillment of many a wish. Her small shining teeth of snowwhite ivory stood close together. I think that nobody could make me get used to kissing such a well-praised mouth: it has rarely come to my knowledge. Her sable cover stopped at her hips; she had pushed it away from her because of the heat; her lord had left her alone. She was well shaped and well made-up; skill had not been wasted on her: God himself had made her sweet body. The lovable lady also had long arms and a white hand. The boy found a ring there that drew him toward the bed where he wrestled with the duchess. Then he thought of his mother and her advice about women's rings. Indeed the well shaped boy soon jumped from the carpet into the bed.

The sweet chaste one was rudely startled when the boy lay in her arms; but she had to wake up in shame, not in jest. The lady well-bred said: "Who has dishonored me? Young man, this is far too much for you: you should set yourself another goal." The lady lamented loudly. He did not care what she said, he forced her mouth to his. After that it was not too long before he pressed the duchess against himself and he also took a ring from her. He then saw a brooch on her shift: he insolently tore it away. The lady was left with a woman's defenses: his strength was a whole army to her. Yet much wrestling was done there. The boy soon complained of hunger. The lady was glowing all over her body. She said: "You shall not eat me. If you knew what is good for you, you would take other food to yourself. There stand bread and wine, and two little partridges as they were brought by a young lady who did not have you in mind."[7]

He did not care where the hostess sat:[8] he ate a good bellyful, and after that he drank long drafts. His being in the pavilion seemed all too long to the lady. She thought he was a boy severed from his wits. She began to sweat in her shame.[9] Yet the duchess said: "Young man, you shall leave my ring here and my brooch too. Take yourself away: when my husband comes you shall have to endure anger, which you might rather want to avoid." Then spoke the boy of noble birth: "Oh, why should I fear your husband's anger? But if this harms you in your honor I shall go away from here." Then he went quickly to the bed: another kiss was given there. That was sorrow to the duchess. The boy rode away without farewell, but he said: "God save you, such was my mother's advice."

The boy was pleased with his robbery. When he had ridden away from there a while, probably close to a mile's distance, then came he

I want to speak of. He noticed by the dew that his lady had been visited. Some of the ropes had been trampled down: a boy had stepped on the grass there. The duke, worthy and well-known, found his wife all sad under the tent. Then the proud Orilus said: "Alas, My Lady, why have I directed my service toward you! Much knightly fame has come to an end for me in shame. You have another lover." The lady offered her denial with eyes rich with water: she was innocent. He did not believe her story. Yet she spoke to him fearfully: "A fool came riding here: however many people I have known, I have never seen a body so well shaped. He took my brooch and my ring without my consent." "Oh, his body pleases you well. You joined yourself with him." Then she said: "That may God forbid. His shoes, his javelin were far too close to me. That talk should seem contemptible to you. It ill behooves a lady to take love there."

The quarrel goes on. The duchess looked at the duke: her mouth then spoke piteously: "Now honor your knight's praise in me. You are loyal and wise, and you have such power over me that you could give me great pain. You should first accept my justification. Let it please you for the sake of all women. You may do harm to me still afterwards. If I lay dead at another's hands, so that your praise would not be debased, how quickly would I then suffer death. It would be a sweet time for me since your hatred lies on me."

But the duke said more: "My lady, you are becoming far too proud for me: I shall therefore bring you down to good measure. Companionship will be left behind, with drinking and with eating; lying together will be forgotten. You shall not receive a single garment except the one I found you sitting in. Your reins shall be a rope of bark, your horse shall hunt for hunger's share, and your saddle well adorned shall be brought to shame." Very soon he tore and broke the samite off it. When that had happened he destroyed the saddle she rode in (her chastity and her womanhood had to endure his hatred), but he tied it together again with ropes of bark. To her his hatred came all too soon. Then he said: "Lady, we shall ride now. If I meet him who took a share of your love here I shall be happy for it. I would take my chance and stand up to him even if his breath gave off fire like that of a wild dragon." Crying, without laughter, the lady rich in sorrow sadly rode away from there. She did not regret what had happened to her, except for her husband's distress. And so sorrow gave her such great grief that she would rather have been dead. Now you shall lament her for loyalty's sake: she begins to endure great sorrow. Even if the hatred of all women stood prepared for me, I regret the lady Jeschute's suffering. So they rode after him along the trail. The boy before them was also fast. Yet the undaunted one did not know that they were chasing him, for when he began to come close to whoever his eyes could see, the good boy gave them greetings and said: "Such was my mother's advice."

So our simpleminded boy came riding down a slope. He heard a woman's voice before the edge of a rock. A lady was weeping with true sorrow; true joy had been broken to pieces for her. The boy soon rode toward her. Now listen to what the lady did. The lady Sigune tore her long brown braids out of her head for sorrow. The boy began to look closer: Schianatulander the prince he found there dead in the young lady's lap. She had been robbed of joy.

"Be they sad or of joyful color, my mother told me to greet them all. God save you," spoke the boy's mouth. "I have found a sorrowful find here in your lap. Who gave you the wounded knight?" The boy undaunted said: "Who hit him? Was it done with a javelin? It seems to me, My Lady, that he lies dead. Would you like to tell me something about it? Who has slain the knight? If I can ride up to him I shall gladly do combat with him." *Parzival tells the story of Jeschute.*

Now let me tell you about Sigune, too. She knew how to lament her hardship with sorrow. She said to the boy: "You have virtue.[10] All honor be to your sweet youth and your lovable face. In truth you shall be rich in blessings. The javelin spared this knight: he lay dead in a joust. You are born from loyalty, that you can take pity on him like this." Before she let the boy ride off she asked him what he was called and said he bore God's stamp on him. "Good son, dear son, beautiful son is what they used to call me who knew me at home." When that reply was given she soon recognized him by his name. Now listen as I name him more precisely, so that you may know well who is the lord of this adventure. He kept himself by the young lady's side. Her red mouth spoke without hesitation: "In truth you are called Parzival. The name stands for straight through the middle. Great love plowed such a furrow through your mother's heart with loyalty. Your father left her sorrow. I do not tell you this so you can boast; your mother is my aunt and I am telling you the real truth, who you are, without false artifice. Your father was an An-schevin, your mother a Waleis.[11] You were born from her at Kan-voleiz. I know the real truth about it. You are also king in Norgals, your head should bear a crown in the capital at Kingrivals. This prince was slain on your account because he always defended your country; he never harmed his honor.[12] Young, devoted, sweet man, two brothers have done much harm to you. Lehelin took two countries from you; Orilus killed this knight and your father's brother in a joust. He also left me in sorrow like this. This prince from your kingdom served me without any shame. Your mother had charge of me then. Dear good cousin, now listen what these stories are. A spaniel's leash gave him his pain.[13] In both our service he has hunted down death and sorrow's distress for me through his love. My senses were diseased that I did not give him love:[14] so the cause of all my grief has cut up my joy. I love him now, dead."

Then Parzival said: "Cousin, I regret your hardship and my great shame. If I can avenge them I shall gladly do so." He was eager to go to battle. She showed him the wrong way to follow: she was afraid that he would lose his life and that she would taste more harm. Then he found a road that went to Brittany. It was paved with flagstones and wide. Whoever walked or rode up to him, knight or merchant, he greeted them all at once, and that was his mother's advice: she had given it to him without wrongdoing. The evening began to come close. Great tiredness came quickly over him. Then the companion of simplicity saw a house, built in good measure. In it was a greedy host, as there are more born from base lineage. He was a fisherman, and devoid of all goodness.[15] Hunger taught the boy that he should turn toward the house and lament hunger's need to that host. The host said: "I shall not give you half a loaf of bread in thirty years. Whoever hopes that I shall give freely of my generosity is wasting his time.[16] I care for nobody except for me, and after that for my children. You will not get in here all day. If you had coins or a pledge I would be your keeper at once." The boy immediately offered him the lady Jeschute's brooch. When the oaf saw it his mouth laughed and he said: "My sweet young man, all who are in this house will do you honor if you want to stay here." "If you want to feed me well today and show me tomorrow how I can truly get to Artus (I am drawn to him), the gold can stay with you." "That I shall do," said the oaf. "I have never seen a body that well shaped. I shall bring you

to the king's Round Table: one wonder deserves another." That
night the boy stayed there. In the morning they saw him elsewhere:
he hardly waited for the day. The host also prepared himself and
walked in front of him; the boy rode behind. There was an urge in
both of them. My lord Hartman von Ouwe,[17] your lady Ginover
and your lord Arthur, the king, are now receiving a guest of mine in
their house. I ask you to keep him from ridicule. He is no fiddle, and
no Welsh harp: they should take another toy and let it please them
for the sake of their good breeding. Otherwise your lady Enite and
her mother Karsnafite will be put through the mill and their fame
brought low. If I have to use my mouth in mockery, well then, I shall
defend my friend with it.

Then the fisherman and the fighting boy came so close to a capital
city that they saw Nantes. The host said: "My boy, God save you.
Now look: that is where you have to ride in." Then said the boy
devoid of wit: "You must direct me farther." "I shall take great care
not to. The household is of such lineage that it would be a very great
wrong if a lowborn man would ever come near them." The boy rode
on, alone, on a meadow not too wide: it stood painted bright with
flowers. No Curneval had educated him:[18] he did not know courtly
life as happens to a man who has not traveled. *Parzival meets Ither,
the red knight, who lays claim to Artus's kingdom. He rides on,
promising to deliver Ither's message to Artus.*

The boy said: "I shall be the messenger of what you have said to
me." He rode away from him, into Nantes. The pages followed him
to the courtyard in front of the palace where there was a group of
many different people. Soon a crowd began to gather around him.
Iwanet jumped closer to him; the page free of falsehood offered him
company. The boy said: "God save you, my mother asked me to say
that before I went away from her house. I see many an Artus here;
who is going to make me a knight?" Iwanet began to laugh. He
said: "You do not see the right one, but that will happen very soon
now." He led him into the high hall where the worthy household
was. Parzival said—as well as he could, on account of the noise—
"God save you lords all, especially the king and his wife. My mother
ordered me on my life to greet them in particular, as well as those
who have a place at the Round Table, because of their rightful fame.
She ordered me to greet them. But one skill is lacking to me in this: I
do not know who is the host here. A knight (I saw him: he was red

all over) has sent this message to him: he wants to wait for him outside. It seems to me he wants to do combat. He also regrets that he spilled wine on the queen. Oh, if only I had received his armor from the king's hand I would be rich in joy because it looks so fit for a knight."

The carefree boy was pushed about very much, jostled here and there. They observed his color. They could see it for themselves. No more lovable fruit was ever made into a man by woman. God was in a sweet mood when he created Parzival who had very little fear of fear. So was brought before Artus the boy in whom God conceived His highest wish. Nobody could be an enemy to him. Then the queen also looked at him before she went away from the high hall where wine had been spilt on her.[19] Artus looked at the boy: he then spoke to the simpleminded one. "Young man, may God give you great reward. I must serve you gladly with love and with goods. That is well settled in my mind." "If God wills it, when will that come true? It seems to me it has been the time of a year since I have wanted to be a knight: that does me more ill than good. Now do not make me wait any longer, treat me according to a true knight's honor." "That I shall do gladly," said the host, "if worth has not passed me by. You are so delightful. The gift I put at your disposal shall be rich for you in worthy help. In truth, I should not gladly leave it undone. You must wait until the morning: I want to prepare you well." The wellborn boy walked up and down like a bustard. He said: "I will not ask for anything here. A knight came riding towards me: if his armor cannot become mine I do not care who talks about kingly gifts. My mother can give them to me anyway: I think she is a queen after all."

Artus soon said to the boy: "A man has on him that armor I would not dare to give to you. I have to live with grief without any guilt on my part since I am without his homage. He is Ither of Kahaviez, who pierced my joy with mourning." "You would be an ungenerous king if such a gift were too much for you. Give it to him," said Keie, "and let him ride to the other one on the meadow." "I would not gladly deprive him of it, except that I am afraid that he will be slain, whom I should help to knighthood," said Artus with the power of loyalty. Yet the boy received the gift, from which sorrow did come since. There was an urge in him to go away from the king. Young and old pressed behind him. Iwanet pulled him by the hands toward a gallery not too high. There he could see forward and backward: the gallery was so low that he heard and saw from there what became sorrow to him. The queen also wanted to be by the window herself with knights and ladies. They all began to look at him. There sat the Lady Cunneware, proud and pure. She would not laugh at all unless she saw him who had obtained, or would obtain the highest praise; she would rather die without laughter otherwise. She avoided all laughing until the boy rode past her: then her lovely mouth laughed. Her back was battered for that.[20]

Keie the marshal took the lady Cunneware of Lalant by her wavy hair: he wound her long fair braids around his hand and held them together without a bolt. Her back had not taken an oath on a judge's staff:[21] yet a staff was held to it in such a way that it cut through her clothes and through her skin before its whirring was completely done. Then the unwise one[22] said: "Your worthy fame has been given a shameful end: I am the net that catches it, I shall beat it back into you until you feel it in your limbs. So many a worthy man has come riding to king Artus in his courtyard and into his house for whom you have avoided laughter, and now you laugh for a man who does not understand the ways of knights." In anger many wondrous things happen. The right to beat this maiden had not been given to Keie before the king. Cunneware was pitied by many friends (even if she had carried a shield, as knights do, the unseemly blows would have been struck) and yet she was a princess by nature. If Orilus and Lehelin, her brothers, had seen this, fewer blows would have been struck.

There was also the silent Antanor, who seemed a fool because of his silence. His speaking and Cunneware's laughter were beholden to the same rule: he never wanted to say a word, she did not laugh, who had been beaten. When her laughter was done his mouth soon spoke to Keie: "God knows, lord marshal, that Cunneware de Lalant is beaten because of the boy. Still, your joy will be destroyed yet by his hands unless he appears to be devoid of all courage."

Parzival rides out and kills Ither. Iwanet helps him to put on the red armor and takes his javelin from him, since it is not a weapon for a knight. Parzival mounts Ither's horse.

As the adventure tells us, no painter from Cologne or Maastricht could paint Parzival better than he sat on the horse there. Then he said to Iwanet: "Dear friend, my companion, I have received here what I asked for. You shall tell King Artus in the city of my service, and also lament the great insult done to me. Bring him back his golden goblet. A knight forgot himself before to the extent that he beat a young lady because she thought of laughing for my sake. Her sad words grieve me. They do not just touch the edges of my heart; the lady's undeserved pain must be in the middle of it. Now do as I ask because you are my companion, and let the insult done to me sadden you too. God save you. I want to go away from you. He will keep us both well."

Sadly he let Ither of Kahaviez lie. He was lovable even in death. In life he was rich in blessings. If true knighthood had brought him to his end, in a joust with a spear through his shield, who would then have lamented this strange affliction?[23] He died from a javelin. Iwanet brought bright flowers to him as a roof. He pushed the javelin's shaft down next to him, in the manner of Christ's passion. The page, flawless and proud, pushed a piece of wood through the javelin's blade in the manner of a cross. He did not want to avoid his task. In the city he said what disheartened many a woman and made many a knight cry, who showed his loyalty in his lament. Great sorrow was endured there. The queen rode out of the city: she asked that the sacrament be taken to the king of Kukumerlant whom Parzival's hand had killed. The lady Ginover, the queen, spoke words of sorrowful import: "Alas and alack, Artus's honor shall break in half through this strange wonder, that he who should have had the highest praise among the knights of the Round Table lies slain before Nantes. He desired his inheritance where they gave him death. He was of the household here, and no ear ever heard of his wrongdoing. He was tamed of wild falsehood: it had been pared from him altogether. Now I have to bury all too soon who was a lock on praise. His heart, wise with high breeding, the seal on that lock, gave him the best advice indeed when he had to show a man's loyalty in true noble spirit: in the pursuit of woman's love. A new fruit of sorrow that bears its own seeds has been sown among women. Sorrow drifts from your wounds. Your hair was so red that your blood could not make the bright flowers redder still. You have wiped out a woman's laughter."

Ither rich in fame was buried like a king, whose death thrust sighs upon the women. His armor lost his body: the simpleminded Parzival's desire brought him to his end for it. *Parzival rides on until he sees a castle.* Gurnemanz of Graharz was the name of the lord of the castle toward which he rode. In front of it stood a broad linden tree on a green meadow, neither wider nor longer than the right measure. The horse and the road carried Parzival where he found him sitting who owned the castle, and the country too. A great tiredness forced him to swing his shield wrong: too far back or front, not at all as requested by the way they measured praise there. Gurnemanz the prince sat alone. The bulk of the linden tree gave its shadow to this captain of true breeding, as it should. His nature was a flight from falsehood. He received the guest, as was his right. With him was neither knight nor servant. Out of his dim wit Parzival spoke to him without hesitation as follows: "My mother asked me to take advice of him who has gray hair. I want to serve you accordingly, since my mother told me that." "You have come here for the sake of advice. Then leave me your goodwill before I give you my advice."

The well-known prince threw a molted sparrow hawk up from his hand. It swept down to the castle: a gold bell rang from its talon: that was his messenger. Then many well-bred young pages soon came to him. He asked them to lead away the guest he saw there and to give him comfort. Parzival said: "My mother spoke the truth: an old man's speech should not be feared." They led him away all at once to where he found many a worthy knight. They all asked him to dismount on a place in the courtyard. Then said whose simple-mindedness was obvious: "A king asked me to be a knight: whatever happens to me after this, I shall not come down from this horse. My mother advised me to give you greetings." They thanked both him and her. When the greeting was done (the horse was tired, and also the man) they invented many a request before they brought him off his horse into a chamber. They all began to advise him: "Let the armor be taken away from you and your limbs made light."

He had to be disarmed quickly. When they saw the rough shoes and the fool's garment those who attended to him were startled. They mentioned it with great hesitation; the host was almost disheartened with shame. A knight spoke with good breeding: "In truth the light of my eyes has never chosen such a worthy fruit. On him lies the look of bliss with a pure, sweet, exalted nature. Why is the very look of love dressed like this? I shall always be distressed that I have found such clothing on the joy of the world. Yet hail to the mother who bore him: the plenitude of wishing lies in him. His helmet is well adorned and the armor looked knightly before it came off the fair one. I quickly noticed on him the bloody stain of a great bruise." The host soon spoke to the knight: "That is done by a woman's command." "No, my lord, he is given to such manners that he could never ask a lady to accept his service. But his color is fitting for love." The host said: "Now let us go see him of the wondrous clothes."

They went where they found Parzival, wounded by a spear that had stayed whole. Gurnemanz devoted himself to him. Such was his devotion that a father who devoted himself to loyalty could not have offered more of it to his children. The host washed and bound up Parzival's wounds with his own hand. Then the meal was laid out; the young guest was in need of it since great hunger had not avoided him. He had ridden away from the fisherman that morning, fasting. His wound and the heavy armor he had obtained before Nantes had caused him weariness and hunger, and the day's far journey from Artus the Briton, during which they had let him fast altogether. The host asked Parzival to eat with him: the guest refreshed himself there. He kept so close to the trough[24] that he made much food disappear. The host took it altogether in jest: then Gurnemanz rich in loyalty asked him eagerly to eat his fill and to forget his weariness.

They lifted the table when the time had come.[25] "I think you are tired," said the host. "Were you up early?" "Certainly, my mother was still asleep. She cannot stay awake that long." The host began to laugh. He led him to the bedrooms. The host asked him to undress; Parzival did not like to do it, but it had to be. An ermine cover was laid over his naked body. A woman never gave birth to such a worthy fruit. Great tiredness and sleep taught him to rarely turn himself on his other side. So he could wait for the day. Then the well-known prince ordered that a bath be prepared at the midtime of the morning at the foot-end of the couch where Parzival lay. That had to be done every morning. They threw roses over him. No matter how little they raised their voices around him, the guest who slept there woke up. The young worthy sweet man soon went to sit in the bathtub.

I do not know who asked them to do this: young ladies came in, wearing rich dresses and lovely with their fair skins, true to their breeding. They quickly washed and rubbed his bruises away from him with white hands. He who was an orphan of wit did not have to be a stranger to them. So he endured joy and comfort, and little harm came to him from his simplemindedness. The young ladies, chaste and bold, cared for him in this way. He knew how to be silent on the things they talked about. It could not seem too early for him: a second day shone from them. Brightness did combat against brightness there; his color extinguished their light since his body was not without light of its own. They offered him a bath sheet; he did not accept it. He knew how to be shamed among ladies, and he did not want to wrap it around him before them. The ladies had to go: they did not dare to stand there any longer. I think they would have liked to have seen if anything happened to him down there. Womanhood walks with loyalty: it knows how to grieve over a friend's sorrow.

The guest walked over to the bed. A garment all white was prepared for him. *Parzival dresses himself.* Then came the host with power vested in loyalty: behind him walked proud knighthood. Gurnemanz welcomed the guest. When that happened every one of the knights said they had never seen such a well shaped body. With loyalty they praised the woman who had given the world such a fruit. In truth and because of their breeding they said: "He will be well favored wherever his service desires reward: love and greetings will be prepared for him. May he enjoy his worth." Every one said the same of him, as did every one who saw him afterwards.

Gurnemanz takes care of Parzival's formal education. He teaches him how to behave at mass, and gives him the following rules of knightly behavior while they eat. The host said to his guest: "You speak like a little child. When will you be silent about your mother and listen to other words? Heed my advice: it will keep you from wrongdoing. I begin as follows: let it please you never to be without shame. A shameless man, what is he good for? His life has fallen in a state of molting because his honor always falls away from him and guides him towards hell. You have beauty and radiance in your bearing, you may well be the ruler of people. If you are of high lineage and if you want to go higher still, let your will be endowed with pity for the host of the needy. Be their shelter against care with generosity and goodness: devote yourself to humility. The worthy man who is plagued by cares is able to wrestle well with shame (it is a bitter task): you must be prepared to come to his aid. If you free him from care God's blessing will be near to you. Things are worse for such a man than for those who yawn for bread before a window.[26] You shall be poor and rich with discretion. For when a lord spends everything he does not have a lord's sense. If he gathers too much treasure that is dishonor too. Give good measure its due. It has entered my mind that you are in need of advice: let misconduct fight its own battles. You should not ask much. Thoughtful answers aimed straight at the question asked by whoever wants to probe you with words should not displease you. You can hear and see, taste and smell: that should bring you close to wisdom. Let mercy accompany courage. Show me the effect of my advice in that way. If a man promises surrender in battle, accept it and let him stay alive unless he has caused you such pain that it is sorrow to your heart. You have to wear armor often: when it comes off you it is time to wash under your eyes and about your hands, so you are clean of iron rust. Then shall you be of love's color and women's eyes notice that. Be like a man, and be of good cheer: that is good for worthy praise. And let women be dear to you: that enhances a young man's person. Never waver toward them, not a single day: there is a man of good sense. If you want to lie to them you can deceive many of them, but false deceit has only a short time of praise against true love. The prowler will lament that the dry wood in the park breaks and cracks and wakes the watchman. Many a fight breaks out on inaccessible roads and close by fences— measure this against true love. It is worthy and its sense prevails against false, deceitful artifice. If you earn its displeasure you must be dishonored and suffer shameful pain forever. You must hold these teachings close to yourself: I want to tell you more about the ways of women. Man and wife are all one, like the sun that shone today and the name that is called day. Neither can be separated from the other: they flower from one and the same seed. Observe that with understanding."

Gurnemanz further teaches Parzival how to ride and fight well. Gurnemanz also wants Parzival to marry his daughter Liaze, but to no avail. When Parzival asks for leave to depart Gurnemanz laments the loss of his three sons. The guest observed the host's sorrow since he had revealed it to him so clearly. Then he said: "My lord, I am still untested. If I ever obtain a knight's praise so that I may desire love properly, then shall you give me Liaze, your daughter, the beautiful maiden. You have lamented too much for me: if I can free you of your sorrow I shall not let you bear so much of it." The young man soon took his leave of the loyal prince and his whole household. The three the prince had thrown on the dice of sorrow had sadly grown to four: he had suffered his fourth loss.

Book Four

And so Parzival went away from there. His well shaped body displayed a knight's nature and a knight's build; alas that many an unsweet bitter thought touched him. The width of the land was too narrow for him and the breadth altogether too confining; anything green seemed faded to him, and his red armor seemed white: his heart forced his eyes to look that way. Gahmuret's nature[1] had taken his simplemindedness away from him; it would free him from thoughts of the beautiful Liaze, the young lady rich in blessings who had offered him honor as companions do, but not love. Wherever his horse wanted to turn now, he could not hold it back for sorrow, whether it wanted to jump or trot. Crosses and hedges of woven bushes avoided his way through the woods,[2] as did the imprint of wagons' tracks: he rode along many unbeaten paths where there was little in the way of roads. Valley and mountain were unknown to him.

But he did not ride astray much, since he arrived that day from Graharz in the kingdom of Brobarz, riding straight across wild high mountains all the way. The day drew close to evening when he came to fast-running water: it was loud with its own noise, the rocks gave it back and forth to each other. He rode along the water, downstream; then he found the city of Pelrapeire. King Tampenteire had left it to his daughter as her inheritance; many people are now enduring hardship because of her. The water moved as arrows do that are well feathered and well cut as the tautness of a crossbow moves them on with the whirr of its string. A drawbridge led across it; many layers of woven wicker lay on it: the river flowed straight into the sea there. Pelrapeire stood well defended. Children ride on swings when we do not want to keep them from doing so. That bridge also swung, but without a rope, and it was not as happy in its youth.[3]

On the other side stood sixty knights or more with their helmets tied on. They all shouted: "Go back, go back." These weaklings wanted combat, with their swords held high. They thought he was Clamide, whom they had often seen before, since he rode so regally up to the bridge on the wide field. When they shouted at the young man with great noise, his horse avoided the bridge out of fear, no matter how he cut it with his spurs. He from whom true cowardice fled always, dismounted and pulled his horse on to the swaying bridge. A coward's mettle would have been all too weak if he had had to go into such combat. Moreover, he had to guard against one other thing: he was afraid the horse would fall. Then the noise on the other side abated; the knights carried their helmets, their shields, and the shining of their swords back inside and closed their gates. They were afraid of a bigger army.

So Parzival went across and rode up to a battlefield where many had chosen their death, who had lost their lives in search of a true knight's praise before the gate in front of the hall that was high and well adorned. He found a ring on the gate and touched it quickly with his hand. Nobody noticed his shouting, except a young lady of fair skin. From a window that young lady saw the knight halt, undaunted. The beautiful one rich in breeding said: "Have you come here in a hostile manner, my lord? There is no need for that. They already offer us much hatred without you, from the land and on the sea, an army angry and brave." Then he said: "My Lady, here you have a man who will serve you, if I can. Your greeting shall be my reward: I hold you in a servant's affection." *The young lady takes Parzival to the queen. On the way the defenders of the city come to greet them. They are all weak with hunger.*

Want had brought them to hunger's hardship. They had no cheese, meat, or bread, they left toothpicks aside and they did not grease any wine with their mouths when they drank.[4] Their bellies were sunken; their hips high and lean; shriveled like Hungarian leather was their skin to their ribs: hunger had chased their flesh away. They had to endure this because of want. Very little dripped on the coals for them.[5] A worthy man had forced them into this, the proud king of Brandigan: they suffered for Clamide's request. The double-handed jar or pitcher rarely spilt any mead there. A pan with cakes from Trüheding never crackled there: for them that sound was cracked. If I wanted to scold them for this I would have very little sense. For where I have often dismounted and where they call me lord, at home in my own house, a mouse is rarely overjoyed. Mice steal their food; nobody would dare to hide it from me, but I do not find it out in the open. It happens all too often to me, Wolfram von Eschenbach, that I endure such comfort.[6]

Much has been heard of my lament: now the story should come back to how Pelrapeire stood full of sorrow. The people there paid taxes on their joy. The heroes rich in loyalty lived in distress. True manliness ordered them to do so; their distress should now move you to pity: their body is now a pledge[7] unless the Highest Hand releases them from it. Now hear more about the poor people: they should move you to pity. They shamefully received their guest rich in courage. He seemed so worthy to them that he should not have desired their hospitality as things stood with them: their great misery was unknown to him. They put a carpet on the grass where a linden tree was walled around and had been made to grow in a certain direction so that it could give shade. He was of a different color than they when he had washed the iron rust off him in a well. Then he almost weakened the sun's bright radiance. He therefore seemed a worthy guest to them. They soon offered him a robe made in the same way as the coat that lay around him before: its sable gave off a wild new odor. They said: "Do you want to see the queen, our lady?" The steadfast hero said he would gladly do so. They went to the hall, to which high stairs gave access. The radiance of a lovely face, sweetness also to his eyes, a bright light shone forth from the queen before she welcomed him. *Parzival is impressed by the beauty of Queen Condwiramurs.*

Condwiramurs had to have the prize. She showed the right *bea curs,* or "beautiful body." They were noble women indeed who gave birth to the two who were together there. Then women and men did no more except look at those two sitting together. He found good friends there. The guest was thinking, I shall tell you what. "Liaze is there, Liaze is here.[8] God wants to temper my distress: now I see Liaze, the worthy child of Gurnemanz." Liaze's beauty was mere air

compared to the young woman who sat here; God had not forgotten
a single wish in her (she was the lady of the land), as the rose
prompted by the dew shows a new bright radiance from its small
bud, a radiance both white and red. That caused her guest great
hardship. His breeding as a man was now complete since the worthy
Gurnemanz had freed him from simplemindedness and advised him
against asking questions, except discreet ones. Next to the rich
queen he sat, without a single word in his mouth, now close here,
now not far there. Many know how to leave off speech who have
been among ladies more often. The queen soon thought: "I think
this man holds me in contempt because my body is without
strength. No, he does it because it is a ruse: he is the guest, I am the
hostess: the first speech should be mine. He has been looking at me
kindly since we have come to sit here: he has revealed his breeding to
me. I have saved my speech for too long: there should be no more
silence here." The queen spoke to her guest: "My Lord, a hostess
must speak. A kiss earned me your greeting; you offered your service
when you came here: a young lady of mine told me so. Guests have
not accustomed us to this: my heart has yearned for it. My Lord, I
ask of you the story of where your travels began." "My Lady, I rode
this day away from a man I left in lamentation, with loyalty un-
broken. The prince's name is Gurnemanz, he is called of Graharz. I
rode from there into this land." The worthy young lady spoke to
him as follows: "If anybody else would have told me, nobody would
agree that this could have been done in one day: my messenger
could not accomplish the journey in two days, even if he rode as fast
as he could. His sister was my mother, I mean your host's sister.[9] His
daughter's radiance may also dim with sorrow. We have lamented
many a bitter day with wet eyes, I and the young lady Liaze. If you
are fond of your host, accept sorrow as we have long endured it here,
woman and man: you shall serve him in part in this. I want to
lament our distress for you: we have to bear great hardship."

Then spoke her father's brother Kyot: "My Lady, I shall send you
twelve loaves of bread, three shoulders and three hams, and I shall
put eight cheeses with them, and two small vats of wine. My brother
shall also give you gifts tonight: there is need of them." Then said
Manpfiljot: "My Lady, I shall send you as much." Then the young
lady sat on the borderline of joy: she could not avoid great gratitude.
They took their leave and rode to their hunting lodge. The old men

lived without defense in a narrow pass on a wild high mountain; yet they had peace from the army. Their messenger came galloping back, and so the weakened people were refreshed. Food had been limited for the people of the town, except for these supplies: many were dead of hunger before the bread came to them. The queen ordered it to be shared among the weak people, and the cheese, the meat, and the wine as well; Parzival, her guest, gave this advice. Therefore hardly a slice remained for the two of them: they shared it without stooping to an argument.

The supplies were consumed also and with them was fended off the death of many a man hunger had left alive. They then guided the guest to his bed, a soft one, I am inclined to think. If the citizens had been birds used for the hunt, their crops would not have been overstuffed, as the food on the table will attest.[10] They all bore the mark of hunger, except young Parzival. He took leave to go to sleep. Were his candles made of straw tied together? No, they were much better. The young man fair of skin stepped into a rich bed, royally adorned, not as poverty would have chosen it; a carpet was spread in front of it. He asked the knights to go back; he did not let them stand there any longer.[11] Pages took off his shoes and soon he was asleep until true sorrow called him and the heart's rain from bright eyes: they soon woke the worthy hero. That came to pass as I want to tell you now. It did not go beyond the limits of womanhood. The young lady I shall tell you a little about here showed chastity with steadfastness. The hardships of war and the death of dear helpers had forced her heart to burst so that her eyes had to wake. Then went the queen, not in pursuit of such love that calls forth the name that names virgins women; she was looking for help and a friend's advice. On her was worthy clothing: a shift of white silk. What could be more combatlike than a woman coming to a man like that? The lady had also swung around her body a long robe of samite. She went where distress forced her to go. Young ladies, chambermaids, whoever was there with her, she let them sleep all over her chamber. Then she slipped softly, without any sound, into the chamber where those who took care of these things had arranged for Parzival to sleep alone. Light of candles there was before his sleeping place, bright like the day. Her path went to his bed: she knelt before him on the carpet. They both had a weak sense, he and the queen, of the love that lies together. Here the wooing was done as follows: the young lady was forsaken by joy; therefore shame forced her. Would he have taken her into the bed? Alas he did not know how. And yet it happens anyway, without knowledge. They gave assurances[12] that they would not join together the limbs that bring reconciliation. They did not really contemplate doing so.[13]

The young lady's sorrow was so great that many tears flowed from her eyes on the young Parzival. He heard the sound of her crying, so that he woke up and looked at her. Joy and sorrow came to him. The young man sat up and soon said to the queen: "Lady, am I the butt of your jokes? You should kneel before God like this. Allow yourself to sit by me here (that was his request and his desire); or lay yourself down here where I was lying, let me stay where I can." She said: "If you want to do honor to yourself and treat me with good breeding so that you do not wrestle with me, I shall lie down by you." Assurances were given; she soon nestled herself in the bed. *The queen tells Parzival she is ready to kill herself rather than to become Clamide's bride, because Clamide has killed one of Liaze's brothers. When Parzival hears Liaze's name his high spirits fall.*

He spoke to the queen: "Lady, would any man's comfort help you?" "Yes, sir, if I might be delivered from Kingrune the seneschal. His hand has felled many a knight for me in good jousting. He will be coming back here tomorrow and he thinks that his lord will be lying in my arms. You have seen my hall: nowhere has it been made so high that I would not rather fall in the moat before Clamide would have my virginity by force. In this way I intend to rebuff his boasting." He said then: "Lady, whether Kingrune is a Frenchman or a Briton, or whether he comes from any other land, you shall be defended by my hand if my body is able to accomplish the task." The night had an end and the day came. The lady got up and bowed, she did not keep her great gratitude silent. Then she slipped back quietly. Nobody was so wise that he noticed her going there, except bright-skinned Parzival. *Parzival overcomes Kingrune in combat. He will not accept Kingrune's oath of submission but* he bade him bring his oath to Gurnemanz. "No, my lord, you would be better advised to give me death. I have slain his son, I have taken the life of Schentaflur. God has given you much honor: if they say that you showed forth your power on me, that you have overcome me, success has come to you." Then spoke young Parzival: "I shall leave you another choice. Take your oath to the queen, to whom your lord has caused great pain in anger." "Then I would be lost. My body would be wasted with swords in pieces so small that they dance in the sun's rays, for I have caused pain to the heart of many a courageous man in there." "Then go from this field to the land of Britain. Bring your oath to a young lady who suffers on my account what she should not be suffering if another had been willing to recognize what is right. Tell her that whatever may happen to me, she shall never see me happy before I avenge her where I shall pierce a shield. Tell Artus and his wife from me, both of them, and the whole household too, that I am in their service and that I shall never come there again before I have freed myself of the shame I bear in common with her who offered me her laughter. Her body suffered great distress because of it. Tell her I am the knight who serves her, her subject in humble service." A consequence arose from that speech: the onlookers saw the heroes part.

Back now came Parzival, the man who comforted the burghers in battle, to where his horse had been caught. They were liberated by him later: doubt now seized the outer[14] army because Kingrune had been crushed in combat. Now Parzival was led to the queen. She gave him her embrace for all to see, she pressed him close to her body and said: "I shall never be the wife on earth of any man, except the one I have embraced." She helped to disarm him and gave her service unstinted. After his great work meager hospitality was shown. The citizens now acted to pledge their full allegiance to him, and they said he should be their lord. Then the queen also said he should be her lover since he had won such a great victory over Kingrune. Two brown sails they saw as they looked down from the ramparts: a strong wind pushed them fast into the harbor. Their keels were weighed down, and the citizens rejoiced: the ships carried nothing but food; God, who is wise, had ordered it so.

The hungry crowd rushed down from the ramparts and hurried to the ships to plunder them. They could have flown like leaves, the thin and the withered, light of flesh: their bellies were not distended with food. The queen's marshal gave the ships protection: he ordered that no one should touch them, on pain of the noose. He led the merchants before his lords in the city. Parzival ordered that their goods should be bought and paid for double the price. The merchants were pleased: their goods were paid for in this way. Fat dripped in the citizens' coals. I would like to be a soldier there now:

nobody drinks beer, they have much wine and much food. Then Parzival the pure did what I shall tell you. First he divided the food in small portions with his own hand. He seated the worthy ones he found there. He did not want to let their empty stomachs bear overmuch: he gave them their shares according to good measure. They became happy because of his advice. Closer to night he gave them more, the artless one who had no pride.

Asked about sleeping together, both he and the queen said yes. He lay with such modesty that would not satisfy many a woman now, if a man were to treat her that way. With a mind to aggravate men[15] they add evil to their good breeding and give themselves airs! In front of guests their behavior is flawless, but the will of their heart destroys what may be present in their attitude. They give their lover secret pain with their tenderness. The loyal steadfast man who always proved himself of good breeding is able to treat his lover with consideration. He thinks, as is probably true, "I have served this lady all these years for love's reward. She has offered comfort to my body: I am lying here now. Once it would have been enough for me if I could touch her dress with my bare hand. If I wanted to be greedy now disloyalty would act in my stead. Should I aggravate her, increase both our shame? Sweet stories before sleep are fitting to a woman's nature." So lay the man from Waleis: he had little fear. The man they called the red knight[16] left the queen a virgin. Yet she thought she was his wife: in the morning she covered her head according to the love of his body.[17] Then that virgin bride gave him both castles and her land because he was dear to her heart.

They were together in such a way that they were happy in love for two days. The third night he kept thinking that his mother had advised embracing; Gurnemanz had also made clear to him that man and wife were all one. They entwined arms and legs. If I have to tell you: he found the nearness sweet. The old custom and the new dwelt there between both of them. All felt good to them and not sad at all. *Clamide arrives before Pelrapeire, to continue the siege. His knights tell him about Kingrune's defeat, and his spirits begin to sink. Still, he keeps ordering fresh attacks on the city, but to no avail. In the meantime Kingrune has reached Artus's court and told all there what Parzival ordered him to. Cunneware is pleased. When he sees he is getting nowhere, Clamide challenges Parzival to knightly combat. Parzival accepts.* Either of them did not mind looking for fire in the other's helmet.[18] They were not allowed to rest; they were given work to do. The shields sprang to pieces on them as if someone had thrown feathers into the wind, as a joke. Yet Gahmuret's son was not tired anywhere in his body, not in any limb. Then Clamide thought the truce was broken from the city: he asked his fellow combatant to do honor to himself and to put an end to the throwing of so many stones.[19] Big blows fell on him: they must have felt like many stones indeed. The lord of the land answered him as follows: "I think many a stone misses you:[20] my loyalty is a pledge for that. If you had peace from my hand many a sling would not break your chest, your head or your thighs."

Tiredness rushed towards Clamide: it was too soon for him. Victories gained, victories lost were chosen there with combat. Yet King Clamide was seen in defeat now, brought low by Parzival's strength. Blood gushed out of his ears and nose: it made the green grass red. He quickly uncovered his head of helmet and coif of mail. The conquered man sat waiting for the blow. The victorious one said: "My wife may now stay free of you. Now learn what it is to die." "Oh, no, worthy hero bold. This way your honor will be shown forth threefold by me. Now that you have bowed me down, what higher praise could come to you? Condwiramurs may say that I am the unblessed one and that your luck has gain. Your country is delivered. As when a man hoses out his ship (and it becomes much lighter), my power is more shallow; a true man's joy has grown thin with me. Why would you make me die? I must give shame to all my offspring as their inheritance. You have the praise and the advantage. There is no need to do more to me. I bear a living death since I was separated from her who ever locked my heart and my senses in her power and I never enjoyed anything from her. Therefore I, unhappy man, leave her body and her land freely to you."

Then he who had victory soon thought of Gahmuret's advice, that courageous men should be prepared for mercy. And he followed the advice like this. He said to Clamide: "I do not want to set you free until you bring your oath to Liaze's father." *Like Kingrune, Clamide also refuses to bring his oath to Gurnemanz, because Kingrune has helped him to kill another of Gurnemanz's sons. Parzival also sends Clamide to Arthur, to tell Cunneware how sorry he is. Clamide and his armies move away from the city. The siege is lifted.* Those of the Round Table were in Dianazdrun with Artus the Briton. If I[21] have not lied, the field of Dianazdrun had to be inhabited by more tent poles than there are trees in Spehtesart;[22] with such a household Artus lay encamped, and with many ladies at the feast of Pentecost. You could also see many a banner and shield there, on which many special coats of arms were raised, and many well-adorned tents arranged in circles. Those things would seem extraordinary now: who could make the travel gear for so many ladies? A lady would have been quick to think that she had lost her reputation if she did not have her lover there. I would not have gone there at all (there was many a simpleton there); even now I would not gladly bring my wife into such a big crowd: I would be afraid of the jostling of people I do not know. Many a one might say to her that love of her had stung him and turned his joy to nothing, and that he would serve her early and late if she turned this grief away from him. I would be in a hurry to go away from there with her.

I have spoken about matters of my own. Now listen how Artus's circle of tents was set apart from the others. First, the household ate before him, rich with many a joy, many a worthy man without falseness and many a proud young lady for whom a joust was just like an arrow: they shot their lovers against the enemy.[23] If combat taught the knights great distress there, the ladies' mood was so disposed that they would reward them with kindness. Clamide the young man rode into the middle of the ring. Artus's wife saw his horse saddled and his body armed, his helmet and his shield battered; all the ladies saw this too. Clamide had come to court like this. You have heard before that he was forced to do so. He dismounted. He was pushed around much before he found the lady Cunneware de Lalant sitting down. Then he said: "My Lady, is it you I have to serve without hatred? Hardship forces me to do so, in part. The red knight offered you his service. He wants to take upon him all the shame that has been done to you; he also asks you to lament it before Artus. I think you must have been beaten. My Lady, I bring you my oath. So commanded he who fought with me: I give it to you gladly, if you want it. My body was forfeit to death."

The lady Cunneware of Lalant took him by his ironclad hand to where the lady Ginover sat who ate with her, without the king. Keie stood also before the table where this story became known to him. It upset him greatly: the lady Cunneware was happy because of it. Then he said: "Lady, that man, whatever he has done to you, he must have been forced to do it. But I think he must have been lied to.

I did it[24] according to courtly fashion and wanted to better you by it: that is why I have your hatred for it. Yet I want to advise you to order this captive to be disarmed: he may think the standing a little long." The proud young lady ordered Clamide's helmet and his coif of mail removed. When they pulled them off him and untied them Clamide was soon recognized. Kingrune often looked at him with knowing looks. At that moment his hands were wrung so that they began to crack like dry wood.

Clamide's seneschal immediately pushed the table away from him. He asked his lord for news; he found him empty of joy. He said: "I was born for shame. I have lost such a worthy army that a mother never offered her breast to one who knew higher loss. The death of my army does not grieve me as much as the hardship lack of love imposes on me; joy is a stranger to me, high spirits too. Condwiramurs is driving me gray. Oh, Pilate of Poncia[25] and poor Judas who was there with a kiss on the faithless errand where Jesus was betrayed. I would not refuse the hardship of their creator's revenge if the lady of Brobarz herself would be my wife in free affection so that I could embrace her, no matter what might happen to me afterwards. Alas her love is far away from the king of Iserterre. My country and my people of Brandigan must have sorrow of it for ever. My uncle's son Mabonagrin[26] lies there too in long pain. Now, King Artus, I have ridden to your house, compelled by a knight's hand. You know well that much shame has been done to you in my country: forget that now, most worthy man. Leave me free from such hatred as long as I am a captive here. The lady Cunneware should also free me from fear,[27] who received my oath when I went before her a captive." Artus's most loyal mouth forgave him his guilt at once.

Then woman and man heard that the king of Brandigan had ridden into the ring. Now push, push closer still! The story spread fast. With good breeding joyless Clamide asked for companionship: "You must deliver me to Gawan, my lady, if I am worthy of it. I know well that he desires it too. If he does your bidding he shall honor you and the red knight." Artus asked his sister's son to give the king companionship; that would have come to pass anyway. The vanquished one free of falsehood was well received by the worthy household. Kingrune said to Clamide: "Alas, that a Briton ever saw you vanquished in his house! You were richer still than Arthur in help and possessions and you had your youth with you. Should

Artus now have praise because Keie has beaten a noble princess in anger since with the knowledge of her heart she had chosen him with her laughter, who is in truth reckoned for the highest praise, without lying?[28] The Britons now think they have planted the branch of their praise on high: without their labor it was done that the king of Kukumerlant was sent back here, dead, and that my lord conceded victory to him who was seen against him in combat. The same man has vanquished me without any artful cunning. They saw fire blowing from the helmets and swords turning around in the hands."

Then they said all together, both poor and rich, that Keie had done wrong. Here we shall leave this story and come back to the main road. The ruined country where Parzival bore the crown was rebuilt: they saw joy and merriment there. His father-in-law Tampenteire left him shining stones and red gold in Pelrapeire; Parzival divided it in such a way that they held him in affection because of his generosity. With many banners and new shields was his land adorned and many tournaments were held by him and his people. He often showed courage at the border, the limits of his land, the young hero unafraid. His deeds against strangers were proved the best.

Now listen also to news from the queen. How could she ever be of better cheer? The young, sweet, worthy woman had her wish fulfilled on earth. Their love was established with such power, ungrafted by the slightest wavering. She had recognized her husband as such and each one of them had found love in the other. He was as dear to her as she was to him. When I take the story into my hands so that they must part, there grows sorrow for them both. The worthy lady grieves me too. His hand freed her people, her country, and her body from great distress; for this she offered him her love. One morning he spoke with good breeding (many a knight heard and saw it): "If you will allow me, my lady, I shall go see how things stand with my mother—with your permission. Sadly enough it is unknown to me whether she is well or not. I want to go there for a short time and also for adventure's sake. If I serve you well your worthy love shall reward me." So he wanted to take his leave. He was dear to her, as the story goes: she did not want to deny him anything. From all his vassals he parted, alone.

Book Five

Whoever wants to know where the man whom the adventure has driven away now goes will see many things of great wonder. Let Gahmuret's son ride. Wherever loyal people are now, they wish him well, since it has to be that he endures great pain, but also joy and honor. One thing hurt him much, that he was parted from her. No mouth ever read or spoke about a woman who could be better and more beautiful. Thoughts of the queen began to weaken his senses: he would have lost them altogether if he had not been such a courageous man. The horse carried the bridle on its own across tree trunks and through marshes, since no one's hand guided it. The adventure lets us know how far he rode that day: a bird would have had to work hard to have flown that distance. If the adventure has not deceived me his travels were not nearly that long on the day when he ran through Ither or when he came from Graharz into the country of Brobarz.

Do you now want to hear how things stood with him? He came to a sea that evening. Fishermen had anchored there; the water obeyed them. When they saw him riding they were so close to the shore that they heard well what he said. Parzival saw a fisherman on the ship: he had such clothes on him that they could not have been better if all countries had served him. His hat was lined and adorned with peacock feathers. Parzival began to ask that same fisherman for advice: that he might tell him in God's name and by the standards of his own good breeding where he might find lodging. The sad man replied as follows: "My lord," he said, "I do not know of any water

or land within thirty miles that is inhabited. Only one house is close
by: in all loyalty I advise you to go there: where else could you go at
this time of day? Turn to your right at the edge of the cliff. Ride on
until you come to a moat; I think you will have to stop then. Ask
them to lower the bridge and to open the roads for you." Parzival
did as the fisherman advised him to: he took his leave and rode away.
The fisherman said: "When you arrive there, as you should, I shall
take care of you myself tonight: thank me then in accordance with
the hospitality you will have received.[1] Be careful: unknown roads
go there; you may well ride the wrong way on the slopes and that I
truly do not wish on you." Parzival rode off then; he began to trot
jauntily down the straight road to the moat. The bridge was pulled
up there, the castle not outdone in walls.[2] It stood straight as if it
had been turned on a lathe. A charge would not bring anyone inside,
except if he could fly or was blown by the wind. Many towers, many
a high hall stood there with marvelous battlements. If all armies
came to besiege them, they would not give a loaf of bread[3] in thirty
years if subjected to that kind of hardship.

A page noticed him and asked him what he was looking for, or
where his journey had begun. Parzival said: "The fisherman sent me
here. I have bowed to his hand only in the hope of lodging. He asked
for the bridge to be lowered and told me to ride inside to you." "My
Lord, you shall be welcome. Since the fisherman said so they will
offer you honor and comfort for the sake of him who sent you here,"
said the page, and he let the bridge down. The brave one rode into
the castle, on a courtyard wide and broad. It was not trampled by
tournaments (short green grass stood everywhere: charges of groups
of knights were avoided there) and it was rarely ridden upon with
banners like the meadow of Abenberc.[4] The work of joy had rarely
been done there for a long time: they understood sorrow well in
their hearts, although Parzival did not grow cold towards them.[5]
Knights young and old received him. Many little pages jumped up
to get his bridle: every one of them tried to seize it before the others
could. They held his stirrup, and so he had to get down from the
horse. Knights asked him to go further: they led him to his room.
He was disarmed very fast, and in the right manner. When they saw
the young man without a beard, so lovely, they said he was rich in
blessings.

The young man asked for water; he soon washed off the rust

under his eyes and on his hands. Old and young thought another day shone from him. So sat the lovely loved one, free of all reproach. They brought a robe for him there, made of furs of Arabia; the well-shaped one put it around him with the belt open. It brought praise to him. Then said the good chamberlain: "Repanse de Schoye wore it, my lady the queen: it is to be lent to you by her, since no clothes have yet been cut for you.[6] I could ask her this with honor: you are a worthy man if I have judged you right." "May God reward you, my lord, that you say so. If you have observed me well my body has obtained happiness: God's power gives such reward." They poured for him and took care of him in this way. The sad ones were happy with him. They offered him honor and worth: they had more provisions than he had found in Pelrapeire, which his hand had delivered from sorrow. *Parzival is taken to a magnificent hall where the fisherman appears again, this time as the lord of the castle.*

The host asked to be seated by the middle fireplace on a cot. He had been cut off from joy: he lived only for dying. Into the hall walked bright-skinned Parzival, who was well received by him who had sent him there. The host did not leave him standing there long; he asked Parzival to walk up closer and to sit down: "Close beside me here. If I were to sit you far away over there, that would be treating you too much like a stranger." So spoke the host rich in sorrow. Because of his illness the host had big fires going and he wore warm clothes. Many a good knight was seated there, and they showed sorrow for themselves.[7] A page leaped in through the door. He was carrying a lance (a custom seemly for mourning): blood rose from its blade and ran down the shaft on his hand, from where it turned back at the elbow. There was crying and wailing in the wide hall: the people of thirty countries could not order their eyes to do the same. The page carried the lance in his hands along the four walls and then again back to the door. He leaped out again through it. The people's hardship was stilled, that sorrow had imposed on them before; the lance the page had brought in his hand had reminded them of it. *The banquet is described in great detail. Particular attention is paid to the various young ladies who carry in various implements. None is as beautiful as the queen.* Behind them came the queen. Her face gave off such a brightness, they all thought day was about to break. They saw the young lady wear her silk from Arabi. On a cushion of green silk she bore paradise fulfilled, both root and branch. That was a thing that was called the grail,[8] which is beyond all earthly wishing. Repanse de Schoye was the queen called, and by her the grail allowed itself to be carried. The grail was such that a woman's chastity had to be well preserved if she wanted to serve it well: she had to move away from falsehood.

In front of the grail came lights: they were not of poor cost; six glasses long, clear, well made, and in them balsam[9] that burned well. When they had come the right distance away from the door, as they should, the queen bowed with good breeding as did all the young ladies who carried the vessels of balsam. The queen devoid of falsehood set the grail down before the host. The story goes that Parzival often looked at her and thought of her who had brought the grail: he was also wearing her robe. *The ladies withdraw to another part of the hall. The banquet goes on.* Parzival noticed full well the riches and the great marvel: he shrank from asking because of his good breeding. He thought: "Gurnemanz advised me loyally and not in jest that I should not ask much. What if my being here is measured by the same standard as there with him? I would then understand how it stands with this household, without asking any question." With that thought a page who carried a sword walked up to him: its scabbard was worth a thousand marks, its hilt was a ruby and the blade might well be the cause of great wonder. The host gave it to his guest. He said: "My Lord, I carried it into the hardship of battle in many places before God wounded me in my body.[10] Enjoy it now, in case they did not take good care of you here. You may well carry it everywhere: when you have tested its nature you will be protected by it in combat."

Alas, that he did not ask then! I am still unhappy about it for his sake. For when he received the sword in his hand he was reminded by it to ask. I am also sorry for his sweet host, whom unspeakable illness does not avoid. A question would have been of good cheer to him. They had given enough there: those whose duty it was took the utensils and carried them away again. They loaded four carts there. Every lady performed her service, the first in rank now first, the youngest last. Then the most exalted tended to the grail, the host, and Parzival. The queen and all the young ladies bowed with good breeding. With the same good breeding they carried out again through the door what they had carried in before. Parzival gazed after them. Before they closed the door behind them he saw on a cot

in a chamber the most beautiful old man he had ever gained knowledge of. I may well tell you so without exaggeration: he was grayer
even than fog.

Who that man was you shall have tale of later. The host too, his
castle, his country, they will be named for you later when it is time
for them, each in their own place, without contradictions and
without dragging things out. I tell the string without the bow. The
string is an example. You may think the bow is fast, but what the
string drives on is faster. If I have told you right, the string resembles
a straight story: they seem right to people too. Whoever tells you of
what is bent wants to lead you astray. Whoever sees the bow strung
will give the string its due: it is straight except when a man wants to
pull it back to bend the bow when it has to power the arrow. But
whoever shoots his story at someone he has vexed with this aggrava-
tion (for then it has no place to stay, and a very roomy path to travel:
in one ear, out the other) would lose all his labor, as I would if I
pressed my story on him: whether I speak or sing, a goat would
understand it better, or a rotten tree trunk.[11]

I want to explain more about those people who showed such
sorrow. Where Parzival had ridden men rarely saw the merriment of
joy, be it tournament or dance: their state of lamentation was so
complete that they did not turn to joking. Where you see fewer
people a little joy does them good; all nooks were full there, and
also the hall where you could see them. The host spoke to his guest:
"I think a bed has been made for you. If you are tired, my advice is
that you go lie down to sleep." Now I should cry "alas"[12] because of
their parting even as they part: great shame will be known to them
both. Before the cot stepped well-shaped Parzival, on a spot on the
carpet. The host wished him good night. The knights all jumped up
then; some of them pushed closer to him. They soon led the young
man into a chamber. It was so well adorned with a worthy bed that
my poverty gives me grief always since the earth makes such riches
bloom.

Poverty was a stranger to that bed. A pfeffel-silk blanket in bright
colors lay on it, as if glowing in a fire. Parzival asked the knights to
go back to their rest since he did not see more beds there.[13] They
took their leave and went away. Another kind of service begins here
now. Many candles and his own color vied with each other to give
light. How could the day be brighter? Another bed stood before his,

with a quilt on it, where he sat. Many young squires, fast and not too slow jumped close to him then: they took off his shoes and leggings from his white legs. Many a wellborn squire also pulled more of his garments off him. Handsome were those young men. Afterwards four fair young ladies walked through the door; it was their task to see to it that the hero was treated well and that he was lying in comfort. As the adventure told me a page carried a candle that burned well in front of each. Parzival the fast man jumped under the cover. They said: "You must stay awake for us a while longer." He played a game with speed to the very end. No color could be called lighter than his; that began to sweeten their eyes before they received his greeting. Thoughts also brought them into hardship, because his mouth was so red and because he was so young that you could not find half a hair near it. *The ladies give Parzival something more to eat and drink, and withdraw.*

Parzival did not lie alone: harsh anguish was his companion until day came. Future suffering sent him its messengers in his sleep, so that the well-shaped young man rivaled the dream his mother had of Gahmuret. His dream was stitched for him with sword-strokes around the hem and rich with many jousts closer to the middle. He suffered great grief in his sleep from the hurtling run of horses. If he could have died thirty times he would have rather endured that while awake. As it was, suffering paid him the reward for these harsh things.

He was forced awake by grief. His veins and bones were in a sweat. The day already shone through the window. Then he said: "Alas, where are the young men that they are not here before me? Who is to hold my clothes for me?" And so the hero waited for them until he fell asleep again. Nobody spoke there, or shouted: they were altogether hidden. Around the middle of the morning the young man woke up again; the brave one sat upright soon.

The worthy hero saw his suit of armor and two swords lying on the carpet. One the host had ordered to be given to him, the other was that of [Ither of] Kahaviez. He said to himself: "Alas, why has this been done? In truth I shall arm myself with them. I suffered so much pain in my sleep that some ordeal has probably been prepared for me today when I am awake. If the host has come to hardship because of war I shall gladly answer his call, and in good faith shall I answer the call of her who lent me this new robe out of her goodness. If only she were well disposed to accept service! That would please me for her own sake, and yet not for her love, since my wife the queen is as fair of body as she is, or more so, in truth.[14] He did what he had to do: from the feet up he armed himself well; to counter every blow he girded on the two swords. The worthy hero walked out the door: there was his horse tethered to the stairs and his shield and spear leaning against them too. That was as he desired.

Before Parzival the hero got his horse under him he ran through many of the rooms to call for the people. He heard or saw no one, and uncommon suffering came to him.[15] That aroused anger in him. He ran to where he had dismounted the evening when he had come. There earth and grass had been touched by footsteps and the dew scattered altogether. Screaming, the young man ran back to his horse. With words of insult he sat on it. He found the gates standing wide open, and many tracks going out through them: he did not linger there any longer, he trotted briskly on to the bridge. A hidden page pulled the rope, so that the end of the drawbridge had almost struck the horse down. Parzival looked back, he wanted to ask more. "May the sun hate you as you ride," said the page. "You are a goose. You could have moved your mouth and you could have asked the host! You did not want to earn great praise."

The guest called for an explanation; the answer was lacking altogether. No matter how much Parzival called, the page behaved as if he was sleeping as he went and slammed the gates shut. Parting came too soon to Parzival at the time that brought him loss and to which he now pays the interest of his joy that is taken from him. The dice had been thrown for the throw of sorrow when he found the grail with his own eyes, with no hand throwing and with no dice falling and showing its eyes.[16] If sorrow spurs him on now, he was not much used to it before: he would not have longed for it at all. Parzival rode off then, following hard on the tracks he saw. He thought: "I think those who rode before me must be fighting for my host's cause today, like true men. If they accepted me I would not put their group to shame. Things would not be left undone, I would help them in the same distress so that I could earn my bread and this wondrous sword their worthy lord gave me. I carry it now unearned by any service. They may well think I am a coward."

He who withstood falsehood turned towards the tracks of the

hoofbeats. His parting gives me grief. Now for the first time the adventure shapes itself.[17] Their tracks began to grow weaker: those who rode before had gone away. The track that had been wide before became narrow. To his regret he lost it altogether. The young man heard news there from which he earned grief in his heart. The hero rich in bravery heard the voice of a woman lamenting. Things were still wet with dew. Before him against a linden tree sat a young lady to whom her loyalty had brought grief. A balsamed knight, dead, was leaning between her arms.[18] Whoever would not take pity who saw her sitting like this I would call unkind. Parzival's horse turned toward her, but he did not recognize her. And yet she was his mother's sister's child. All earthly loyalty was thin air compared to what showed forth in her. Parzival greeted her and said: "My Lady, I am very sorry for this ordeal that brings suffering to your soul. If you have any need of my service people will see me in it."

She thanked him, interrupting her lamentation, and asked him where he had come riding from. She said: "It is improbable that anyone should take it on himself to travel through this wasteland. Great harm may come here to ignorant strangers. I have heard and seen many people lose their lives here, who found death with their weapons in their hands. Go back if you want to stay alive. But tell me first, where were you last night?" "It is a mile or more from here that I never saw a castle so sumptuous with all kinds of riches. I rode away from there a short time ago." She said: "If someone is prepared to believe you, you should not deceive her willingly. You are carrying a stranger's shield. The forest may have been too much for you if you rode here from cultivated land. Within thirty miles no wood or stone was ever cut for any building, except for one castle that stands all alone: it is rich in all the earth can wish for. Whoever looks for it eagerly, alas he does not find it. Yet you see many people looking for it. Whenever a man sees the castle, that should happen without his knowledge.[19] My Lord, I think it is not known to you. It is called *Munsalvaesche*.[20] The kingdom of the castle's lord is called *Terre de Salvaesche*.[21] Old Titurel bequeathed it to his son. That worthy hero was called King Frimutel, and his hand gathered great praise. He lay dead in a joust when love ordered him to be there. The same man left four worthy children behind. In spite of their riches three are caught in lamentation. The fourth one suffers from poverty, which he chose before God on account of his sins. That same man is called Trevrizent. Anfortas, his brother, leans: he can neither ride nor walk, lie nor stand. He is the lord of Munsalvaesche. God's punishment does not miss him." She said: "My Lord, if you had come to that lamentable company, the host would have been freed from much suffering he has endured for so long." The man from Waleis said to the young lady: "I saw great wonder there, and many well shaped ladies." By the voice she recognized the man.[22]

Then she said: "You are Parzival. Now say it, did you see the grail and the host devoid of joy? Let me hear pleasant news. If his torment has been turned away, how fortunate you are in that journey of salvation! You will tower over everything the air encompasses: wild and tame alike shall serve you, riches and power shall reach their outer limits for you." Parzival the hero said: "How did you recognize me?" She said: "Because I am the young lady who lamented her sorrow to you before, and who told you your name. You must not be ashamed of our kinship: your mother is my mother's sister. A flower of womanly chastity she is, purified without dew. May God reward you because you felt such sorrow then for my friend, who lay dead in the joust for me. I have him here. Now taste the grief God has given me for his sake: that he should not live any longer. He did all the good a man can do. His death was heavy on me then, and since I have known new and stronger lamentation from day to day." "Alas, where did your red mouth go? Is it you, Sigune, who told me who I was, without a lie? Your head is shorn of your wavy, long brown hair. I saw you very lovely in the forest of Prizljan, even though you were rich in lament. You have lost color and strength. Your grim company would annoy me if I were to have it: let us bury this dead man."

Then her eyes wet her gown. And the lady Lunete's advice had never been with her.[23] That lady advised her mistress: "Let this man live, who slew yours: he may compensate you enough." Sigune did not desire compensation, as women do whom you observe in fickleness—many whom I want to leave unmentioned. Listen how more is told about Sigune's loyalty, who said: "Of all that could bring me joy, only one thing would: that his slow death would leave the man of many sorrows.[24] If you left there as one who helped, your person is worthy of praise indeed. You also carry his sword girded around you: if you know that sword's magic power you may engage in combat without fear. Its edge is made just right: Trebuchet's hand made it. He belonged to a noble lineage. A spring stands by Karnant, and the king is called Lac after it. The sword can stand one blow only, with the second it falls to pieces altogether: if you want to bring it there again it will become whole through the water's flow.[25] You must have the original spring, under the rock, before day has shone on it. That same spring is called Lac. If the pieces are not scattered, and if somebody puts them together well, the sword's edge and its grooves will be whole and stronger still as soon as the spring wets them and the markings will not lose their shine. The sword also needs a word of blessing: I fear you left it behind there. But once your mouth has learned it, the power of salvation will grow and bring fruit for you forever. My dear nephew, believe me, whatever you found of wonders there must serve your hand: you may also freely wear the crown of eternal salvation high above the worthy. Your wishes on earth shall be granted to you in full: nobody is so rich that he could have wealth greater than yours if you treated the question right."[26]

He said: "I did not ask anything." "Alas that my eyes see you," said the lady of lamentation, "since you were without courage to ask! You did see such great wonders (that asking should have failed you then!); you were close to the grail, to many women free of falsehood, the worthy Garschiloye and Repanse de Schoye, to the silver that cuts, and to the bloody spear. Alas, why do you come to me here? Dishonored creature, accursed man! You must have had the poisonous wolf's tooth that the gall of falsehood should have taken such strong root in you so soon. Your host should have moved you to pity, by whom God did such wonders, and you should have asked about his grief. You are alive, and dead to salvation." Then he said: "Dear niece of mine, show a better disposition toward me. I shall atone for what I may have done." "You shall be spared atonement," said the young lady. "I know well that a knight's honor and a knight's praise vanished from you in Munsalvaesche. You shall now find no more answers in me, in any way." And so Parzival parted from her.

The hero rich in valor regretted bitterly that he had been so slow to ask when he had been sitting next to the sad host. Because of his lamentation and because the day was so hot, sweat began to make him wet. To get some air he untied his helmet and carried it in his hand. He untied his visor: his radiance was bright through the rust of the iron. He came unto a new track, for before him there went a horse that was well shod, together with a horse unshod that had to carry a woman, whom he saw. He happened to be riding behind her. Her horse had been sold to sorrow: you could have counted each one of its ribs through its skin. *The wretched horse is described in more detail, as is the near naked woman riding on it.* When Parzival spoke a greeting to her she looked at him with recognition. He was the most handsome in all the land, and therefore she had suddenly recognized him. She said: "I have seen you once before. Suffering has come to me from it, but may God always give you more joy and honor than you have deserved on my account. Because of that my dress is now poorer than when you last saw it. If you had not come near me at that time I would now have honor without any doubt." He said: "Lady, observe better at whom you direct your hatred. Never has shame come to you or any other woman on my account (I would have dishonored myself if it had), since I first acquired the shield and learned the ways of knights. But I grieve for your sorrow otherwise." The lady rode on, weeping, so that she watered her breasts. They stood white and high and round as if they had been turned on a lathe: there never was a turner so skillful that he could have turned them better. The lady sat there so lovely that Parzival had to pity her. She began to cover herself with her hands and her arms before Parzival the hero.

Then he said: "Lady, in God's name take my fur cape as a token of my service, true and without mockery." "My Lord, if it were beyond doubt that all my joy rode on it, I still would not dare to lay hands on it. If you want to save us both from death, ride until I am far from you. And yet I would little regret my death, except that I am afraid you may come to grief." "My Lady, who would take our life away? God's power has given it to us, and even if a whole army wanted it you would see me fighting for us." She said: "A worthy hero wants it. He is so determined on combat that six of you would be in great travail. I am sorry about your riding with me. I once was his wife; now my withered body could not even be the hero's servant: so obvious is his anger against me." Then he said to the woman: "Who is here with your husband? For if I would now flee on your advice, that could easily seem a crime to you. When I learn to flee I would just as well die." Then said the naked duchess: "He has nobody here except me, but that is cold comfort for victory in battle." Nothing except the knots and the hem were whole in the lady's dress, but she wore womanly chastity, the crown of praise, in her poverty. She lived so much for true goodness that falsehood had vanished from her. Parzival tied the visor before him: he wanted to carry it into battle. He adjusted his helmet with its straps so that he could see comfortably. In the meantime his horse bent its head towards the lady's horse and did not neglect to neigh. He who rode there in front of Parzival and the naked lady heard it and wanted to see who was riding with his wife. *Parzival and Orilus, Jeschute's husband, engage in combat. They fight for a long time because* I shall explain the one knight's anger to you: his highborn wife had been violated once, and yet he was her true protector, and she was to look to him for refuge. He thought her woman's sense had turned away from him and that she had dishonored her chastity and her renown with another lover. He took the shame to heart. His judgment on her was such that no woman could have suffered more hardship, except for death, and all without any guilt on her part. He could have withheld his favor from her whenever he wanted to, nobody would have gone against that since a man has power over his wife.[27] Parzival the bold hero wanted to restore Orilus's favor to the lady Jeschute by means of the sword. I have often heard people ask for this in a friendly manner, but here they were far removed from the ways of flattery. It seems to me they are both right. If He Who created both the crooked and the straight is able to decide, let Him arrange matters for both of them in such a way that the combat may come to an end without anyone dying. They are hurting each other enough even so. *Parzival eventually succeeds in unhorsing Orilus. When Orilus still refuses to surrender* Parzival the worthy hero pressed him against himself until a rain of blood spurted through his visor. Then the prince was suddenly forced to grant what was asked of him. He did it as one who was unwilling to die. He spoke to Parzival: "Alas, brave strong man, where did I ever deserve this hardship, that I should lie dead before you?" "I shall very gladly let you live," said Parzival, "if you will honor this lady." "I cannot do that: her guilt toward me is too horrible. She was rich in honor, but she destroyed it altogether and sank me into grief. I shall do anything else you want if you grant me life. I held it once from God, now your hand is the messenger of the word[28] and I shall owe it to your praiseworthy deed." So spoke the wise prince: "I shall buy my life at a good price. My brother, who is rich, wears the crown in two countries, as a mighty ruler; you can take the one you want if you do not strike me dead. I am dear to him, he will ransom me according to the conditions I negotiate with you. In addition I shall take my duchy as a fief from you. Your praiseworthy fame has won honor in combat with me. Absolve me now, brave hero bold, of reconciliation with this woman and impose upon me anything else that may bring honor to you. I cannot enter into reconciliation with the dishonored duchess, no matter what else may happen to me."

Parzival the high-minded said: "People, land, or movable riches, none of those can help you if you do not give me this assurance: that you will travel to Britain and no longer delay the journey to a young lady whom a man struck on my account; my judgment against him will not be lifted without her intercession. You shall pledge your allegiance to that highborn young lady and tell her that I am at her service, or else you shall be struck dead here. Tell Artus and his wife, both of them, that I am at their service and that they should reward my service by making amends for the blows.²⁹ In addition I want to see this lady in your favor with true reconciliation, without deceit, or else you must ride from here dead on a bier if you want to deny me this. Mark my words and be wise enough to do these deeds: give me your assurance of it here." Duke Orilus then spoke to king Parzival as follows: "If nobody can give anything except what you want, I'll do so, because I still want to live." For fear of her husband the lady Jeschute, the well shaped, had hesitated to separate those in combat. She lamented her enemy's hardship. Parzival let Orilus get up after he had promised reconciliation with the lady Jeschute. The vanquished prince said: "My Lady, since it happened on your account, this dishonorable defeat of mine in combat, come here, you shall be kissed. I have lost much honor through you; what of it? It is in the past now." The lady with her naked skin was very quick to jump from her horse on the grass. Even though the blood from his nose had made his mouth red she kissed him as he had ordered her to.

There was no more waiting there: both of them and the lady rode to a hermit's dwelling hacked out from the wall of a rock. Parzival found a reliquary³⁰ there, and also a painted spear leaning against the wall. The hermit was called Trevrizent. Parzival acted in good faith: he took the reliquary and swore an oath on it. In so doing he repeated his own oath after himself.[31] He said: "Upon my knight's honor, whether I have it or not, whoever sees me with my shield will judge me according to the ideals of knighthood. As befits its order[32] the power of this name has often hunted down high praise; the calling of the shield tells us so, and it is an exalted name still. May my body ever be bowed to the shame of this world and may all my praise be spoiled. Let the pledge of these words indeed be my salvation before the Hand of the Most High, which, I believe, God bears. Now let me suffer scorn to my detriment in both lives,[33] for ever, as inflicted by His power, if I have done this lady wrong when I happened to snatch her brooch from her. And I took more gold away with me then. I was a fool and not a man, not grown into my wits. Her body suffered much, much crying and the sweat of anguish. She is truly an innocent woman. I do not exempt anything more from this statement.[34] Let my salvation and my honor be the pledge for this. If you also think she must be innocent, take this, give her back her ring. Her brooch was given away; you have my stupidity to thank for that."

The good hero Orilus received the gift. Then he wiped the blood from his mouth and kissed his heart's true love. Her naked skin was also covered. Orilus the famous prince slid the ring back on her hand and gave her his fur cape: it was made of rich skins, wide, and hacked to pieces by a hero's hand. I have rarely seen women wearing a warrior's dress so cut to strips in combat. No tournament was assembled by her battle cry, nor was ever a spear broken in two where such a tournament had to take place.

But then Prince Orilus spoke to Parzival as follows: "My Hero, your unforced oath gives me great happiness and little suffering. I have suffered shameful defeat, which has given me joy. May my body now make honorable amends to this worthy woman I cast out of my favor. Since I had left the sweet one alone, what could she do against what happened to her? But when she spoke of your beauty I thought there was a friendship there. May God reward you now, she is free of falsehood. I have done base things to her. I had ridden to the forest of Prizljan then, where the young saplings are." Parzival took the spear from Troys and carried it away with him. The wild Taurian, Todine's brother[35] had forgotten it there. Now tell me how or where shall our heroes be at night? Their helmets and their shields had suffered: you could see they were hacked to pieces. Parzival took his leave from the lady and from her lover. Then the wise Prince Orilus invited Parzival to stay with him by his fire: to no avail, no matter how much he begged. The heroes parted there. The adventure tells me that Orilus the famous prince came to where he found his tent and a part of his retinue. The people were altogether overjoyed that reconciliation had obviously taken place between him and the duchess, the bearer of happiness.

There was no more delay then: Orilus was disarmed and he washed the blood and the rust off him. He took the lovely duchess, led her to the place of reconciliation, and ordered two baths prepared for them. There lay the lady Jeschute crying next to her beloved, for love and not for suffering, as still happens to good women. It is also known to many people that eyes that weep are set above a sweet mouth. I want to speak some more of this. Great love leads to joy and suffering both. If a man were to put the things of love on the scales as if he wanted to weigh them, they could not alternate in any other way. And so reconciliation took place, I believe. They went to take their separate baths. You could see twelve fair young ladies with her. They had cared for her ever since she had incurred her dear husband's wrath without her fault. She had had a cover at night, no matter how bare she had ridden during the day. They then bathed her with joy. Would you now like to hear how Orilus came to know the story of Artus's travels?

A knight began to tell him: "I saw a thousand tents or more pitched on a plain. Artus, the rich high king, the lord of Britain is encamped not far from us here—a mile's riding through rough country—together with a group of lovely ladies. There is also a great number of boisterous knights. They are encamped down by the Plimizoel, on both banks." Then Duke Orilus stepped out of his bath. This is what Jeschute and he did: the soft, sweet, well shaped one also stepped out of her bath soon and came to his bed. There came deliverance from sorrow. Her limbs earned better clothing than she had worn for a long time. In close embrace their love—the princess's and the wise prince's alike—acquired the prize of joy. Young ladies quickly dressed their lady. His armor was brought there for the man. You should praise Jeschute's dress. Birds caught in snares they ate with joy. As they sat on their bed the lady Jeschute received many a kiss. Orilus gave them to her.

Jeschute's dress is described in some detail, as is Orilus's armor. They ride off to Artus. In Artus's camp Orilus immediately looks for Cunneware de Lalant. She recognizes his coat of arms and concludes that he must be one of her brothers, either Lehelin or Orilus.

The prince knelt before the young lady. He said: "You spoke the truth: it is I, your brother Orilus. The red knight forced me to give you assurance. I bought my life with that promise. Accept my assurance: then all shall be done here as I promised him." She received assurance in her white hand from him who wore the dragon,[36] and set him free. When that had happened he stood up and said: "I shall and must lament out of my loyalty for you. Alas, who has struck you? The blows you received bring no happiness to me. When the time comes that I should avenge them I shall show whoever wants to look that great suffering has come to me on their account. The bravest man a mother ever brought into the world also helps me in my lament: he calls himself the red knight. My Lord King, My Lady Queen, he sends you this message: he offers his service to both of you together, and in addition also to my sister. He asks that you should reward his service by making amends to this young lady for the blows she has received. I would also have benefited in my combat against the fearless hero if he had known how close she stands to me and how her suffering touches my heart."

Keie then earned new hatred from knights and ladies, whoever was sitting there on the banks of the Plimizoel. Gawan and Jofreit, the son of Idoel, and him whose hardship you have heard of before, the captive king Clamide, and many another worthy man (I can mention their names, except that I do not want to make this too long), began to press closer. Their service was accepted with good breeding. The lady Jeschute was taken down from her horse, where she sat. King Artus did not forget, nor did the queen his wife: they received Jeschute well. Many a kiss was given by ladies there. Artus said to Jeschute: "I came to know your father Lacken, the king of Karmant, so well that I lamented your sorrow from the moment they first told me of it. And you yourself are so well shaped your friend should have spared you that, for the radiance of your loveliness won the prize at Kanadic. Because of your glorious beauty the hawk remained yours, and he rode away on your hand. Even though Orilus did me wrong I did not wish this sorrow on you, nor shall I wish on you whatever may happen. I am happy that you have his favor now and that you are wearing a woman's clothes after your great hardship." She said: "My Lord, may God reward you for this: you increase your fame by it." The lady Cunneware de Lalant led Jeschute and her lover away from there at once. To one side and outside the king's circle, above a spring stood her tent on the plain. It was as if a dragon above had half of the apple-shaped tent in his claws. Four ropes pulled the dragon, just as if he had been flying there alive and well, and as if he had been drawing the tent up into the sky. Orilus recognized it by this, since his own coat of armor was the same. He was disarmed. His sister knew how to offer him honor and comfort. Everywhere the retinue said that the red knight's valor had taken fame as his companion.

They said so without whispering. Keie asked Kingrune to serve Orilus in his stead. He knew how, the man he asked,[37] since he had often done it for Clamide in Brandigan. Keie abandoned his service because his evil star had ordered him to give the prince's sister too much of a hiding with his staff. Out of good breeding he withdrew from service. Also, his guilt was not forgotten by the highborn young lady. But Kingrune made enough food there; he carried it before Orilus. Cunneware, wise to what earns praise, cut his food for her brother with her white, soft hands. The lady Jeschute of Karnant ate like a woman of good breeding. Artus the king did not forget to come to where those two were sitting, eating lovingly. Then he said: "If it goes badly with you here, that was not my will. You never sat over a host's bread who offered it to you with a better will and so completely without fear of treachery. My Lady Cunneware, you must care well for your brother here. May God's blessing give you a good night." Artus went to sleep then. Orilus was bedded so that his wife Jeschute treated him to her company until the next day.

Book Six

D o you want to hear now how Artus parted from his home in Karidol, and also from his country, as his household advised him to? He rode with the worthy of his country and of other lands, as the story says, for eight days in search of him who called himself the red knight and who had brought him such honor in that he had freed him of great care when he ran through king Ither, and also when he sent Clamide and Kingrune, each separately, to the Britons and to his court. He wanted to invite him to join the Round Table.

Artus orders his knights not to enter into any jousts without his express permission, but he pledges to help them should the need arise.[1] You have heard that pledge well. Would you now like to hear where Parzival of Waleis had gone to? A fresh coat of snow had fallen thick on him at night. And yet it was not time for snow if things are as I have been told. Artus is a man who belongs to May: whenever he was talked about it happened on Pentecost or in the flower time of May.[2] The sweet air they give him all the time! The story here is cut from different pieces of cloth,[3] it agrees well with snow and its ways. *Artus's falconers lose their best falcon.*

He stayed that night near Parzival because the forest was unknown to both of them and they both were badly frozen there. When Parzival saw the day, the path he had been following was snowed under. He rode away from there through much rough terrain, over fallen tree trunks and many a stone. The day began to shine brighter and brighter, and the forest began to grow thinner as well, to the point where a tree trunk had been felled on a plain. He slowly rode toward it. Artus's falcon kept him company all the time. At least a thousand geese were there, and there arose a great cackling. The falcon threw himself among them and struck one of them so that she could hardly break away from him under the branches of the fallen tree trunk. Flying high had become pain to her now. From her wounds three drops of red blood fell on the snow. They brought grief to Parzival. That happened because of his true love. When he saw the drops of blood on the snow (which was all white), he thought: "Who has used his skill on this pure color? Condwiramurs, this color may indeed liken itself to you. God must want to make me rich with happiness since I found something here that is like you. Honored be the Hand of God and all His creatures. Condwiramurs, here lies your image: the snow has offered the blood its whiteness and it makes the snow red like this. Condwiramurs, your beautiful body likens itself to this, and you cannot deny it." As things had come to pass there, the hero's eyes measured two tears for her cheeks, the third one for her chin. He showed true love toward her without wavering. And so he began to lose himself in thought until he stayed there without his senses: mighty love wielded her power over him there. Such grief did his wife bring to him. The queen of Pelrapeire showed that same color on her own skin. She robbed him of his conscious mind.

Parzival stays in a trance. One of Cunneware's squires discovers him, on the way back from an errand. The squire wakes up the whole camp, shouting that the Round Table has been disgraced by the undetected presence, so near, of a knight in arms. Great noise arose among the knights: they began to ask everywhere if knightly combat had taken place. Then they heard that a single man kept himself ready for combat. Many now regretted the promise[4] Artus had received from them. Segramors, who was always spoiling for a fight, did not really walk, but ran and jumped at once. Whenever that one thought he had found a fight they had to tie him down or he wanted to be in the middle of it. Nowhere is the Rhine so wide that when he saw fighting on the other shore he did little to try the water first, whether it was warm or cold: he just jumped into it, the hero bold.[5] Quickly the young man came to the court in Artus's circle.[6] The worthy king was sound asleep. Segramors ran through the tent ropes and pushed his way in through the entrance of the tent. A sable cover he pulled off those who lay there and were in sweet sleep, so that they had to wake up and laugh about his boorish behavior. Then he said to his aunt: "Ginover, my lady Queen, our kinship is known; they know in many lands that I can count on your favor. Now help me, Lady, and speak to Artus, your husband, so that I may get permission from him (an adventure is close by) to be the first at the joust."

Artus said to Segramors: "Your assurance told me that you would act according to my will and renounce your stupidity. If you ride a joust here, many another man will want me to let him ride and to fight for praise also. My defenses will be weakened by this. We are approaching Anfortas's army that comes out of Munsalvaesche to defend the forest in battle. Since we do not know where it stands we could easily come to grief." Ginover implored Artus in such a way that Segramors became very happy when she got him his adventure. All good things happened to him there, except for his dying for joy.[7] On that occasion the proud young man without a beard would not have relinquished his share in his coming praise to anyone else. His horse and he were armed, and out rode King Segramors, galloping through the young forest. His horse jumped over tall underbrush. Many a golden bell sounded, on its gear and on the man. They could have thrown him into the thornbushes together with a pheasant.[8] If anyone had been in a hurry to look for him, he would have found him by his bells: they knew how to jingle loudly. So rode the unintelligent hero to him who had been conquered by love. He did not strike nor stab before he had uttered his challenge to him. Parzival stayed there, lost to his senses. The marks of the blood did that to him and also that harsh love that often takes my senses away and touches my heart without softness. Oh, a woman is setting hardship on me: if she wants to conquer me like this and never come to my aid I shall declare it's all her fault and flee from her comfort. Now hear also of both of these, their coming together and their parting.

Segramors spoke as follows: "You act, My Lord, as if you were pleased that a king and his people are camped here. No matter how little weight this has for you, you must repay him for this or I shall lose my life. You have ridden too close, looking for combat.[9] Yet I want to ask you, as good breeding requires, to surrender yourself to me; or else you shall soon be paid by me in such a way that your falling will disturb the snow. Then you would wish you had done the former with honor." Parzival did not speak in spite of the threat: Lady Love spoke of other cares to him. To get ready for the joust the valorous Segramors turned his horse away from Parzival. The Castillian on which Parzival the well shaped sat without his senses also turned around, so that Parzival looked away from the blood. His sight was turned away from it, and so his fame was increased. When he no longer saw the drops, lady Reason spoke sense to him again. Here came King Segramors. Parzival began to lower the spear from Troys, firm and tough, with his hand—the spear with beautiful colors he had found in front of the hermit's dwelling. He received a blow from the spear through his shield. His own blow in its turn was aimed in such a way that Segramors the worthy hero had to leave his saddle and that the spear that had taught him falling was still there and whole. Parzival rode without asking questions to where the drops of blood lay.[10] When he found them with his eyes Lady Love bound him with her bond. He spoke neither this nor that when he took leave of his senses.

Segramor's horse runs back to its stable, and Segramor follows, on foot. Back in the camp he is not terribly depressed by his defeat. Keie then asks for Artus's permission to fight Parzival. The permission is granted and Keie arms himself. Lady Love, why do you act like this, to make the sad one happy with a joy that does not last long? You make him almost waste away. What does it look like to you, Lady Love,[11] that you make manly minds and heartfelt high spirits come to shameful defeat? You have quickly overcome both the worthy and the worthy of contempt, and anything on earth that enters into any kind of combat with you. We must admit that your powers exist, in full truth without falsehood. Lady Love, you have one thing that brings you honor, and not much else besides. Lady Lovely keeps you company, otherwise your power would be full of holes. Lady Love, you show faithlessness in old ways always new. You take many a woman's good name away and advise her to take lovers among her own kin. Many a lord has done his vassal wrong on account of your power, many a friend his companion (your manner has a way of making itself known), and many a vassal his lord. Lady Love, it should grieve you that you addict the body to desire, which makes the soul harm itself. Lady Love, since you have the power to make the young old, even where one counts only very short years, your works are ambush and deceit.

These words would not be fitting for any man who had ever received comfort from you.[12] If you had helped me more, my praise for you would not be so slow. You have earmarked loss for me and you have treated my eyes so badly (and also those on my dice) that I cannot trust you. The weight of my grief was always that of many light trifles to you. But you are too wellborn for me that my weak anger would ever bring a word of accusation against you. Your thrust has such a sharp point and you weigh down the heart with a heavy burden. My lord Henric van Veldeke has measured the tree of his poetry against your nature with great artistry. If he had only taught us more of how people should keep you! He has cut[13] off the piece on how to win you. Many a fool's high find must go bad with stupidity. If that was, or will be known to me, I blame you for it, Lady Love: you are a lock around the senses. No shield or sword helps against you, no fast horse, and no high castle with worthy towers: you are powerful beyond all defenses. What can escape the fight with you, on land or on sea, whether it swims or flies? Lady Love, you also used your power when Parzival the hero bold took leave of his senses on your account, as his true love advised him. The worthy, sweet, radiant lady, the queen of Pelrapeire, sent you as a messenger to his body. You also took the life of Kardeiz, the son of Tampenteire, her brother. If people have to pay you such tribute I am pleased that I have nothing from you, unless you were to leave me something a bit softer. I have spoken the words of all of us.[14] Now listen also to what happened there.

Parzival beats Keie in the same absentminded manner. He then goes back to his trancelike state. His true love taught Parzival, who makes falsehood disappear, to find the three drops of snowy blood that set him free of his senses. Both his thoughts about the grail and the image in the queen's likeness were a major hardship. The weight of love was heavy on him. Sadness and love break tough minds. Can this be adventure? They may both be called pain. Valorous people should lament Keie's grief. His manliness commanded him to go bravely into many a combat. They say in many lands, far and wide, that Keie, Artus's seneschal, was a boorish man without breeding. My story absolves him of this: he was a companion of honor.[15] No matter how small the following I have, Keie was a true and brave man: that say I with my own mouth. I shall tell more about him still. Artus's court was a destination where many strangers came, both the worthy and those worthy of contempt. Those of cunning manners, who were used to deceiving people, were of small weight to Keie. But he knew how to honor those who had courtesy about them and were worthy company, and he would direct his service toward them. I tell this story about him: he was a keen observer. He showed a very rough disposition in the protection of his lord: deceitful and false people he separated from the worthy. He was a sharp hailstorm to their behavior, sharper even than the bee's sting. Look, these people have undermined Keie's reputation.[16] He was wise in manly loyalty; he earned much hatred from them. My lord Herman von Düringen,[17] many of those I observed belonging to your court had better be outside of it. You could also use a Keie, since true generosity brought you such a variegated following, some a band worthy of contempt and some a worthy group. That is why my lord Walther[18] has to sing "Good Morning, Good and Bad." Where they sing such a song the false are honored.

Gawan visits the fallen Keie and laments his fate. He then sets out to look for Parzival, unarmed. When he finds Parzival: The son of King Lot said: "My Lord, you want to do combat since you refuse to greet me. But I am not so devoid of courage that I should not bring up another question.[19] You have dishonored man, and kin, and the king himself, and you have increased our dishonor here. If you want to live according to my advice, if you want to give me your company to go before the king, I could earn you the favor of the king's pardoning your offense." Threats and pleas were thin air to King Gahmuret's son. The highest praise of the Round Table, Gawan, was wise to all such hardship: he had experienced it in a harsh manner when he stabbed through his hand with a knife. The power of love had forced him to do this, and the company of a worthy lady.[20] A queen had kept him from death when the brave Lehelin[21] vanquished him so completely with a magnificent joust. The soft and sweet one, fair of skin, set her head as a pledge there, Queen Inguse of Bahtarliez was the loyal lady's name.[22] Then my lord Gawan thought: "What if love has conquered this man as it did conquer me then, and his thoughts of true love have to yield love its victory?" He observed the way the man from Waleis looked, what his eyes focused on. Then he threw a scarf of faille from Syria, lined with yellow silk over the drops of blood.

When the faille had become a roof for the drops of blood, so that

Parzival did not see them, the queen of Pelrapeire gave him back his senses here, but she kept his heart there. Now please listen to his words. He said: "Alas, my lady and my wife, who has taken your body away from me? Did my hand not acquire your worthy love, crown, and land in a true knight's manner? Am I the one who freed you from Clamide? I found oh and woe there, and many a courageous heart sighing when I came to your assistance. A mist before my eyes has taken you away from me here, in bright sunlight, I don't know how." He said: "Alas, where did my spear go that I brought here with me?" Then my lord Gawan said to him: "My Lord, it was wasted in the joust." "Against whom?" asked the worthy hero. "You do not have a shield here, or a sword: what kind of praise could I earn from you? But I must bear your mockery; maybe you will be friendlier to me after this. Whenever I have jousted I sat firmly in my saddle.[23] If I do not find combat with you, the lands are so wide I can get praise and handwork there, and endure both joy and fear."

My lord Gawan then said: "What was done here to you with words was done without falsehood and in friendship, and not rich in deceit. I ask what I shall earn by my service. A king is encamped here, and many knights, and many a lady fair of skin. I shall bear you company there if you let me ride with you. I shall protect you there from all combat." "My thanks to you, My Lord: you speak well. I gladly offer you my service for that. Since you offer me company, who is your lord and who are you?" "I call lord a man of whom I hold much good. A part of it I shall name here. He always was of such disposition toward me that he treated me as a knight. King Lot has his sister in marriage. She brought me into the world. All that was in God's thoughts for he is pledged to service in His Hand.[24] He is called King Artus. My name is also not hidden, not kept secret in many places: people who know me call me Gawan. My person and my name are at your service, if you want to keep shame away from me."

Then said Parzival: "Is it you, Gawan? What weak praise do I have of it that you are such a friend to me here! I have heard people say about you always that you are a friend to all men. I should like to receive your service after all, if only I can repay you with my own. Now tell me, whose are those tents, many of which are pitched there? If Artus is encamped there I must lament that I cannot see him with my honor safe, nor the queen. First I must avenge a beating that has made me ride in sorrow ever since. This is how it happened: a worthy young lady offered her laughter to me. The seneschal beat her on my account until the twigs fell off her." "That has been avenged," said Gawan, "and none too gently: his right arm and his left leg have been broken.[25] Ride over here, look at the horse and at the stone. Splinters are also lying here in the snow, of the spear you asked about before." When Parzival saw the truth he asked more and said: "I leave it to your judgment, Gawan, if that was the same man who set insult as the goal of my travels. I shall ride with you wherever you want." "I do not want to practice lying on you," said Gawan. "Segramors was thrown on the ground here after the joust, a hero in combat, whose deeds were always chosen for praise. You did it before Keie was felled: you have earned praise from them both."

They rode with each other then, the man from Waleis and Gawan. Many people on horseback and on foot offered them worthy greetings there, to Gawan and to the red knight, because their breeding ordered them to do so. Gawan went where he found his tent. The lady Cunneware de Lalant's tent ropes came close to his. She was happy; with great joy the young lady received her knight who had avenged her for all that had ever been done to her by Keie. She took her brother and the lady Jeschute of Karnant by the hand; that is how Parzival saw them coming. His skin shone through the marks of iron rust as if dewy roses had flown there. His armor had been removed. He jumped up when he saw the ladies. Now hear how Cunneware spoke.

"To God first, and then to me be welcome since you have remained a man in deed. I had avoided laughter altogether until my heart recognized you when Keie took my joy away from me, who beat me so, then. You have avenged that enough. I would kiss you if I were worth kissing." "That I would have desired at once today," said Parzival, "if I had dared to do so, for I am very pleased with your welcome." She kissed him and made him sit down again. She sent a young lady back to her tent and told her to bring rich clothes. *Parzival is dressed in the new clothes Cunneware gives him. After mass Artus and the knights of the Round Table come to greet Parzival and to ask him to join them. Parzival agrees and a banquet is held. During the banquet queen Ginover forgives Parzival for the killing of Ither. All those at the banquet are very impressed with Parzival's beauty and bearing.*

Men and women loved him, and so he was treated with dignity until the end that brought sighs. Here came of whom I want to speak, a young lady rightly praised for her loyalty, even though she had lost her breeding. Her story did many people harm. Now listen how the young lady rode. A mule tall like a Castilian, colorless and yet done up in the following manner: it had its nostrils slit and it was branded;[26] it could be taken for a Hungarian mare. Her bridle and her harness had been made with good work, expensive and rich. Her mule stepped in full gear. She did not have the looks of a woman. Alas, why did she have to come there? And yet she came: so it had to be. To Artus's army she brought pain. The young lady's knowledge allowed her to speak almost all languages: Latin, Heathen,[27] French. She was well-bred in knowledge (dialectics and geometry), and she was also privy to the art of astronomy. She was called Cundrie, sorceress (*la surziere*) was her nickname, not lame of mouth, since it spoke well enough for her. She struck down much high joy.

In appearance the young lady rich in knowledge was unlike those they call people of beauty. The destroyer of joy had put on a bride cloth from Ghent, bluer still than lapis lazuli. That was a cape well cut in the French style. Under it good pfeffel-silk was on her body. A London hat with peacock feathers lined with cloth of gold (the hat was new, the ribbon not old) was hanging on her back. Her story was a bridge: it carried sorrow across joy. She robbed them of joy altogether. A braid swung above the hat, down from her to the mule, so long was it, and black, hard, and not too shiny, soft as the hair on a pig's back. She had the nose of a dog. Two boar's teeth protruded out of her mouth, a hand's-breadth long. Each eyebrow, braided, pushed itself up to the ribbon that held her hair. I lost my breeding because of the truth, since I have to speak of women like this. No other woman can say that of me.[28]

Cundrie showed the ears of a bear. Her face was rough to look at, not fashioned after the desire of a friend's love. She was carrying a whip in her hand: its thongs were of silk and its handle was a ruby. The hands of this charming and faithful lover showed the color of a monkey's skin.[29] The nails were not clean at all: as the adventure tells me, they stuck out like a lion's claws. Seldom had a joust been ridden for her love. So the mainspring of sorrow, the oppressor of joy came riding into the circle. She went to where she found the host. The lady Cunneware de Lalant ate with Artus; the queen of Janfuse ate with the lady Ginover. Artus the king sat in state. Cundrie held still in front of the Briton; she spoke to him in French. Even though I have to tell it in German her story does not make me too happy. "Son of King Utpandragun, your actions here have cast shame on yourself and on many a Briton. The best of many lands would be sitting here with dignity if there were no gall mixed in with their praise. The Round Table is brought to nothing: falsehood has gained part in it. King Artus, you stood high above your peers in praise; your rising praise sinks now, your swift worth limps, your high praise bends low, your honor has shown itself false. The company my lord Parzival brought to it has lamed the strength of the Round Table's honor, even though he also bears the trappings of a knight. You call him the red knight, after him who lay dead before Nantes. Both their lives were unalike, for the mouth of a knight never read of one who showed such utter dignity." From the king she rode to the man of Waleis. She said: "You make my manners so bad that I withhold my greeting from Artus and his household. May dishonor come to your fair face and your manly limbs. If I had reconciliation or peace to offer they would both be lacking for you. I seem unnatural to you, and yet I am more natural than you are. My lord Parzival, why do you not speak to me and tell me a story: why did you not free the sad fisherman of his sighs when he sat without joy and without comfort?

"He displayed the burden of his grief for you. You most unfaithful guest! His grief should have made you take pity. May your mouth grow empty yet, I mean of the tongue within it, as your heart is empty of good sense.[30] You are earmarked for hell in heaven before the Hand of the Highest, as you are on earth if the worthy come to their senses. You barrier to salvation, you curse of bliss, true contempt of perfect praise! You are so shy of manly honor, and so ill in dignity that no physician can cure you of it. I want to swear on your head, if someone wants to administer that oath to me, that greater falsehood was never available to any man so fair.[31] You baited hook, you adder's fang! And yet the host gave you a sword your honor never was worthy of. Your silence earned you the highest sin. You are the plaything of the herders of hell. Dishonored flesh, my lord Parzival! You also saw the grail carried before you, and the silver knives and the bleeding spear. You barrier to joy, you bastion of grief! If only a question had accompanied you to Munsalvaesche—there is a city in heathen lands called Tabronite, that contains the height of all earthly wishes—asking would have earned you more here. Feirefiz Anschevin conquered the queen of a country in hard knightly combat.[32] In him the manliness that both your father showed did not go to ruin. Your brother is a great marvel of a man: he is both black and white, the son of the queen of Zazamanc. Now I think of Gahmuret whose heart was always weeded of falsehood. Of Anschouwe your father was called, who left you another inheritance than the one you have acquired. You are spoiled for praise. If your mother had ever done wrong I would gladly believe that you were not his son. No, her faith taught her pain; believe good words of her, that your father must have been wise in manly loyalty, and that he gathered high praise far and wide. He knew how to join in merriment. Great heart and small gall, and his breast a roof above them. He was a weir and a dam to catch fish. His manly courage knew how to catch praise. Now your praise has come to falsehood. Alas, that it ever came to my ears that Herzeloyde's son has done his honor such wrong!"

Cundrie herself was the pledge of care. Weeping, she wrung her hands, so that many a tear followed another. Great sorrow pressed them out of her eyes. Her loyalty taught the young lady to well lament the distress of her heart. She went back to the host and added to her story there. She said: "Is there no worthy knight here who has desired the praise of valor and of high love as well? I know of four queens and four hundred young ladies you might like to see. They are in *Schahtel marveil*, the castle of wonder. All adventure is like thin air compared to what you may earn there: the worthy conquest of high love. Even if I shall have pain of the journey, I want to be there tonight." Sad, not cheerful did the young lady ride from the circle, without taking her leave. She often looked back, weeping. Now listen to the last words she spoke: "Oh, Munsalvaesche, target of grief! Alas that no one will comfort you!" Cundrie the sorceress, not lovely but proud, had saddened the man of Waleis. What help was the advice of his brave heart now, or of true breeding and manliness? Shame was with him more than any other one of his virtues. He had avoided real falsehood, for shame gives praise as a reward and is yet the crown of the soul. Shame surpasses other virtues when it is practiced. Cunneware began the first weeping because Parzival the hero bold had been so insulted by Cundrie the sorceress, a very strange creature indeed. The grief of their hearts gave many worthy ladies the juice of their eyes and you had to look at them weeping.

After Cundrie leaves, a knight rides up to Artus and Gawan. He accuses Gawan of having treacherously killed his lord, and challenges him to combat forty days from the day in the city of Schanpfanzun. Artus promises that Gawan will come. Beacurs, Gawan's brother, asks for permission to fight in his brother's place, but to no avail. The knight, Kingrimursel, a famous warrior, rides away. To Artus's army had come joy and lament on that day: such a checkered life was given to the heroes. They stood up everywhere; there was sorrow without number. The worthy ones soon went to where the man of Waleis and Gawan stood together: they comforted them as best they knew. Clamide, the highborn one, thought he had lost more than anyone who might be there, and that his pain was too sharp. He spoke to Parzival: "Even if you were by the grail now, I must still say without mockery: Tribalibot in heathen lands, and also the mountains of the Caucasus, and whatever wealth a mouth might speak of, together with the value of the grail would not compensate for the suffering of my heart that I earned before Pelrapeire. Woe is me, poor unhappy man! Your hand separated me from joy. Here is the lady Cunneware de Lalant: but this noble princess also wants to be subject to your command so much that she does not allow anyone to serve her, even though she has the means to reward service well. And yet she might get tired of me having been a prisoner to her here for so long. If I am ever to recover my joy, it would help me if she would do what brings honor to her, so that her love would restore to me a part of what I lost through you when the object of my joy walked past me, unseeing. I would have kept her well, if it had not been for you.[33] Now help me with this young lady.

"That I shall do," said the man from Waleis, "if she accedes to requests as courtesy demands. I shall gladly compensate you, since she is mine anyway, for whom you say you live in sorrow. I mean she who shows the body beautiful, Condwiramurs." Janfuse, the pagan lady, Artus and his wife, and Cunneware de Lanant, and the lady

Jeschute of Karnant also went to comfort him. What more do you want them to do? They gave Cunneware to Clamide,[34] since he was in pain for her love. He gave her his body as a reward, and a crown for her head. The lady of Janfuse observed this. The heathen lady said to Parzival: "Cundrie named a man for us who is a brother to you, I think. His power rules far and wide. The wealth of two crowns stands fearful in his care, on water and the roads of the earth. Azagouc and Zazamanc: the countries are strong, and not weak at all. Nothing compares to his riches, except the Baruc's, when people speak of wealth, and Tribalibot. They worship him like a god. His skin has a very beautiful glow. He is a stranger to the color of all men, since his skin is seen to be both white and black. I traveled here through one of his lands. He would have liked to have turned back my travels to this place. He tried to, but he was unable to. I am the daughter of his mother's sister; he is a high king indeed. I shall tell you more wondrous things: no man ever sat in the saddle after a joust with him.[35] His praise is very highly valued. No lips more generous ever sought the breast, and his virtue is lost to falsehood. He is Feirefiz Anschevin, who knows how to endure pain indeed on a woman's account.

"As strange as things are here for me, I too came here to learn new things and to know adventure. The highest gift now lies with you. All baptized folk separated themselves from evil by praising you. Good bearing is an advantage to you, and the radiance of your skin, and the manly virtue they say you have, and they speak the truth. And strength and youth go together with the rest." The rich, wise heathen lady had earned this fruit of knowledge: she spoke French well. Then the man from Waleis replied to her. Such were his words: "May God reward you, My Lady, that you give such friendly comfort to me here. I am not freed from sorrow and I shall tell you why. I cannot tell my suffering as it tells itself to me, so that many a person now sins on my account, who does not know of my sorrow, and I have to bear his mockery too. I do not want to allow myself any joy until I have seen the grail, first of all, whether the time be short or long. My thoughts drive me towards that goal. I shall never separate myself from it, not ever in my life. If observing the commands of my good breeding now forces me to hear the world's contempt, Gurnemanz's advice cannot have been wholly sound.[36] That worthy man advised me to avoid impertinent questions and always to fight against low behavior. I see many a worthy knight here. Advise me now through your good breeding how I can come closer to your favor. A stern, sharp judgment has been passed against me here with words. If I have lost any man's favor on that account I shall little reproach him for it. If I were to take praise after this, treat me accordingly then. Leaving you is a pressing obligation for me now. You all gave me your company while I stood in the strength of praise. Of that be now absolved until I set right what turned my verdant joy gray. Great sorrow shall be with me too, so that my heart shall give rain to my eyes, since I left at Munsalvaesche what thrust me away from true joy and from so many a fair young lady! Whatever anyone has said of wonder, still the grail has more to show. The host drags on a life of sighs. Oh helpless Anfortas, what did it help you that I was with you?"

They could not stay there any longer: they had to part now. The man from Waleis spoke to Artus the Briton and to the knights and the ladies: he wanted to see and hear how they gave him permission to take his leave. It did not please anyone that he rode away from them so sadly. I think it caused them all pain. Artus shook Parzival's hand and promised him that if ever his country would come to such hardship as it earned from Clamide, he would have that hardship as his own. He also regretted that Lehelin had taken two rich crowns from him. Many a man offered him much service there; the grief of sorrow drove the hero away from them. Cunneware the fair young lady took the hero without fear by the hand and led him aside. My lord Gawan kissed him. The manly one spoke to the hero rich in valor: "I know well that your travels will not be without combat. May God give you luck, and may He help me too, that I may still give you the service I am able to wish for. May His power grant me that."

The man of Waleis said: "Alas, what is God: if He were mighty he would never have given such mockery to us both. If God were able to live in power I would be subject to Him in service since I would understand His grace. Now I want to renounce my service to Him; if He has hatred, I want to bear it.[37] Friend, when the time comes for you to do combat, may a woman take up combat for you: may she guide your hand, and may she be a woman in whom you have recognized chastity and womanly virtue. Let her love guard you there.[38] I do not know when I shall see you again. May it go with you according to my wishes." Their parting gave them both bitter companions in sorrow. The lady Cunneware de Lalant guided him to where she found her tent. She ordered his armor to be brought there. Her soft hands with their fair skin armed Gahmuret's son. She said: "It is right that I should do this, since the king of Brandigan wants me because of you. Great concern for your honor brings me suffering with many sighs. As long as you are not able to defend yourself against sadness your grief weakens my joy."

Now was his horse saddled, and his own grief awakened. The well-shaped hero also wore a light, white, iron suit of armor. Without lying of any kind I say his coat and surcoat were adorned with precious stones. Only his helmet did he not yet have tied on. Then he kissed Cunneware the fair young lady. So I was told of them. A sad parting came to both affectionate friends. Gahmuret's son rode away. Whatever adventures have been told, nobody may measure them against this one without you all first hearing what he did now, where he turned and where he went; he who spares his body knightly combat should not think of him for a while, even though his proud mind may advise him to do so. Condwiramurs, your lovely body beautiful is often thought of now. What an adventure is brought to you! He whom Herzeloyde bore now follows the calling of the shield without delay, on account of the grail. He was also one of its heirs.[39]

Part of Artus's retinue sets out on an expedition to Schahtel marveile, to see the four queens and the four hundred ladies. They do not meet with success. Gawan also departs to fight King-rimursel. He ponders well which weapons he is going to use. Eckuba the young one left to go on board her ship; I mean the rich heathen lady. The people at the Plimizoel went this way and that. Artus went to Karidoel. Cunneware and Clamide also took their leave of him. Orsilus the well-known prince and the lady Jeschute of Karnant soon took their leave of him too, but they stayed on the plain with Clamide for three days because he celebrated marriage, not the real wedding, that would come at home in great style. Because his generosity guided him, many knights, a sorry band, stayed in Clamide's household[40] and also many of the wandering singers. He took them home to his country. With honor and without shame his possessions were divided among them, and nobody was turned away in deceit. Then the lady Jeschute and Orilus her lover went with Clamide to Brandigan. That was done in honor of the lady Cunneware, the queen. They crowned his sister there.

I know full well that any intelligent woman who is inclined to loyalty, and sees this story written, will tell me in truth that I am able to speak better of women than I sang to one[41] in measured tones. Belakane the queen was without wrongdoing and devoid of all falsehood when a dead king laid siege to her soul. Later a dream gave the lady Herzeloyde images that brought sighs to her heart. What was the lady Ginover's lament on Ither's last day? In addition it was great sorrow to me that the king's daughter of Karnant, the lady Jeschute whose chastity was well-known, rode in such a shameful way. How was the lady Cunneware threshed while she was held by the hair! They have now really found compensation for this: both their shame has gained victory. Now let a man take up this story and go on making it who is able to tell adventures and speak in rhyme, both the kind of rhyme that ties lines together and the kind of rhyme that breaks them off. I would gladly tell you more if only a mouth would order me to do so, a mouth set above other feet than those that move in my stirrups.[42]

Book Seven

He who never did a shameful deed shall now hold this adventure in his hands for a while—the worthy, renowned Gawan. The adventure judges many without hatred who are next to, or even above Parzival, the lord of the story. He who always drives his hero with words to the highest mark is slow with praise for the other side. The people's goodwill shall be given to him who takes the truth to all sides. If he does not, his words will remain without a roof above them, no matter what he says or said. Who shall have his words of sense well received unless wise men give them shelter? A false and lying tale, I think, would be better off in the snow without a host,[1] so that pain comes to the mouth that spreads it as the truth. In that case, God will have treated the teller as is the wish of good people brought to grief because of their loyalty.[2] There are those who are eager for such work that is doomed to mishap. If a worthy man takes part in this, bad sense must teach him so. He should stay away from it if he is able to feel shame.[3] He should take these words for guidance.

After he has ridden for a few days, Gawan encounters a mighty army. The coats of arms the knights display are unknown to him. He decides not to flee, but to ride straight through the army, ready to do battle. Nobody stops him.

The army had now marched and ridden past. Gawan had been waiting for that. It happened as he had thought it would: whoever saw the hero waiting there thought he belonged to the same army.

Prouder knights never rode, neither on this side of the sea nor on the other: they had the power of high minds.

Now a squire altogether devoid of baseness rode very soon after them, hard on their tracks (haste was upon him). A riderless horse ran next to him; it carried a new shield. With both spurs he urged on his horse, without much consideration. He wanted to hurry to the battle. His clothes were well cut. Gawan rode to the squire. After greetings he asked for news: whose retinue this was. The squire said: "You mock me. My Lord, if I have deserved such pain from you through my baseness, it would have been reckoned better against my honor if I had suffered other hardship. By God, now soften your hatred. You know each other better than I do: what help is it then to ask me? That knowledge should come one and a thousand times better to you than to me."

Gawan offered many an oath that he had not recognized the people who had ridden past him. He said: "My many travels come to shame, since in truth I cannot say that I have ever seen any of these in any place before this day, wherever my services were asked for." The squire spoke to Gawan: "My Lord, I have done wrong. I should have told you before. My better sense was slow then. Judge my guilt according to your favor. I shall gladly tell you afterwards: let me lament my baseness first." "Young sir, tell me who they are, by the pain your breeding causes you." "My Lord, such is the name of him who rides before you, and no obstacles come to him in his travels: King Poydiconjunz, and with him rides Duke Astor of Lanvarunz. There also rides a reckless person to whom no woman ever offered love: he wears the wreath of baseness and is called Meljacanz. Woman or virgin, whenever he was hunting for love he took them in dire distress: they should kill him for it.[4] He is Poydiconjunz's son and he also wants to do a knight's combat here. He is rich in valor and he often did show himself undaunted in combat before. But what help is his manly behavior? If her little swine were running along with her, a mother sow would defend them too. I never heard a man praised when his courage was without courtliness. Many will follow me in this.

"My Lord, listen to another wondrous thing. Let me tell it to you especially. A man driven by baseness, King Meljacanz of Liz, leads a great army that rides behind you. He has cultivated an eagerness for proud anger[5] without need: improper love ordered him to do so."

The squire spoke on in good breeding: "My Lord, I'm telling you because I saw it. King Meljacanz's father summoned the lords of his land to him on his deathbed. His valorous life stood with one unredeemed pledge: he had to surrender to death. In that sorrow he commended Meljacanz the fair to all who were there, on their honor. Then he chose one especially for him: the prince was his highest man. That prince had proved himself in loyalty and he had been emptied of all falsehood. The king asked him to educate his son. He said: "You can now give proof of your loyalty to my son. Ask him to hold in esteem both strangers and those who belong to the household, and ask him to share his possessions when those who know hardship want him to do so." And so the young man was commended to him.

Prince Lippaut did all that his lord, King Schaut, had agreed with him on his deathbed. He did not neglect any of it: it was all done, to the very end. The prince took the young man with him. He had lovely children at home, who are still dear to him: a daughter lacking in nothing, to be a knight's lover, except time. She is called Obie, her sister is called Obilot. Obie has brought this grief to us. One day things came to the point that the young king asked her for love in reward for his service. She cursed his sentiments and asked him what he was thinking of and why he had rid himself of his senses. She said to him: "If you were so old that you would have earned the right to take a prize under a knight's shield, in time passed with honor, with your helmet tied on your head, on hard travels for five years of your days, and if you had then come back and been here at my command, I would say yes for the first time to what your will desired, and I would still oblige you all too soon.[6] Your are dear to me (who denies it) as Galoes[7] was to Annore, who later chose death on his account when she lost him in a joust." "Not gladly," said he, "My Lady, do I see you so in love that your anger goes out to me. Mercy belongs with service if you want to measure true love right. My Lady, it is truly excessive for you to scorn my sentiments in this way: you have run ahead of yourself. I could still take advantage of the fact that your father is my vassal[8] and that he has received many a castle and all his lands from my hand." "If you give somebody a fief, that person will have to serve you," she said. "My goal is set higher than that. I do not want to hold a fief from anyone: my freedom is such that it is high enough for any crown an earthly head ever wore."[9] He said: "You were taught this so that your pride would increase in this way. Since your father gave this advice he shall make amends for this evil deed. I shall bear arms here after all, there will be thrusts and blows, in combat or in tournament: many a spear will remain here in two pieces." He went away from the young lady in anger. His anger was much lamented by all his retinue. Obie lamented it too. To deal with this imminent hardship Lippaut, who bore no guilt, offered to submit to court, and he offered many other kinds of compensation besides. Right or wrong, he wanted justice done by his peers,[10] a court where the princes would be, and he had come to this business without guilt. He much implored his lord for the favor of his mercy. That anger brought loss of joy to him.

They could not prevail on Lippaut to want to take his lord captive since he was his host—a loyal man would still avoid this now.[11] The king went away from there without taking leave, as his sick mind advised him. His squires, the children of princes who had been there with the king, showed their grief by crying. To their minds Lippaut should prosper, since he had educated them in true loyalty and he had not cheated them of worthy living. Only my lord was angry, and yet the prince's loyalty had revealed itself to him too. My lord is a Frenchman, the burgrave of Beaveys. He is called Lisavander. They had to stand against the prince, one and all, since they had to follow the calling of the shield. Many princes and other young men became knights at the king's court today.[12] King Poydiconjunz of Gors, a man who is able to do combat with sharp weapons, leads the first army: he leads many a well-armed horse. Meljacanz is his brother's son. They are both capable of arrogance, the young one and the old one too. May baseness hold sway over them! Anger has shown itself to such an extent that both kings want to come before Bearosche where they must serve ladies with great travail. Many a spear must they break there, both in charge and in thrust. Bearosche is so well defended that we would have to leave it undestroyed if we had twenty armies, each of them bigger than those we have. My journey is hidden from the army that follows. I have brought this shield along in stealth, away from the other squires, in case my lord might find a joust through his first shield, aimed there in the turmoil of the charge."

The squire then looked behind him: his lord was riding quickly after. Three horses and twelve white spears hurried along with him. I think his desire did not deceive anyone: he dearly wanted to seize the first joust there by rushing ahead. That is what the adventure told me. The squire said to Gawan: "My Lord, let me have your leave." He turned himself toward his lord.

What do you want Gawan to do now, except to find out what these tales mean? Yet doubt taught him sharp pain. He thought: "If I watch the fighting, and if I do none of it, all my praise will be extinguished. If I go to the appointed place to fight and if I am delayed, all my worldly praise will be truly destroyed. I will not do it: I must fight my combat first." His distress rolled back on itself. When he thought of the journey to his combat, staying here was much too dangerous. Yet he could not just ride on. He said: "Now God must keep the power of my manliness." Gawan rode toward Bearosche.

Gawan rides toward the city, but when he gets close enough, he sees that all its gates have been walled up. His eyes also had to see many worthy ladies. The hostess herself had come to watch from the high hall, together with her two beautiful daughters, who shone with bright radiance indeed. Soon he heard what they said: "Who may be coming to us here?" said the old duchess: "What kind of group could this be?" Her eldest daughter said quickly: "Mother, it's a merchant."[13] "But they are carrying shields along for him anyway." "That is the way many merchants travel." Her younger daughter said: "You accuse him of what never was, Sister, you should be ashamed: he never earned the name of merchant. He is of such lovely shape that I want to have him for my knight. His service may desire reward here: I want to give it to him in love."

Gawan's squires then observed a linden tree and an olive tree standing below the wall. That seemed a welcome find. What more do you want them to do now? Nothing more, except that King Lot's son dismounted where he found the best shade. His steward immediately brought a cover there and a mattress on which the proud worthy one sat. Above him sat a flood of women, like an army. The squires who had come there unloaded his clothes and his armor from the packhorses, and sought shelter under other trees.

The old duchess soon remarked: "My daughter, what merchant would behave like this? You should not speak so ill of him." Then spoke the young Obilot: "More discourtesy has come over her: she turned her proud temper against King Meljacanz of Liz when he asked for her love. Dishonored is such a mind!" Then said Obie, not free of anger: "His behavior does not matter to me: there sits a merchant who lives off barter.[14] His business shall be good here. His pack boxes are well watched—your knight's, my silly sister. He wants to stand guard over them himself." *Gawan then observes an allied army come to help the city.*

When the burghers[15] saw that help wanted to reach them, what had been their common resolve before seemed a wrong decision. Prince Lippaut himself said: "Alas, that Bearosche's gates should be walled up! But if I follow the culling of the shield against my lord my best breeding is the prey of death. His favor would help me and be better to me than his great hatred. What of a joust through my shield, aimed there by his hands? Or what if my sword would hack my worthy lord's shield to pieces? If an experienced woman were ever to praise this, she would be too free of her person. And what if I had my lord in my tower?[16] I would have to let him go, and go with him into his. No matter how he wants to torture me, I am wholly at his command. But I should gladly thank God that he has not taken me captive, since his anger will not leave him until he lays siege to me here. Now advise me with wisdom," he said to the burghers, "in these difficult matters."

Many a wise man said: "If your innocence had counted for anything at all, things would not have come to this pass." They gave him urgent advice that he should open the gates and ask all of his best men to ride to battle. They said: "We are able to fight like this; we do not have to defend ourselves against Meljacanz's two armies from the ramparts. Those who have come here with the king are mostly youngsters: we should be able to seize a hostage rather easily, and once that is done great anger often disappears. Perhaps when he has done a knight's combat here the king might be inclined to free us from distress and mitigate his anger. Combat in the field should be more fitting to us than that they take us down from the walls. We should be confident that we can fight there among their tent ropes, except for the power of Poydiconjunz: he leads the core of knights, the captive[17] Britons Duke Astor leads, and they are our greatest fear; you will see him in the forefront of battle. His son Meljacanz is there too. If Gurnemanz had educated him his praise would have been higher still; and yet you see him among the group of fighters.

Great help has come to us against them." You have heard their advice well.

The two armies fight on the plain before the city. Meljacanz of Liz performs great feats of bravery. Obie comments: "Now look," she said, "Sister mine: it is true that your knight and mine are doing different work. Yours thinks we shall lose the mountain and the castle. We shall have to choose another kind of defense." The young one had to suffer her mockery. She said: "He can make up for it yet. I still give my trust to him because of his courage, so that he may be freed from your mockery. He should direct his service to me and I shall increase his joy. Since you say he is a merchant he shall pay the market price for my reward." Gawan clearly heard their combat of words. He thought it proper to put it behind him as much as he could. If a pure heart is not ashamed of itself death must have taken it away from shame already. *King Poydiconjunz reproaches both Meljacanz and the duke of Lanvarunz for their overeagerness to do battle.*

Now hear me speak of Obie. She offered enough of her hate to Gawan, who bore it without guilt. She wanted to bring shame on him. She sent a boy to Gawan, where he sat. "And be sure to ask him whether the horses are for sale and whether any good dresses are for sale in his pack boxes. We ladies will buy them all at once." The boy came on his errand; he was received with anger. The looks in Gawan's eyes taught fear to his heart: the boy became so frightened that he neither asked nor said anything of all his lady had asked him to say. Gawan also did not let words be. He said: "Go away, you rascal. You will receive blows to the face of me, many, if you want to come closer to me." The boy then ran away. Now listen to what Obie did next.

She asked a young knight to speak to the burgrave of the city, who was called Scherules. She said: "You must ask him to do something because I want him to, and to tackle it in a manly way. There are seven horses by the moat under the olive trees; those he should seize, and much wealth besides. A merchant wants to deceive us here: ask him to prevent it. I expect this to be done by his hands: he should take the goods without payment and seize them without blame." The squire reported all his lady's lament down in the city. "I must save us from deceit," said Scherules; "I shall go there." He rode to where Gawan sat, who rarely forgot courage. Scherules found lack of weakness in him, a fair face and a high chest, and a knight fair of skin. Scherules observed his arms and each of his hands and what beautiful bearing he found there. Then he said: "My Lord, you are a stranger. Good sense has been lacking to us since you do not have lodging. Count this as an oversight on our part. I shall now be seneschal myself: people and goods, all that is called mine, I offer it to you in the manner of good service. Never did a guest come riding to a host who was as devoted to him." "By your leave, My Lord," said Gawan, "I have not deserved this yet, but I shall gladly follow you."

Scherules, adorned with praise, spoke as his loyalty taught him: "Since it has fallen to me, I am now your protector against loss, except if the army outside were to take things from you. Then I shall stand with you in the fight." He spoke with a laughing mouth to all the squires he saw there: "Load up your harnesses all, we shall ride down to the valley." Gawan rode with his host. Obie did not give up: she sent a woman minstrel whom her father knew well, and she sent these tidings with her: that a counterfeiter was traveling by. "His possessions are rich and many. Since my father has many mercenaries who want horses, silver and clothes, ask him on his true honor as a knight to give the merchant's possessions to them as their first reward. It will make seven men take to the field."[18] The woman minstrel spoke to the duke as his daughter had instructed her to. It is always great hardship to him who wages war that he must have rich booty to defray the cost. The mercenaries put pressure on Lippaut the loyal man, so that he suddenly thought: "I shall acquire these goods, in anger or in friendship." He did not avoid pursuing Gawan. Scherules rode up to him; he asked where he was riding in such haste. "I am riding in pursuit of a swindler: they told me tidings of him: he is a counterfeiter."

My lord Gawan was innocent: nothing had directed suspicion at him except the horses and the other things he carried along. Laughter touched Scherules. He said: "My Lord, you have been deceived. Whoever told you this lied, be it maid, man, or woman. You shall judge him differently: he never possessed any tool to mint coins. If you want to hear the right story, his body never carried a money changer's purse. Observe his bearing, listen to his words. I just let him in my house. If you are able to detect a knight's bearing, you must admit that he does the right things. His body was never bold to falsehood. Whoever does violence to him in spite of this, even if he were my father or my child, my kinsman or my brother, or any man who is in anger against him, will have to turn the rudder of combat against me: I shall defend him and save him from unjust combat wherever I can, My Lord, without losing your favor. I would rather abandon the calling of the shield for sackcloth and flee so far away from my land that nobody would recognize me before you, My Lord, did anything to him that would bring you shame. It would be better to receive them well, all who have come here and have listened to your sorrow, than to want to rob them. You should refrain from this." The prince said: "Let me see him now. Nothing bad can come of that." He rode to where he saw Gawan. The two eyes and the heart Lippaut had brought with him there told him that the stranger was fair of skin and that right manly virtue dwelt with his behavior.

Whomever true love brought to the point of suffering heartfelt love will be known by heartfelt love for this: that the heart is a pledge to true love, so pawned and sold that no mouth can ever fully tell what wonders love can work. Woman or man, heartfelt love will very often weaken a high mind. Obie and Meljacanz, both their love was so complete and rooted in such faith that you should be sorry for his anger. His riding away from her in anger brought her sorrow and such pain that her flawless nature was emboldened to anger in its turn. Innocent Gawan was chilled by this, as were others who suffered from it with her there. She often lapsed from womanly virtues because her flawless nature was so entangled in anger. It was a thorn to both her eyes whenever she saw a worthy man. Her heart decreed that Meljacanz had to be the highest, above all. She thought: "If he teaches me sorrow, I shall gladly endure it for his sake. I love the young, worthy, sweet man more than the whole world: the sentiments of my heart compel me to it." Much anger is still caused by love: do not condemn Obie on that account.

Lippaut greets Gawan and asks him to fight on his side. Gawan regrets that he has to decline the invitation: he has to fight his own combat first. Lippaut thanked him and rode away. He found his daughter in the courtyard, and the burgrave's little daughter too. They were tossing rings. Then he spoke to Obilot: "My daughter, where are you coming from?" "Father, I came down here. I trust the foreign knight will grant me this: I want to ask him to serve me for a reward." "My daughter, you are to be pitied: he told me neither yes nor no. Take up my request with him." There was haste for the maiden to go to the guest. Gawan jumped up when she came into the chamber. He welcomed her. He sat next to the sweet one. He thanked her that she had not forgotten him where they had treated him wrong.[19] He said: "If ever a knight suffered grief because of such a little lady, I should be in such grief because of you."

The young, sweet, fair one spoke without any falsehood: "God will surely know, My Lord, you are the first man who ever became companion to my speech: if my breeding is safeguarded in this, and also my sense of propriety, that gives me a gain in joy, for my teacher told me that speech is the roof of the mind. My Lord, I ask for you and for myself. True suffering teaches me to do so. I shall name it for you, if that is acceptable to you. If you think less of me therefore, I still travel on the path of good measure, for when I asked you I asked myself. You are me, in truth, even though the names are separate. You shall have my name: be now both maiden and man. I have begged for you and for me. If you, My Lord, let me go from you now unrequited and in shame, your praise must stand judgment before the court of your own breeding since my virginal fear looks to you for mercy. If it is pleasing to you, My Lord, I shall give you love with heartfelt sentiment. If you have manly virtue I think you will not neglect to serve me: I am worthy of service. My father also asks for help from friends and kinsmen, but do not let yourself be deceived by that. You serve us both for my reward alone." He said: "My Lady, the sound from your mouth shall pry me loose from loyalty. Disloyalty should be abhorrent to you. My loyalty suffers one hardship: it has been pledged. If the pledge is not redeemed I shall be dead. But let me turn my service and my senses toward your love: before you are allowed to give love you must live five more years—that is the number for the time of your love." He now remembered how Parzival put more trust in women than in God: his advice was this maiden's messenger into Gawan's heart. Then he promised the little· lady he would bear arms on her account. He began to tell her more still: "Let my sword be in your hands. If anyone desires a joust against me you must ride into the thick of battle and do combat for me there. People may think they see me in battle, but the fighting must be done by you."

She said: "That will not be too much for me. I am your protection and your shield, your heart and your comfort since you have freed me from doubt. I am your leader and your companion against mishap, a roof against the storms of misfortune and a comfortable rest for you. My love shall bring peace to you and be your happy defense against danger so that your courage will not be lost, even though you may have to defend yourself down to the very soul that is your body's host.[20] I am host and hostess and I shall be with you in battle. As long as you have confidence in that, salvation and courage shall not desert you." Then said the worthy Gawan: "My Lady, I want to have both; since I live in obedience to your command you must give me your love and your comfort." All the while her little hand was between his hands. Then she said: "My Lord, now let me go. I must also see to this: how could you ride out without a keepsake from me?[21] I would be far too dear to you for that. I should take pains to prepare a gift for you. When you wear it no other praise shall be higher than yours in any way."

Then he left the maiden and her friend. They both offered all their service to Gawan the guest. He bowed in gratitude for their favor. Then he said: "When you grow old enough for love, if the forest would grow nothing but spears in the way it now grows wood, that would be a small seed crop for the two of you.[22] If your youth can rule people like this and you carry this across into later life, your love will yet teach a knight's hand how a shield always vanishes against a spear." Then both maidens went away with joy and without sorrow. The burgrave's little daughter said: "Tell me, My Lady, what do you have in mind to give him? Since we have nothing but dolls, if mine are in any way more beautiful, you can give them to him without any displeasure on my part. There will be very little argument about this." Prince Lippaut came riding by when they were halfway up the hill.[23] He saw Obilot and Clauditte walk up it before him. He asked them both to stand still. Young Obilot said: "My father, I was never in such need of your help: give me advice, the knight has accepted me." "My daughter, whatever your will desires: it shall be given to you if I have it. Oh praise be the fruit that came to us in you! Your birth was a day of bliss." "My father, I will tell you then, and lament my distress in secret; speak to me about it as your good grace allows." He asked her if he could set her on the horse in front of him. She said: "Where should my friend go then?" There were many knights who stood around him. They argued about who should take her. It would have been a pleasure for any one of them; yet they offered her to one only. Clauditte was also fair of skin.

As they were riding her father said to her: "Obilot, now tell me part of your grief." "I have promised a gift to the foreign knight. I think my mind must have spoken madness. If I have nothing to give him, what good is it that I am alive? Since he offered me his service I have to blush shamefully because I have nothing to give him. A man was never so dear to a maiden." Then he said: "My daughter, count on me: I shall prepare it well for you. Since you desire service of him I shall give you what you may reward him with, if your mother will let you. May God grant that I enjoy it. Oh, such a proud, worthy man, what confidence I have in him! And yet I did not speak a word to him when I saw him last night in my dream." *Obilot's mother has a new, rich dress made for her. One of the sleeves is given to Gawan. He nails it to one of his shields. Under the cover of night the allied armies move into the city. The battle begins at the break of dawn. Gawan and Scherules hear mass and go to their post on the ramparts.*

What can I say more? Maybe that Poydiconjunz was superb: he rode up there with such power of men that if every bush in the Black Forest was a tree, whoever wanted to observe his host could see no more of a forest there. He rode up with six banners; they began the battle early in front of them. Trumpeters gave a ringing sound like the thunder that has always accompanied much fear and trembling. Many a drummer worked there together with the sound of the trumpeters. If any blade of grass was not trampled there I could not help it. The vineyards of Erffurt[24] still show the grief they came to from trampling: the feet of many horses left tracks there. Then Duke Astor came up in battle against those of Jamor.[25] Sharp jousts were ridden and many a worthy man unseated behind his horse on the field. They were eager for battle. They shouted many battle cries in foreign tongues. Many a battle horse ran without its master: its lord stood there on foot. I think he knew what it is to fall.

My lord Gawan saw that the plain consisted of woven strands of warriors: his friends were intertwined with the opposing army. He also got into the thick of battle. It was hard to see him: even though Scherules and his men little spared their horses Gawan put them to shame. The knights he thrust down there and the strong spears he broke! If the worthy messenger of the Round Table had not held his power from God, he would have gathered much praise there. Many a sword was made to sound. Both armies against which his hand was lifted in defense were the same to him: that of Liz and that of Gors. He quickly pulled away many a horse from either side and brought them to his host's banner. He asked if anybody wanted them there. Many said yes. They all grew rich on his friendship.

Then a knight came riding toward him who also knew how not to spare the spear. The burgrave of Beavoys and Gawan the courteous one came toward each other until the young Lisavander lay on the flowers behind his horse as if he had practiced falling in a joust. That makes me feel sorry for the squire who rode with good breeding the other day, and told Gawan the story of where all this began. He dismounted and stood over his lord who lay down on the field. Gawan recognized him and gave him back the horse that had been taken there. The squire bowed to him, so it was told to me. Now look where Kardefablet himself stands on the field; he had been taught to do so by a violent joust Meljacanz's hand had guided.[26] His men pulled him away then. "Jamor"[27] was often shouted there among powerful strokes of the sword. Things got tight there, without much room for maneuver, where onslaught pushed against onslaught. Many a helmet rang in his bearer's ears. Gawan assembled his companions. Then his charge rode with great power. With his host's banner he protected the worthy men of Jamor at the last moment. Then many knights were felled to earth. Believe it if you want to: I have no witnesses, except for what the adventure says.

The battle goes on. Gawan rides to another part of the field because he will not do battle against the captive Britons who are fighting for Poydiconjunz. He rides against Meljacanz's army that has pushed the defenders back to the moat.

A knight red all over offered many a joust to the burghers there. He was called the unnamed since nobody there knew him. I am telling you what I have heard. He had come to Meljacanz three days before. The burghers came to grief on his account. He had decided to help Meljacanz. Meljacanz gave him twelve squires from Semblidac who took care of him in the jousts and in the thick of battle. Whatever spears their hands might offer, they were completely wasted by him. His jousts sounded loud when they hit, for he made King Schirniel a captive there, and his brother too. And he did still more. He did not absolve the duke of Marangliez from giving him assurance. They were men of great valor, each on his post. Their soldiers fought on regardless. Meljacanz the king did battle there himself. Whether he brought them happiness or pain in the heart, they had to admit that any man that young had rarely done more than he had done then. His hand hacked many strong shields in two. What strong spears shattered in his hands where charge locked into charge! His young heart was so great that he had to lust for combat; nobody could oblige him there completely (to his distress) until he challenged Gawan to a joust.

Gawan unseats Meljacanz and takes him prisoner. Prince Lippaut, the ruler of the land, did not shrink from manly courage. Against him fought the king of Gors. There both men and horses had to endure pain because of the bows and arrows, where the Kahetins and the foot soldiers of Semblidac both exercised their skills.[28] The Turks of Kahetin knew how to retreat. The burghers had to think about ways to keep the enemy away from their defenses. They had foot soldiers: their ramparts were as well guarded as the best. Whatever worthy men lost their lives there, they felt the harshness of Obie's anger, since her stupid arrogance brought many people in distress. What crime had Lippaut committed? His lord the old King Schaut would have absolved him of it altogether. *The combatants are worn down by the battle, but Gawan manages to unseat Meljacanz before it ends. The red knight sends his prisoners into the town to plead for Meljacanz's freedom. He then rides off, leaving fifteen horses to his squires. Gawan returns the tattered sleeve to Obilot. Lippaut invites his knights to eat, but they all remain standing until Meljacanz, their king, has eaten, even though they are very tired.*

Then said young Meljacanz: "Your breeding was always perfect, all the while I lived here, so that your counsel never failed me. If I had followed you better then, they would have seen me happy today. Now help me, Count Scherules, since I trust you in this matter, with my lord[29] who keeps me captive here (they will both heed your advice) and Lippaut, my second father, let him now reveal his breeding to me. I would not have lost his favor if his daughter had refrained from this: she tried mockery fit for a fool on me, that was unwomanly behavior." Then spoke the worthy Gawan: "A reconciliation is taking place here that no one shall undo, except death."

At this moment the red knight's prisoners enter the room. Gawan understands that the red knight must have been Parzival. Gawan then pledges his own prisoners to Scherules.

Gawan sent word through Scherules to his lady Obilot that he would like to see her, and declare in truth that he was her bondsman, and that he also wanted to take leave of her. "And tell her I leave a king for her here. Ask her to ponder how she will receive him so that praise will rule her behavior." Meljacanz heard these words. He said: "Obilot will become the crown of all womanly virtue. It softens my heart that I must give assurance to her and that I shall live here in her peace." "You should know her here for this: nobody took you captive here except her hand." So spoke the worthy Gawan. "She alone shall have my praise." *Scherules rides ahead, Meljacanz and Gawan enter the hall together. Lippaut greets Meljacanz as follows:* "If it would not displease you, your old friend would like to receive you with a kiss: I mean my wife, the duchess." Meljacanz quickly replied to the host: "I shall gladly receive the kiss and the greeting of two ladies I see here. I offer no reconciliation to the third." The parents wept because of this. Obilot was very happy. The king was welcomed with a kiss, he and two other beardless kings, as was the duke of Marangliez. They also did not begrudge Gawan a kiss, nor that he took his lady in his arms. He pressed the child fair of skin to his breast like a doll. A friend's affection drove him to do so. He said to Meljacanz: "Your hand pledged assurance to me; be absolved of it now and pledge it here. The bulwark of all my joy sits in my arm here: you shall be her prisoner."

Meljacanz went up to her to do so. The young woman pulled Gawan to herself. Obilot was given assurance there, where many a worthy knight saw it. "My lord King, if my knight is indeed a merchant, as my sister argued so vehemently against me, you have done wrong to pledge him your assurance." So spoke the maiden Obilot. After this she ordered Meljacanz to pledge assurance to her sister Obie, and that the pledge should be given in her hand. "You shall have her for your lover because of your praise as a knight; she shall always gladly have you for her lord and her lover. I do not wish to absolve either of you from this." God spoke out of her young mouth. Her bidding was done on both sides. Lady Love fashioned their love all new with her powerful senses and her heartfelt loyalty. Obie's hand slid out of her cloak where it took hold of Meljacanz's arm. She wept as her red mouth kissed him who had been wounded in the joust. Many a tear that flowed from her bright eyes made his arm wet. Who made her so bold before the people? Love did, young and old. Lippaut then saw his wish fulfilled. Nothing so dear had ever happened to him. God did not withhold the honor of calling his daughter "My Lady" from him.[30]

How did the wedding go? Ask that of those who received gifts there. I cannot tell you exactly where many a man rode, whether to comfort or to combat. They told me that Gawan took his leave from the high hall where he had come to do so. Obilot wept much because of this. She said: "Take me with you now." The young, sweet maid had her request denied by Gawan. Her mother could hardly break her away from him. He then took his leave from them all. Lippaut offered him all his service since he bore fondness in his heart for him. Scherules, his proud host, and all his people did not shy away from riding out with the hero bold. Gawan's road led to a forest. Scherules then sent a huntsman and food along with him. The worthy hero took his leave: Gawan was given over to grief.

Book Eight

*G*awan leaves Bearosche. Now the time of his combat also drew
near. The forest was long and wide. He had to make his way
through it if he did not want to avoid combat. He had been chosen
for this without any guilt on his part. Now Ingliart was lost, too, his
horse with the short ears. Never had a better horse jumped in
Tabronit among the Moors. Now the forest became mixed, here a
few trees, there a field, so wide that a tent could stand on it only
with great difficulty. He then saw and came to know cultivated land
that was called Ascalun. There he inquired about Schanpfanzun
from the people who traveled past him. He crossed many high
mountains there, and many a marsh. And there he saw a castle. Oh,
it showed forth such noble radiance. Toward it he turned, a stranger
to that country.

Now hear me tell of adventure and with it help me lament
Gawan's great sorrow. My wise men and my fools all, do so out of
friendship and leave him with me in distress.[1] Alas, I should be
silent now. No, let him sink deeper yet, he who often bowed to good
fortune and now sinks into discomfort. This castle was so magnificent that Aeneas[2] did not find Carthage as impressive where death
was love's pledge to the lady Dido. *Gawan meets King Vergulath
who is engaged in rescuing falcons. The king offers him hospitality.*
Then said King Vergulath: "My lord, I have thought of this: you
must ride into the castle over there. If it finds favor with you I shall
now break the obligation of companionship toward you. But if my
riding on is an offense to you I shall leave off what I have to do."

Then said the worthy Gawan: "My Lord, it is right that you should do whatever you command. That will be done without angering me, and it will be quite forgiven you with goodwill." Then said the king of Ascalun: "My Lord, you see Schanpfanzun. There lives my sister, a young lady. Whatever any mouth said of beauty, she partakes of it altogether. If you would consider it a pleasure she will in truth take pains to entertain you until I return. I would then come sooner than I should. You will also be able to wait a long time for me once you have seen that sister of mine. You will not care if I would be away even longer."[3] "I enjoy seeing you, and her too. But grown ladies have always spared me their worthy hospitality." So spoke the proud Gawan. The king sent a knight and instructed the young lady that she should take care of Gawan in such a way that a long time would seem a short, fleeting moment. Gawan rode to where the king commanded. If you want me to, I can still be silent about his great hardship. No, I will tell you more. *Gawan enters the castle.*

The praise of the castle we shall leave out here, because I have much to tell you about the king's sister, a young lady, and I have told you enough about buildings anyway.[4] I shall describe her as I should. If she was beautiful it became her well. And if she had the right mind with it, that was good to make her a worthy person, so that her virtue and her being were like those of the margravine who often shone over all counties from Castle Heitstein.[5] Good for him who shall experience this side of her in private![6] Believe me, he shall find pleasure there better than elsewhere. I am allowed to say of women what my eyes can see. Wherever I turn my speech toward goodness in a woman she must be guarded by high breeding. Now listen to this adventure, you who are loyal and you who are friendly; I do not care for the disloyal.[7] Their loyalty is riddled with holes; they have lost all their salvation and their soul must suffer torment for it.

Gawan rode into the courtyard, in front of the high hall, toward companionship, as the king had sent him, who would cover himself with shame on his account. A knight who had brought him there guided him to where Antikonie the queen sat, and of fair color was her skin. If womanly honor could bring profit, she had taken great care in the purchase of it and thrust away from her all that was false: her flawless nature earned praise in this. Woe is me that van Veldeke the wise man died too soon! He could have praised her better.[8]

When Gawan saw the lady, the messenger went up to her and said all that the king had ordered him to say. The queen did not hesitate; she spoke: "My Lord, come closer to me. You are the guardian of my breeding: now order and teach. If your pleasure should be increased it must be by your command. Since that brother of mine recommended you so well to me I shall kiss you, if kiss I must. Now command according to your breeding what I shall do or leave undone."

With great breeding she stood before him. Gawan said: "My Lady, your mouth is so made for kissing that I shall have your kiss together with your greeting." The mouth to which Gawan offered his was hot, full, and red. The kiss they exchanged was not one meant for a guest. The highborn guest sat next to the young lady rich in virtue. Sweet talk was not lacking to them on both sides, with loyal affection. They knew how to renew, he his request, she her refusal. He began to lament this heartily, and he also begged much for her favor. The young lady spoke as I shall tell you: "My Lord, if you are wise in other matters this may seem enough to you. I am offering you at my brother's request what Anpflise[9] did not offer in any better way to my uncle Gahmuret, without lying with him. My true affection would weigh a bit more in the end if someone were to weigh us right. And also, My Lord, I do not know who you are, but you want to have my love after such a short time." Then spoke the worthy Gawan: "Knowledge of my kinship teaches me things; I tell you, my Lady, that I am the son of my aunt's brother. If you want to grant me your favor you should not leave that undone because of my lineage:[10] it has been proved against yours in such a way that they both stand on the same level and walk together in right measure."

A serving woman began to pour drinks for them and quickly turned away again. But more ladies[11] were sitting there; they too did not forget to go and work according to their duties. The knight was gone too, who had brought him there. When they had all gone away from him Gawan thought that a very small eaglet often catches the big ostrich. He felt under her mantle there and I think he touched her small hip. His torment was increased by this. From love they got such hardship, both the young lady and the man, that a thing would have happened there if evil eyes[12] had not spotted them. They were both prepared in their will. Now look, here comes the pain of their hearts. A white knight—his hair was gray—walked in through the door. In a call to arms he named Gawan, whom he recognized. He kept shouting in a loud voice: "Alas and alack. You were not satisfied with my lord whom you killed; you are also raping[13] his daughter here." People always answer a call to arms: the same custom was followed there. Gawan said to the young lady: "My Lady, now give me your advice: neither of us has many weapons here to fend them off." He said: "If only I had my sword!" Then spoke the worthy lady: "We shall go to a place where we can defend ourselves, flee to the tower there that stands next to my room. With luck all may be well."

Knights here, merchants there, the young lady soon heard the people coming from the city. She ran toward the tower together with Gawan. Her friend had to suffer hardship. She repeatedly asked the people to leave off; her screams and the noise she made were such that nobody took notice of her. They pushed toward the door to fight. Gawan stood in front of it to defend it. He prevented them from going in. He pulled a bolt that was used to lock the tower clean out of the wall. His evil-minded neighbors often moved away from him with their throng. The queen ran here and there: was there anything in the tower for defense against this disloyal army? Then the pure virgin[14] found a set of stone chess pieces and a board, well inlaid and wide. That she brought to Gawan in his combat. It was hanging from an iron ring; and by that ring Gawan took it. On this square shield much chess had been played. It was sorely hacked to pieces. Now listen to what the lady did. King or rook, she threw them at the enemies all the same: they were big and heavy.[15] They tell the story about her that whomever the swing of her throw hit went down against his will. The rich queen fought there like a knight. Next to Gawan she showed herself so warlike that the merchant women of Tolenstein[16] did not fight better at carnival, because they do it for a laugh and punish their bodies without need. When a woman grows dirty from a suit of armor she has forgotten her rightful place, if we were to measure her womanly virtue, except if she does it out of true love. Antikonie's grief was shown forth in Schanpfanzun and her high spirit bowed. She cried heavily in the fight: she showed full well that the love of an affectionate heart is true. What did Gawan do there? Whenever time was given to him he observed the young lady well, her mouth, her eyes, and her nose. I think you never saw on any skewer a rabbit better shaped than she was here and there, between her hips and her breast.[17] Her body knew full well how to arouse love's lustful desire. You never saw an ant that showed a better waist than she did, where her belt lay. That gave her companion Gawan manly valor. She endured with him in their need. The pledge named for him was death, and no other negotiations.[18] Gawan thought very little of his enemies' hatred when he looked at the young lady; for that reason many of them lost their lives. *King Vergulath comes back and joins in the battle against Gawan. When Kingrimursel sees the battle he is close to despair, since he had pledged himself to insure Gawan's safety. He pushes trough the crowd and fights together with Gawan until they manage to escape. The king wants to fight on, but the people prevail on him to decree an armistice for the rest of the day and the following night. They use the argument that Kingrimursel is the king's cousin and Gawan is his guest. We are told that Gawan never killed the king's father: another knight did. Antikonie thanks Kingrimursel.*

If you want to listen now I shall tell you the story my mouth spoke of before, how a pure mind became troubled. Dishonored be the course of the battle Vergulath fought at Schanpfanzun. He did not owe that to his birth, neither to his father nor his mother. The young man, who had much good in him, suffered great distress for shame when his sister the queen began to insult him. They heard him beg much. Then spoke the worthy young lady: "My Lord Vergulath, if I carried a sword and if I were a man by God's command, so that I could follow the calling of the shield, your combat would be totally eclipsed[19] by now. I was a young lady without defense, except that I still carried a shield on which honor is painted. That coat of arms I shall name for you if you care to know it: good bearing and worthy behavior. Much steadfastness dwells with both of those. That shield I raised for my knight whom you had sent to me: other protection had I none. Even if they see you changing, you still did wrong to me if womanly praise is to have its rightful place. I have heard it said that where it so happens that a man flees to a lady's protection, valorous pursuit should give up its combat altogether, if there were any manly breeding there.[20] My Lord Vergulath, the fact that your guest chose to flee to me for protection against death, shall teach your praise the distress of disgrace."

Kingrimursel said: "My Lord, because of my trust in you I promised my lord Gawan safe conduct to your land, that time on the plain by the Plimizoel. Your assurance was the pledge I gave in your name: if his courage brought him here none would stand up to him, except one man. My Lord, I have been wrecked by this. My peers must look into this. This crime has come much too soon for us. If you cannot spare princes we shall wreck crowns too.[21] If people have to see you with your good breeding, that good breeding must tell them that kinship stretches from you to me. If there had been dishonorable cunning on my part in establishing kinship[22] between us, you would have still gone too far against me in haste, since I am a knight after all, in whom no falsehood has been found yet, and my praise should also gain this for me: that I should die devoid of falsehood. I trust full well in God for that, and may my salvation be my messenger to Him. Also, wherever the story is heard that Artus's sister's son came to Schanpfanzun on the strength of my safe conduct—if Frenchman or Briton, Provençal or Burgundian, Galician or the people of Punturtoys hear of Gawan's distress all the praise I ever had will be dead. His fearful combat brings me much narrow praise, while my blame is wide. That shall turn joy away from me and rob me of my honor."

When that speech was done one of the king's men, who was called Liddamus, stood up. Kyot himself names him so. Kyot was the name of the singer whose art did not allow him not to sing and speak in such a way that many still grow happy from it. Kyot[23] was a man from Provence who saw this adventure of Parzival written in a heathen language. I retell in German what he told about it in French, if I am not without my wits. Then spoke Prince Liddamus: "Why should Gawan be in my lord's house, since he killed his father and brought dishonor so close to him? If my lord is known for his valor, his own hand will settle this here. That way one death will atone for another. I think both kinds of grief are alike." Now you see how it stood there with Gawan: for the first time he had come to know great danger.

Then spoke Kingrimursel: "Whoever is so quick with threats should also hasten into combat. Whether you have to fight in formation or in a wide open space, people can easily defend themselves against you. My lord Liddamus,[24] I trust I can full well save this man from you. Whatever he might have done to you, you would leave it unavenged. You went too far when you spoke. People would do well to believe of you that a man's eyes never saw you in the forefront where warriors fought. Fighting was always so hateful to you that you always began the flight.[25] You were even better versed in other things: wherever people thronged to battle you executed a woman's retreat. Whatever king trusts your counsel wears his crown very crooked. Gawan, the valorous hero, would have been opposed by my hands in the lists of combat. I had pledged myself to him that combat would have taken place here if my lord had allowed it. He bears my hatred with his sins: I had expected other things from him. My lord Gawan, promise here in truth that you will stand to respond to me in combat a year from now to the day, if my lord happens to leave you your life: I shall give you combat there. I challenged you at the Plimizoel; let the combat now take place at Parbigoel before King Meljacanz. I shall bear a crown of sorrows until the appointed day when I come against you in the lists. There your manly hand shall make hardship known to me."

Liddamus defends himself against Kingrimursel's charges of cowardice in the field. Kingrimursel remains unconvinced. The king puts an end to the argument, and asks his councillors to accompany him to another room. The queen, Gawan, and Kingrimursel also leave. The queen serves her two guests supper. Now listen what they advised the king of the country before the council broke up. He had taken the wise ones to him and they had come to his council. Many spoke their intention as their best sense spoke to them. Then they weighed it all on many scales. The king also asked them to hear his words. He spoke: "I was engaged in combat when I went riding in search of adventure in the forest of Laethamris. A knight saw all too high praise in me that week, for he quickly struck me off my horse without delay. He forced me to promise that I would get the grail for him. Even if I were to die for it now I must fulfill the promise his hand won from me in combat. Give me your advice, I have need of it. My best shield against death was that I pledged my hand to that undertaking, which is known to you now through my words. He was great in manliness and courage, the hero who ordered me to do even more: if I did not acquire the grail I was to go without evil cunning to her whom they give the crown in Pelrapeire (her father was called Tampenteire), and I was to do so in a year from now. When she looked into my eyes I was to pronounce my assurance to her. He sent word to her that it would increase his joy if she thought of him, and that he was the one who had delivered her from King Clamide in the past."

When they had heard these words, Liddamus said: "By these lords' leave I now speak. They too may give advice. Let my lord Gawan be your pledge for what that one man forced you to do there. He is beating his wings against the cleft stick you caught him in. Ask him to promise you before us all that he will get the grail for you. Let him ride away from you in good friendship and fight for the grail. We would all have to lament the shame if he were slain in your house. Now forgive him his guilt through your sister's favor. He has suffered great hardship here and now he must turn toward his death. In whatever lands the sea has enclosed there stands no house as well defended as Munsalvaesche. A road rough with battle leads to its location. Leave him in comfort tonight: let them inform him of this counsel tomorrow." All who gave advice followed him. And so my lord Gawan kept his life there.

They took such care of the undaunted hero there at night, I am told, that his comfort was very great. When they saw the middle of the morning and when they had sung mass, there was great jostling in the high hall of common folk and worthy people. The king did as they had counseled him: he had Gawan brought in. He did not want to force him to anything except what you yourselves have heard. Now watch where she brought him, Antikonie of fair skin. Her uncle's son came with her there, and many other vassals of the king. The queen led Gawan before the king, by her hand. A wreath of flowers was her headdress. Her mouth took praise away from the flowers in that wreath: no flower was as red, in any way. If she were to offer her kisses to a man in good favor, a forest would have to waste itself for him in many a joust untold.

With praise we should greet the chaste and sweet Antikonie, free from falsehood, for she lived in such virtue that her praise was never weakened by false words. When people heard her praises, their mouths wished that those praises would remain so upstanding, protected from false foul speech. Life was clear to her on all sides, like a falcon's eye, and balsam burning bright. Her desire for honor counseled her now: the sweet one rich in happiness spoke as good breeding required: "Brother, here I bring the hero you yourself ordered me to take care of. Now let him have profit from me: that will not bring grief to you. Think of brotherly loyalty and do so without sorrow. Manly loyalty suits you better than that you should suffer the world's hatred, and mine, if I were able to hate. Teach me to leave hatred untried toward you."

Then spoke the sweet worthy man: "That shall I do, Sister, if I can: give me your advice in this yourself. It seems to you that a bad deed has come between me and honor, and that it has pushed me away from praise. What should I do as your brother then? If all crowns were to serve me I would forsake them at your command. Your hatred would be my greatest grief. Joy and honor mean nothing to me, except when they agree with your teaching. My lord Gawan, I will ask you for this: you came riding here in search of praise; now do me the favor of your praise. Help me, so that my sister may forgive me my guilt. Before I lose her I forgive you for my heart's sorrow if you will give me assurance that you will earn the grail for me in good faith, without delay."

Reconciliation was brought to an end, and at the same time Gawan was sent in combat to the grail. Kingrimursel also forgave the king, who had lost him before because he had broken his safe conduct. That took place in front of all the lords.

Gawan is reunited with his squires and pages and asks to take his leave. When Gawan had breakfasted (I am telling you the story as Kyot read it) great sorrow arose there because of heartfelt loyalty. He spoke to the queen: "My Lady, if I have my senses and if God spares me my life I must travel in your service and always turn my knightly spirit to the service of your womanly goodness. That you have triumphed over falsehood may teach you happiness: your praise outweighs all other praise. May good fortune preserve your happiness. My Lady, I want to take my leave: grant it to me and let me go. May your breeding safeguard your praise." His going brought sorrow to her. Many a fair young lady cried with her out of friendship. The queen spoke without any deceit: "I wish you had had more profit by me, my joy would have been exalted over my sorrow; now your peace could not have been better. Believe me, when you suffer pain, when knighthood has guided you into the power of sorrowful grief, then know, my lord Gawan, that my heart shall be a part of that, whether it be loss or gain." The noble queen kissed Gawan's mouth. He became ill in his joy because he rode from her in such haste. I think that meant sorrow to both of them.

His squires had seen to it that his horses had been brought into the courtyard before the high hall where the shadow of the linden tree fell. The landgrave Kingrimursel's companions had also come to him (so have I heard it). Kingrimursel rode with Gawan until before the town. Gawan asked him with good breeding to take the trouble to lead his retinue to Bearosche for him. "There is Scherules. They themselves must ask him for an escort to Dianazdrun. There lives many a Briton who shall bring them to my lord, or to Ginover the queen." Kingrimursel promised him that. The hero quickly took his leave. Gringuljet, his horse, was soon armed, as was my lord Gawan. He kissed his kinsmen, the pages, and also his worthy squires. The assurance he had given compelled him toward the grail: he rode alone toward strange hardship.[26]

Book Nine

"**O**pen up." "To whom? Who are you?" "I want to come to you, into your heart." "Then you want too narrow a space." "What of it, I find hardly any room, but you will not have to complain of my pushing you: I want to tell you about wondrous things now." "Yes, is that you, my lady Adventure?[1] How fares the good one? I mean the worthy Parzival whom Cundrie drove to the grail with unsweet words, where many a lady wept that his travels could not be turned back." *The poet briefly alludes to episodes from the previous books.*

The adventure tells us that Parzival the hero soon came riding into a forest, I do not know at what time. There his eyes found a hermit's dwelling of new build, through which a swift spring ran: one side of it was built over the spring. The young hero undaunted was riding for the sake of adventure. God[2] wanted to show kindness to him then. He found a woman hermit who gave her virginity and her joy through love of God. The mainspring of woman's cares welled up out of her heart anew, and yet on account of old loyalty. He found Schianatulander and Sigune. The hero lay buried inside, dead. Her life endured sorrow over the coffin.[3] Sigune the duchess seldom heard mass. Her life was one bending of knees. Her full mouth, hot, and red of color, was faded there and pale since worldly joy had left her altogether. No other young lady suffers such great pain; Sigune must be alone with her lament.

She loved his dead body with a love that had died with him so that the prince had never enjoyed it. As far as I understand these things,[4] whatever wife is bound to companionship and refrains from other love through the power of her breeding grants her husband's dearest wish if she refrains from other love as long as he lives. No waiting suits her so well; I shall swear to that if I have to. Afterwards she may do as she pleases: she will still keep her honor.[5] She will not wear a more radiant crown if she goes to the dance with joy. Why do I mix joy with grief, to which Sigune was bound by her loyalty? I would gladly let that be. Parzival rode up to the window over fallen tree trunks; there was no road in sight. He rode up all too close, which he came to regret. He wanted to ask about the forest, or where his travels would be taking him. He wanted an answer: "Is anybody inside?" She said: "Yes." When he heard that it was a woman's voice he quickly moved the horse on untrampled grass. It seemed all too late for him: he should have dismounted earlier.[6] That shame brought him pain.

He tied the horse securely to the branch of a fallen tree trunk. He hung his shield on it too; it was riddled with holes. When the flawless gentle man had unbound his sword with good breeding he went to the wall and stood before the window. He wanted to ask for knowledge there. The hermit's dwelling was empty of joy and bare of all pleasure: he found nothing there but great grief. He wanted her at the window. The young woman of pale color stood up from her prayers. Yet it was still totally unknown to him who she was or might be. She wore a shirt of hair closest to her skin, under a gray gown. Great grief was her special love: it had laid low her high spirits and awakened many sighs from her heart. With good breeding the young woman went to the window; she welcomed him with sweet words. She carried a psalm book in her hand. Parzival the hero noticed a small ring there, which she had never lost in her grief, but kept by true love's counsel. Its small stone was a garnet: when you looked at it, it glowed through the window just as if it had been a small spark. Her headdress was in keeping with the sorrow of her soul. "Out there by the wall," she said, "stands a bench,[7] My Lord: sit if you like, if your thoughts lead you to it and your leisure too. I have come here in answer to your greeting; may God reward you for that. He rewards the faithful for their actions."

The hero did not forget her advice: he sat in front of the window. He also asked her to sit inside. She said: "I have rarely sat here with any man." The hero began to ask her how she lived and what she ate. "You are sitting so far from the road in this wilderness, My

Lady. It is a marvel to me that you can feed yourself since there is no cultivated soil anywhere around you." She spoke: "My food comes here to me from the grail, without delay. Every Saturday Cundrie the sorceress brings me the food I must have for the whole week. She has thought it out for herself that way." She spoke: "If I were well in other ways I would care little about food: with that I am well provided."

Parzival thinks she is mocking him. He asks her why she, a hermit, is wearing a ring. She assures him that she does not indulge in earthly love and tells him her story again. He recognizes her and takes off his coif of mail. She recognizes him in turn and asks him if he has found the grail yet, or at least understood its real nature. He spoke to the highborn lady: "There I have lost much joy. The grail gives me enough sorrow. I left a country where I wore a crown and also the most lovely wife: never was such a beautiful body born of human fruit on earth. I long for her flawless virtue; I grieve much for her love and even more for my high goal: to see Munsalvaesche and the grail. That has not happened yet. Cousin Sigune, you do me harm by being so hostile to me, since you know my many woes." The maiden said: "All my revenge on you, cousin, must be forgotten now. You have indeed lost much joy since you neglected to ask the worthy question when the sweet Anfortas was your host and your happiness. Asking would have fulfilled your highest wish then: now that joy must be lost and all your high spirits lamed. Care has tamed your heart that would have been wild and unsettled if you had asked to know then."[8]

Parzival asks Sigune for advice. She advises him to find a path back to Munsalvaesche. She suggests the best way may simply be to follow Cundrie's tracks. Parzival rides off. He is challenged by a knight from Munsalvaesche and defeats him. Whoever wants to hear, to him I tell the story of how things stood with Parzival afterward. I shall not check the number of weeks: how long since Parzival rode in search of adventure as before. One morning a thin layer of snow had fallen, and yet so thick as that which still gives frost to people now. It was in a great forest. Toward him walked an old knight, whose beard was all gray in color, but his skin smooth and fair. His wife's skin showed the same color. On their journey to confession they both wore rough gray cloaks on their bare bodies. The knight's children, two young ladies a man would like to look at, went there wearing the same clothes. They did as their flawless hearts counseled: they all walked barefoot. Parzival offered his greeting to the gray knight who walked there. He was to receive happiness from that knight's advice. The knight might well be a lord. Small dogs, such as ladies use for hunting, ran about there too. With humble bearing, and not too proud, more knights and squires with good breeding also walked there on the journey toward God. Many were so young they were without a beard altogether.

Parzival, the worthy hero, had taken such good care of his body that his rich garments suited him as they should a knight. He rode in a suit of armor all unlike the clothing the gray man wore coming toward him. Parzival quickly turned the horse away from the path with the bridle. Then his questioning asked about the good people's journey. He took in the sweet words they answered. Parzival heard the gray knight's lament: why had the holy days not made Parzival ride without a weapon or walk barefoot to observe the holy hours of the day? Parzival spoke to him: "My Lord, I do not know one way or the other how it stands with the beginning of the year, or how the count of the weeks goes. All that is unknown to me. I used to serve one called God before His mercy decreed such miserable mockery over me. My senses never wavered from Him Whose help was promised me. Now His help has failed me altogether."

Then the knight of gray color said: "Do you mean God whom the virgin bore?[9] If you believe in His being human, in what He suffered for us on a day like this, and if you observe the holy hours of this day, your armor does not suit you. Today is Good Friday, for which all the world may rejoice, and at the same time sigh with fear. Where was ever more exalted loyalty seen than what God showed us, Whom they hanged on the cross for us? My Lord, if you live according to the precepts of baptism, you must lament this exchange: He has given His worthy life in death for our guilt, so that man was lost and earmarked for hell. If you are not a heathen, think, My Lord, of these hours. Ride on and follow our tracks. Not too far ahead sits a holy man: he shall give you advice, and absolution for your wrongdoing. If you tell him about your sorrow he shall free you of sin."

The knight's daughters began to speak: "Why do you want to treat this man so badly, father? We have such bad weather now, so what advice are you giving him? Why do you not lead him where he can warm himself? It seems to us that his arms encased in iron are cold, even though they are shaped like the arms of a knight. He would freeze, even if he was three instead of one. You have tents standing near by and a house cut from pilgrim's cloth. If King Artus would come to you, you would have enough food to entertain him. Now do what a host should for this knight, who is with you." The gray man said: "My Lord, my daughters speak nothing but truth. Near this place I travel every year through this wild forest, whether it be warm or cold, always around the time of the martyrdom, which gives steady reward for service. Whatever food I brought, by God I shall share it with you without mockery." The young ladies asked him to stay; they did so with good intentions, and he would have gained honor if he had stayed. Parzival observed that their mouths were red, full, hot, even though sweat was rare because of the frost. Their mouths were not set in sorrow as befitted the holy hours of the day. If I had to reproach them for anything, I would not gladly leave off unless I earned myself a kiss there in reconciliation, if they would agree to it. Women are always women: they have soon conquered the body of a fighting man. Success has often come to them in this.[10]

Parzival decides not to stay with them after all. Away rides Herzeloyde's offspring. His manly breeding counseled chastity and compassion. Since the young Herzeloyde had given him loyalty for his inheritance, repentance began to stir in his heart. For the first time he thought of Him Who had created the whole world, his Creator, how powerful He was. He said: "What if God can give help that overcomes my sadness? If ever He became fond of a knight, if ever a knight earned His reward, or if shield and sword may be so worthy of His help, and true manly combat, so that His help may cure me of grief, and if today is the day of His help, let Him help, if help He can." Parzival turned back to where he had ridden from. They were still standing there, sorry he had gone from them. Their loyalty had taught them this: the young ladies followed him with their eyes. His heart also told him that he liked to see them since looking at them spoke to him of beauty.

He said: "If God's power is so great that it can guide both horses and animals, and people too, then I shall praise His power. If God's power includes help, then let it show this Castilian what is best for my travels. That way His good help will show itself: now go according to God's choice."[11] He put the reins on the horse, over its ears; he egged it on with the spurs. Toward *Funtane la salvatsche* it went, the fountain of salvation where Orilus received the oath. The flawless Trevrizent sat there, who ate badly many a Monday, as he did the rest of the week. He had altogether renounced mulberry wine, other wine, and bread too. Yet his flawless nature compelled him to do more: he had no mind for food, whether fish or meat, that carried blood. So stood his holy life. God had given him a mind to prepare himself to meet the heavenly host. Through fasting he suffered great sorrow; his flawless nature fought against the devil. From this man Parzival will now learn the hidden tales of the grail. Whoever asked me about this before, and was angry with me because I did not tell him, has earned ill praise of it. Kyot asked me to conceal it, since the adventure told him that nobody should think of it before the adventure itself guided it with words to the point where the story would welcome it with a greeting, so that a man has to speak of it anyway.[12]

Kyot, the master well-known, found the foundation of this adventure in Toledo,[13] written in heathen script and discarded. He first had to learn the ABC of the writing, except for the cunning of necromancy. It was a help that baptism was with him: otherwise this story would still be unheard. No heathen cunning could assist us in revealing the nature of the grail and how one is initiated to its secrets.

A heathen, Flegetanis, earned high praise for his knowledge. That same scholar of nature was born of Salomon, begotten of Israelite kin in the old days before baptism became our shield against the fire of hell. He wrote about the grail's adventure. Flegetanis was a heathen on his father's side, and he prayed to a calf as if it were his god. How can the devil bring such mockery on such wise people that they did not and do not separate it from Him Who wields the Hand Supreme and to Whom all wonders are known?[14] Flegetanis the heathen could tell us much about the going down of every star and its future coming back, and how long each of them goes around before it stands at its endpoint again. By the circular movement of the stars all human nature is regulated. Flegetanis the heathen saw secrets hidden among the stars and spoke of them with caution. He said there was a thing called the grail,[15] whose name he had read among the stars, without question as to what it was called. "A host of angels left it on earth; they rose up high above the stars, because their innocence drew them back there. Since then baptized sons of men must guard it with the same flawless breeding. Men who are called forth to the grail are always honorable."

So wrote Flegetanis about these matters. Kyot, the wise master, began to look for this story in Latin books: where might there have been a people suitable to guard the grail and of flawless inclination? *Wolfram then briefly recounts Parzival's genealogy. Parzival rides on, past the spot where he reconciled Orilus with Jeschute, until he finds the hermit.*

The hermit said to him: "Alas, My Lord, that such things happened to you in these holy hours! Has fearful combat driven you into this armor? Or have you remained without combat? Other clothes would suit you better if your pride would leave you that advice. Now may it please you to dismount, My Lord (I think that will not be offensive to you) and warm yourself by a fire. If adventure has sent you forth for love's reward, if you are in favor of true love, love then as love goes now, as this day's love stands, and serve for a woman's greeting later. May it please you to dismount, if I may ask?" Parzival the warrior dismounted at once. With good breeding he stood before the hermit. He told him of the people who had directed him there, how they praised his advice. Then he said: "My Lord, give me your advice now: I am a man who holds sin inside him."

When these words had been spoken the good poor man said: "I shall give you my advice. Now tell me who directed you here." "My Lord, a gray man came toward me in the forest, who received me well, as did his household. That same man, free of falsehood, sent me to you here. I rode along his track until I found you." The host said: "That was Kahenis, he is wise in worthy conduct. The prince is a man from Punturteis; the rich king of Kareis has his sister for a wife. Never was more flawless fruit of love born than his own children who came toward you there. The prince is of royal lineage. Every year his travels take him here to me."

Parzival spoke to the host: "When I saw you standing before me, were you in the least afraid when I rode toward you? Was my coming an annoyance to you?" The hermit said: "My Lord, believe me, the bear and the stag have scared me more often than man. One truth I can tell you: I do not fear what is human. I also have experience of men. If you do not take this for boasting, I still have my virginity where fleeing is concerned. My heart never suffered the disgrace that I turned away from fighting in my fighting days. I was a knight as you are, who also strove after high love. Sometimes I wove sinful thoughts in with chastity. I preened my life so that a woman would grant me her favor. My body has forgotten that now. Give me the reins, into my hand. There, under the overhang of that rock, shall your horse stand to rest. In a while we shall both go and break off twigs and ferns for him: I am poor in other fodder. But we shall feed him very well."

Parzival recognizes the reliquary in the hermit's dwelling. He also asks him about the spear he took from there, and how long he has been on his own. Parzival spoke: "Joy is a dream to me: I am bearing sorrow's heavy reins. My Lord, I shall tell you even more. No eye has ever spotted me where a church or monastery stood where they spoke of God's honor, not since those times. I looked for nothing but combat. I also bear much hatred against God since he is a godfather to my grief. Others he has exalted all too high: my joy is buried alive. If God's power knew how to be of help, what anchor would my joy be then? It now sinks through the bottom of grief. If my manly heart is wounded—and how can it be whole if sorrow puts its sharp crown on the honor the calling of the shield conquered for me against warlike hands?—I count that as shame to Him Who has the power of all help: He does not help me if His help is as bold to help as they vouch for."

The host sighed and looked at him. Then he spoke: "My Lord, if you have good sense you should trust in God. He helps you because he has to help you. God must help us both. My Lord, you must explain to me (may it please you first to sit): tell me with an open mind how this anger began, from which God received your hatred. Be guided by your good breeding and hear of His innocence from me, before you complain to me about anything He did. His help is always unfailing. Even though I was a layman[16] I could read the story of the true book and write how man should remain in service to the great help of Him who never tired of steadfast help against the sinking of the soul. Be loyal without all wavering, since God himself is loyalty,[17] and false cunning has always displeased Him. We should let Him benefit from this: He has done much for us since His high noble nature became man's image for us. God is called truth, and

He is truth: false behavior has always saddened Him. This you should ponder well: He is unable to waver toward any man. Now let your thinking teach you to beware of wavering toward Him.

The hermit further tries to allay Parzival's anger against God by reminding him of man's sins through the ages and God's continued promise of redemption. Parzival's anger abates, and he tells the hermit of his private grief: his failed attempt to help Anfortas and win the grail. The hermit proceeds to explain the meaning of the grail and the rituals connected with it. He says: "You say you are yearning for the grail: I must pity you, you stupid man, since nobody may search for the grail except if he is known to heaven and called to the service of the grail. I must tell you this about the grail: I know it and I have seen it as true." Parzival said: "Were you there?" The host said to him: "My Lord, yes." Parzival was altogether silent about the fact that he had been there too. He asked the hermit for knowledge: how things stood about the grail.

The host said: "It is well-known to me that many a warlike knight lives at Munsalvaesche with the grail. For the sake of adventure they always go on many travels, these same Templars, whether they are looking for care or praise: they endure it for their sins. There dwells a warlike host. I shall tell you about their food. They live off a stone. Its nature is very pure. If you have not recognized it, it will be named for you here: it is called *lapsit exilis*.[18] Through that stone's power the phoenix burns up so that it turns to ashes, but those ashes bring life to it. Therefore the phoenix throws off its molt and gives off a very bright glow afterwards, so that it becomes more beautiful than before. Also, never did such illness overcome a man that if he sees that stone one day he cannot die during the week that comes soonest after it. Also, his color never deteriorates. They must admit that his skin is of the same color as when he saw the stone, man or woman, as if his or her best years had just begun. And if he were to see the stone for two hundred years, nothing would change, except that his hair might turn gray. Such power does the stone give to man that his flesh and bone receive youth without delay. The stone is also called the grail.

"On it descends a message today, in which its highest power lies. Today is Good Friday. In truth you can observe how a dove flies down from heaven. It brings a small white wafer, which it leaves on the stone. The dove is transparently white. It takes its way back to heaven. Always, I tell you, on every Good Friday it brings to the stone that from which the stone receives all that smells good on earth, of food and drink, like the highest perfection of paradise: whatever the earth may bear. Moreover, the stone shall always allow the game that lives under the sky to multiply, whether it flies or runs, and hovers. The power of the grail gives sustenance to the brotherhood of knights.

"But listen how those who are called to the grail become known. On the outer edge of the stone an inscription composed of characters shows the name and the lineage of whoever shall undertake the journey to salvation, be they maidens or squires. Nobody can erase those letters. As soon as you have read the name, it fades before your eyes. They all came there as children, who are adults there now. Hail the mother who bore the child that will take part in service there! Poor and rich alike are happy if their child is called there, and they shall send it to the host. The Templars fetch children from many countries. They are forever protected from the shame that bears sin, and if their reward grows great in heaven they are granted their highest wish there when life dies for them here. Those who did not stand on either side when Lucifer and Trinitas[19] began to do battle, those angels, noble and worthy, must go to earth to this same stone. The stone is always pure. I do not know whether God forgave them, or whether He increased their loss, or if it was His right to take them back again. Since then a man has always taken care of the stone. God appointed him to this task and sent His angel to him. My Lord, so it stands with the grail."

But then Parzival said: "If knighthood can earn praise for the body and paradise for the soul with shield and spear, then knighthood has always been my desire. I always fought where I found battle, that my warlike hand would come closer to praise. If God knows about battle He should call me there, that they may know me there. My hand shall not avoid battle there." But then spoke his flawless host: "You must beware of pride there with humility of will. If not, your youth may easily lead you astray, so that you may break the virtue of moderation. Pride has always sunk and fallen," said the host. Tears welled up in each of his eyes when he thought of the tale he would tell there with words.

He said: "My Lord, there was a king there: he was, and still is, called Anfortas. You and I, poor souls, should always feel compassion for his heartfelt grief: pride gave it to him as his reward. His youth and his wealth brought sorrow to him and to the world, as did his desire for love outside chaste sentiment. Such behavior is not seemly for the grail: there knight and servant must be on their guard against wantonness. Humility has always conquered pride. There lives a worthy brotherhood: with the warlike power of their hands they have turned away people of all lands so that the grail is unknown except to those called to the host of the grail in Munsalvaesche. Only one ever came there uncalled, a stupid man, and he took sin away with him because he did not speak to the host about the grief he observed in him. I should not reprimand anyone. Yet he must atone for the sin of not asking about the host's misery. The host was weighed down with grief; never was such great pain known."

The hermit asks Parzival if he is King Lehelin, a knight of Munsalvaesche, since his horse bears the emblem of that castle. The hermit does not know that Parzival lost his own horse in combat with a knight of Munsalvaesche and that he is now riding that knight's horse. Parzival tells the hermit who he is and that he killed Ither of Kucumerlant. The hermit laments Parzival's misfortune and reveals that he is his uncle, his mother's brother. He then proceeds to tell the story of his brother Anfortas, the present lord of the grail.

"Then my brother had come to the years for the time of the sprouting of the beard. Love has her combat with such youth. She presses her friend so hard that people may say it is to her dishonor. Whichever lord of the grail desires love other than what the inscription allows must come to grief, and to that pain in the heart that produces sighs. My lord and my brother chose a lady love for himself, of good behavior, as it seemed to him. Let it be left unsaid who she was. In her service he acted as a true knight, so that cowardice fled from him. And so by his fair hand the rim of many a shield was riddled with blows. He looked for adventure for the sweet good one's sake. If ever high praise was known in any land of chivalry, he was beyond the telling of it. 'Amor' was his battle cry. That cry is not altogether good for humility.

"One day the king rode alone (much to his people's regret) in search of adventure, to enjoy love's help: his desire for love compelled him to do so. He was wounded in a joust with a poisoned spear in his private parts, so that he never became healthy again, that sweet uncle of yours. It was a heathen who fought there and rode the same joust, born in Ethnise, where the Tigris flows out of paradise. That same heathen was sure that his valor would win him the grail. His name was engraved in the spear: he had been seeking knightly combat in faraway lands; for the grail's power only did he wander through water and land. Joy vanished for us with his combat. Yet your uncle's fighting must be praised. He carried the iron of the spear away in his body. When the young worthy man came home to his people they saw misery revealed. He had slain the heathen; we should lament him, too, but only as is fitting.

"When the king came to us so pale and with his strength all gone, a physician's hand touched the wound until he found the spear's iron. The spear's shaft was made of Spanish reed; part of it was in the wound. The physician reclaimed both point and shaft. I fell down to prayer. I promised God's power that I would never act as a knight again if God would promise on His honor to help my brother out of his grief. I also abjured meat, wine, and bread, and afterwards all that carries blood, so that I would never desire a taste of it again. I took leave of my sword and that meant more lamentation to the people, my dear nephew, I am telling you. They said: 'Who shall be the protector of the grail's wonders?' Then wept clear eyes.

"With God's help they carried the king before the grail without delay. When the king saw the grail, that was his other discomfort: he could not die. Death was not granted to him because I had given myself up to a life of poverty and the dominion of our noble lineage had grown so weak in strength. The king's wound was poisoned, as they read in books of medicine." *But the books turn out to be of little help. The hermit goes on to tell Parzival about several cures that were tried but brought no relief. Finally the grail itself points to a solution.*

"We fell to prayer before the grail. On it we suddenly saw written that a knight would come. If a question were heard there, the misery would have an end. If there were a child, a maiden, or a man who prepared the knight for the question in any way, that question would not help, except that the shame would stay as before and cause more pain in the heart. The writing said: 'Have you understood this? Your attempts to prepare him will only come to shame. If he does not ask the first night, the power of his question fades. If his question is asked at the right time, he shall have the kingdom and the misery shall have an end at the Hands of the Highest. With that Anfortas will be cured, but he shall never be king again.' So we read on the grail that Anfortas's torment would come to an end when the question came to him. We dressed his wound with whatever we could to soothe it: the good salve called nardas, and what was mixed with theriac, and the smoke of lign aloe;[20] but it hurt him at all times. Then I came to this place. Feeble joy is the allowance of my years. Since then a knight did come riding there: he would gladly have avoided it, the man of whom I spoke before, who earned lack of praise there, since he observed real hardship and did not ask the host: 'My Lord, how stands it with your grief?' Since his boorishness commanded him that he should not ask there, great happiness counted little for him."

The hermit invites Parzival to accompany him into the forest to scavenge for food. They find twigs for the horse and roots for themselves. Parzival thinks the food is better than any he has had at Gurnemanz's or at Munsalvaesche.

Food was served there: if they had not wiped their hands that would not have hurt their eyes, as they say of hands that have handled fish.[21] I can assure you for my part that if they wanted to hunt birds with me and if I were taken for a hunting bird, I would gladly fly up from their hands: after such small bites I would show that I can fly.[22] Why do I mock these loyal people? My old boorishness advised me to do so. You have heard full well what scattered their wealth, why they were poor in joy, often cold and rarely warm. They suffered sorrow in their hearts for nothing but real loyalty. They received recompense from the Hands of the Most High, without any mishap. God grew and remained fond of both of them. Parzival and the good man then stood up and went to the horse in the stable. In a tone of weak joy the host spoke to the horse: "The hardship hunger brings you is grief to me because of the saddle that lies on you and shows Anfortas's coat of arms."

When they had taken care of the horse they began a new lament. Parzival said to his host: "My Lord and my dear uncle, if I dared to tell you for shame, I should lament my unhappiness before you. Forgive me by your own good breeding since my trust goes out to you. I have done such wrong: if you want to let me pay for it I shall take leave of comfort and be the one unredeemed from sorrow always. You shall lament my boorishness with loyal counsel. He who rode to Munsalvaesche, and saw the real hardship, and asked no question, that am I, a child unredeemed. So have I sinned, My Lord."

The host said: "Nephew, what are you saying now? We shall both together adopt heartfelt lamentation and let joy slip away, since your understanding cut itself off from salvation.[23] When God gave you five senses they withheld their counsel from you. How was your loyalty guarded by them in those hours near Anfortas's wound? But I do not want to withhold advice from you, and you should not lament too much either. You should lament and be lamented in good measure. Mankind has a wild nature. Sometimes youth wants to take the path of wisdom. If age then wants to show boorishness and confuse pure behavior, white shall become dirty and green virtue gray, in which that might take root which may grow into honor. If I could make it green again, and make your heart so bold that you would want to earn praise from God, and not despair, your success might stand you in such worthy stead that it could be called a retribution. God himself would not abandon you. I am the source of God's counsel for you. Now tell me: did you see the spear in the castle of Munsalvaesche? When the star Saturnus stood at its end-point again, the wound and the snows of summer taught us this: the frost never caused him so much pain, that sweet uncle of yours. The spear had to be in the wound, then, and so one pain helped to heal the other, and the spear became bloodred.

"The days when some stars arrive teach the people there to lament their misery, especially the stars that stand so high above each other and run counter to each other on an uneven course. The changes of the moon also do much harm to the wound. In the time I have named here the king must leave rest behind. Great frost causes him such pain that his flesh grows colder than snow. Since they know that the poison on the spear's iron is hot, they put it on the wound at that time. It draws the cold out of his body. All around the spear glass looks like ice. But nobody was able to take it away from the spear in any way, except Trebuchet, the wise man, who made two knives out of silver. They cut it, they did not avoid it. A charm that was worked into the king's sword revealed that art to him. There is many a man who gladly says that aspinde wood does not burn, but if any splinter of this glass would fall on it, flames of fire would flare up and the aspinde would be burnt. The wondrous things this poison can do!

"The king cannot ride or walk, lie, or stand: he leans, without sitting, with knowledge that makes him sigh. At the change of the moon pain comes to him. Brumbane is the name of a lake; they carry him to it because of its sweet air and the deepness of his bitter wound. He calls that his hunting day. What he can catch there in such painful hurt he needs more of at home. From this came the story that he was a fisherman. He had to endure that story, but he has little salmon and lamprey for sale, that sad man." Parzival spoke at once: "On that lake I found the king, anchored on the water. I thought he wanted to catch fish or look for some other pleasure. I had ridden many a mile to that place that day. I had left Pelrapeire exactly in the middle of the morning. That evening I was worried: where might there be an inn? My uncle gave me advice."

Parzival describes his reception at Munsalvaesche. The hermit explains to him that the king was in great pain then, because of Saturn's position in the sky. Parzival asks more questions about the grail. Parzival said to the host: "Twenty-five young ladies did I see there, who stood before the king and knew all about good breeding." The host said: "Young ladies should take care of the grail (that is what God decided), and they performed their service before it. The grail chooses among the highest. Similarly, knights shall guard it with goodness and chastity. The coming time of the high stars brings great misery to the people there, young and old. God has kept his anger against them all too long. When shall they ever say yes to joy? Nephew, now I shall tell you something you may well believe of me. A double exchange often faces them: they give and take profit. They receive small children there of high breeding and fair of skin. If a country anywhere becomes rulerless, and if they recognize God's hand there so that the people want a ruler from the grail's host, they are given one. They must also treat him with good breeding, since God's blessing protects him there. God provides men in stealth, but they give maidens openly. You may be very sure of this, that King Castis desired Herzeloyde whom they gave to him gladly. They gave him your mother for a wife. But he was not to enjoy her love: death led him into the grave before he could.[24] Before that he had given your mother Waleis and Norgals, Kanvoleis and Kingrivals, all given to her in lawful surrender. The king was not to live much longer. It happened on his journey back that he lay himself down to die. Then she wore the crown over two countries, and there she won Gahmuret's hand.

"And so those of the grail give: young ladies openly, men in stealth, to be fruitful to the service again when their children shall increase the grail's host with service of their own. God can teach them these things well. Whoever has given himself to the service of the grail must not care for the love of women. Only the king shall have one, by right, a pure wife, and other knights whom God has sent as rulers to rulerless lands. I set myself above this command when I observed the service of love. The beauty of my youth and the virtue of a worthy lady advised me that I should ride in her service where I often did hard combat. The wild adventures seemed so suitable to me that I rarely entered tournaments. Her love guided joy into my heart: for her I showed myself in many a combat. The power of her love forced me to wild deeds of knighthood in faraway lands. I bought her love that way: the heathen and the baptized were all the same to me in combat. She seemed to me rich in reward."

The hermit, whose name is Trevrizent, goes on to describe his adventures. On one of them he met Parzival's father, who gave him Ither as a squire. Trevrizent advises Parzival to do penance for both the slaying of Ither and the death of his mother, so that he may find peace. Without any reproach the host began to ask him again: "Nephew, I still have not heard from where this horse has come to you." "My Lord, I won that horse in combat when I rode away from Sigune. I spoke with her in front of her hermit's dwelling. After that I quickly thrust a knight off it and pulled it with me. The man was from Munsalvaesche." The host spoke: "Did he get away with his life, the man whose horse it should be by right?" "My Lord, I saw him walk before me, and I found the horse standing near me." "If you want to rob the people of the grail like this, and if you believe in addition that you shall win their love, your senses divide themselves in contradiction." "My Lord, I took it in combat. Whoever accuses me of sin for that should first find out how things stand. I had lost my horse before."

But then Parzival said: "Who was the young lady who carried the grail? They lent me her cloak." The host said: "Nephew, if it was hers (she is your mother's sister), the loan is not for you to boast of: she thought you would be lord there, the grail's and hers, and mine also. Your uncle also gave you a sword with which you have been abandoned to sin, since your mouth that speaks well unfortunately did not express a question then. Let that sin stand with the others. We shall go rest for the day." No bed and covers were brought to them: they went to lie down on a heap of leaves. That lair was certainly not made up according to their high status. Parzival stayed there like this for fifteen days. The host took care of him as I tell you: herbs and roots had to be their best food. Parzival endured the hard life because of the sweet words, since the host absolved him from sin and also gave him advice for a knight.

One day Parzival asked him: "Who was the man who lay before the grail? He was all gray but with a fair skin." The host said: "That was Titurel. That same man is your mother's grandfather. To him the grail's banner was first entrusted, with orders to protect it. He suffers from an illness called *pograt*, his lameness is beyond help. Yet he never lost his color because he sees the grail so often; and therefore he cannot die. They value the bedridden one for his advice. In his youth he often rode through ford and meadow for a joust. If you want to enhance your life and behave in a right worthy manner, you must spare your hatred against women. Women and priests are known for this: they have unwarlike hands. Therefore God's blessing guards priests.[25] Your service should honor them with loyalty: you will come to a good end only if you are mindful of priests. Whatever your eye sees on earth does not liken itself to a priest. His mouth professes that martyrdom which has shattered our loss.[26] Also, his consecrated hand touches the highest pledge that was ever set for guilt. If a priest has proved himself such that he can redeem that pledge with chastity, how could he live a more holy life?" This was the day of parting for them both. Trevrizent made a decision. He said: "Give me your sin, before God I am the pledge of your conversion.[27] And do as I have told you: remain undaunted in your will." They took leave of each other. You can try to find out how if you want to.[28]

Book Ten

A year has passed since Gawan left King Vergulath. They meet again to do combat, but since they are kin they are not allowed to do so. They each go off, separately, in search of the grail.
One morning my lord Gawan came riding on a green plain. He saw a shield there, shining in the sun—a joust had been aimed through it—and a horse that carried a woman's riding gear: its reins and saddle were expensive enough. It was tied to a branch, next to a shield. He thought: "Who could this woman be, who has such valor that she handles a shield? If she moves against me in combat, how shall I defend myself?[1] On foot I can save myself, but if she wants to wrestle[2] for a long time she may well bring me down, and I may win either hatred or greeting if a joust should take place on foot."

The shield was hacked to pieces. Gawan began to look at it as he came riding closer. The window of the joust[3] had been cut wide in it with a spear. That is how combat paints shields. Who would pay the shield makers if their paint was like that? The trunk of the linden tree was big. A woman lame in joy sat behind it on green clover. Great hardship caused her such pain that she had forgotten joy altogether. Gawan rode around the tree, closer to her. A knight lay in her lap, that was why her hardship was so great.

Gawan was not silent in his greeting.[4] The lady thanked him and bowed. He found her voice hoarse and dulled with weeping because of her fear. And so my lord Gawan dismounted. There lay a man, pierced through. His blood went into his body.[5] Then he asked the hero's wife whether the knight was alive or whether he was fighting death. She said: "My Lord, he is still alive, but I do not think he will be for long. God has sent you to me for comfort; advise me now as your loyalty desires. You have seen more sorrow than I have; let your comfort be given to me, that I my see your help." "That I shall do," said he. "My Lady, I would like to turn death away from this knight: I trust I could cure him very well if I had a reed. You might then see and hear him healthy for a long time, since he is not too badly wounded: the blood is a weight on his heart." He grabbed a branch off the linden tree. He slipped the bark off it like a reed (he was no fool with wounds). He pushed it into the body where the joust had hit, and then he asked the woman to suck, and the blood flowed toward her. The hero's strength opened itself again so that he could speak well, and began to talk. When he saw Gawan above him the knight thanked him much and said it was to Gawan's honor that he had freed him from his weak condition, and asked Gawan if he had come there, to Longrois, in knightly pursuit. "I also rode from far Punturtois, and I wanted to seek adventure here. I shall always lament in my heart that I have ridden so near here. You should avoid it also, if you have good sense. I did not think it would turn out this way. Lischoys Gwelljus has hurt me badly and put me behind my horse with a powerful joust: it went through my shield and through my body with a big shock. Then this good woman helped me on her horse and to this spot." He sorely implored Gawan to stay. Gawan said he wanted to see what kind of harm would come to him there. "If Logroys is so close that I can catch up with him in front of the castle, he shall have to answer me: I shall ask him what he had to avenge on you."[6] "Don't do that," said the wounded man. "I can tell you the truth. The journey that leads there is not for a child: it may well be called dangerous."

Gawan binds up the knight's wounds and rides on. There he saw his joy and his heart's sorrow below him. A spring flowed out of the rock. There he found what he did not regret: a woman so fair he liked to look at, the most beautiful flower of all women's color. Except for Condwiramurs no body more beautiful was ever born. Sweet with beauty was the lady, well behaved and of courtly manner. She was called Orgeluse of Logroys. The adventure also tells us of her that she was a stimulant of love's desire: her eyes sweet without sorrow and a bowstring[7] for the heart.

Gawan offered his greeting to her. He said: "If I may dismount by your leave, My Lady, and if I may observe that you are willing to have me near you, great sorrow will leave for joy. No knight has ever been so happy. My body must die if any woman has ever pleased me more." "Splendid; that is good to know."[8] Such was her speech when she looked at him. Her sweet mouth said more later: "Do not praise me too much: you might easily receive dishonor for it. I do not want every mouth to deliver its verdict on me. If my praise were common, it would be reckoned of small value with the wise and the dumb, the straight and the crooked. How could it rise up beyond the common level of honor? I should keep my praise such that the wise hold sway over it. I do not know who you are, My Lord. The time may have come for you to ride away from me. But my verdict does not set you free: you are near to my heart, but far outside of it, not inside. If you desire my love, how have you deserved love by me?[9] Many a man throws his eyes at a woman,[10] but he would throw them more softly if he avoided seeing what cuts him through the heart. Let your poor desire turn away to another love, not to me, if your hand must serve for love. If adventure sent you to search for love, as is the way of knights, you shall not have reward from me; you may well earn shame here, if I must tell you the truth."

Then he spoke: "My Lady, you speak true to me. My eyes are a danger to my heart: they have looked at your body and I must say in truth that I am your captive. Turn your womanly senses toward me. Even though it may have nettled you, you have locked me in. Untie or tie me now, you shall find me of the same disposition. If I had you as I would like to have you I would gladly endure[11] the fulfillment of my highest wish." She said: "Then take me with you. If you want to share the gain you seek of me with love, you shall lament it later in shame. I would like to know if you are the one who would dare to suffer combat for my sake. Give that up, if you want praise. If I should give you more advice, and if you would say yes to what follows, you would seek love elsewhere. If you desire my love you shall be dispossessed of love and joy. If you lead me away from here great sorrow shall touch you later." Then spoke my lord Gawan: "Who may have love without service? Must I tell you that such a man carries love away in sin? Whoever is eager for worthy love belongs in its service, before and after."[12] She said: "If you want to give me service you must live the warlike life, and yet you may earn shame after all. Ride down that path (it is not a road) there across that high, narrow bridge, into an orchard. You shall look for my horse there. You shall hear and see many people there, who will be dancing and singing songs, and playing the tambourine and the flute. No matter how they guide you, walk through them to where my horse stands, and untie it: it shall walk behind you."

Gawan does as he is asked. The people in the orchard feel sorry for him, and warn him against Orgeluse. An old knight becomes their spokesman. He said: "If you want to accept advice, you should stay away from that horse. Nobody here shall keep you from it, but the best thing you could ever do would be to leave the horse here. My lady be cursed that she is able to part so many a worthy man from his life." Gawan said he would not leave the horse there. "Alas for what will happen after this!" said the gray and worthy knight. He untied the horse's reins and said: "You shall not stand here any more. Let this horse step behind you. Let Him Whose hand salted the sea counsel you in your sorrow. Be on your guard against my lady's beauty, that it does not bring you to shame: with all her sweetness she is sour, like a rainshower glistening in the sun." "May God decide," said Gawan. He took his leave from the gray man, and again from people here and there. They all spoke words of lamentation. The horse stepped behind him along a narrow road, out of the gate and on the bridge. There he found the guardian of his heart. She was the lady of the land. Even though his heart flew to her, she bore much hardship for him in it. With her hands she had untied the ribbons under her chin and put them on her head.[13] A woman you find that way has limbs prepared for battle: she would most probably enjoy the pleasure. What other clothes was she wearing? How could I now think of examining her dress? Her radiant look frees me of this.

When Gawan went to the lady her sweet mouth received him like this.[14] She said: "Welcome, you goose, never did a man drag so much stupidity along as you do, since you want to give me your service. Alas, how gladly you would do without it!" He said: "If you are quick to anger now, mercy must follow. Since you punish me so much you shall have the honor of rewarding me. In the meantime my hand shall be lifted in your service until you are of a mind to reward me. If you want me to, I shall put you on this horse." She said: "I did not want this. Your inexperienced hand may well seize a smaller pledge." She turned away from him and jumped on the horse from among the flowers. She asked him to ride ahead.[15] "It would be a pity if I lost such an honorable companion," said she: "May God unhorse you."[16]

Whoever wants to follow me in this must avoid false words against her. Let no one speak too soon, before he knows what he should avenge and before he gains knowledge of how things stood with her heart. I also could speak words of revenge about that woman fair of skin: how she did Gawan wrong in her anger, or what she will still do to him—I shall take full revenge on her. Orgeluse the rich one did not act like a companion: she came riding up to Gawan with such angry behavior that I am hardly confident that she will free me of my cares. They both rode away from there on a shining heath. Gawan saw a herb standing there. Its root was good for wounds, he said. Then the worthy one dismounted, down on the earth. He grabbed the root and sat in the saddle again. The lady also did not forget to speak. She said: "If my companion is a physician and a doctor, he could earn a good living if he has learned how to offer jars for sale."[17] Gawan's mouth spoke to the lady: "I am riding to a wounded knight; his roof is a linden tree. If I still find him, this root shall cure him well and turn away all his weakness." She said: "I would like to see that. What if I learn the art?"

Soon a squire came after them there: he was in haste because of the message he had to deliver. Gawan wanted to wait for him. Then he thought the squire looked unseemly. Malcreatiure[18] was the proud squire called. Cundrie the sorceress was his well-shaped sister.[19] He had her features entirely, except that he was a man. In his case, too, each tooth stood out as in a wild boar, unlike the image of a man. His hair was also not as long as Cundrie's, that hung down her back until it touched her slipper. It was short, sharp as a porcupine's skin. People become like that of necessity by the water Ganjas in the land of Tribalibot.[20]

Wolfram speculates that monsters are born because women eat the wrong herbs during pregnancy. He goes on to tell us that Queen Secundille, wife to Feirefiz, sent both Cundrie and her brother to Anfortas as a gift, because she wanted to know more about the grail. Anfortas sent Malcreatiure on to Orgeluse. Malcreatiure now proceeds to threaten Gawan with a beating. Gawan said: "My knighthood has never suffered the strength of such behavior. That is how they should beat those who are good for nothing, and not warlike in a manly fashion; I am still empty of such pain. If both you and that lady mine want to offer me shameful words, you alone will have to enjoy something you may well take for anger. No matter how fearfully you are built, I would rather do without your threats." Gawan grabbed him by the hair and threw him under the horse. The squire wise and worthy looked back at Gawan in fear. His porcupinelike hair took revenge: it cut Gawan so in his hand that it showed all red with blood. The lady laughed about this. She said: "I like to see you both very much in such anger." They turned around then; the horse ran along.

They came where they found the knight lying wounded. With loyalty Gawan's hand bound the root on the wound. The wounded one said: "How did it go with you since you parted here from me? You have brought a woman who has planned shame for you. It is her fault that I am in such pain. In *Av'estroit mavoie* she helped me to a sharp joust to the detriment of my body and my wealth. If you want to keep your life let this treacherous woman ride and turn away from her. Now you yourself should see what her advice did to me. Yet I could heal very well if I could be at rest. So help me, faithful man." Then my lord Gawan said: "Choose from all my help." "Close by here stands a hospital," said the wounded knight. "If I were to come there within a short while I could rest there for a long time. We still have my lady love's horse standing here, and it is quite strong. Now lift her on it, and me behind her." Then the wellborn stranger untied the lady's horse from the branch. He wanted to pull it closer to her. The wounded one said: "Away from me! Why are you in such a haste to step on me?" He pulled it farther away for her. The lady followed him, soft and yet not in haste, according to her man's advice. Gawan put her on the horse. In the meantime the wounded knight jumped on Gawan's Castilian. I think that was done wrong. He and the lady rode away: that was a sinful gain.

Gawan lamented it much. The lady laughed more about it than seemed fitting to him for any joke. Since they had taken the horse from him her sweet mouth spoke to him like this: "I took you for a knight; after that, in a short while, you became a physician for wounds. Now you have to be a page. If anyone has to prosper by his skill, you may trust in your senses. Do you still desire my love?" "Yes, My Lady," said my lord Gawan: "If I could have your love it would be dearer to me than anything. If whoever lives on earth

without a crown, and all those who wear crowns and strive for
joyful praise, would share their gains with me in exchange for you,
the sense of my heart advises me that I should leave it be: I want to
have your love. If I cannot earn it a bitter death must soon show itself
to me. You lay waste your own property. Even if I should ever earn
freedom, you would still have me for your own. That seems to me
your uncontested right. Now call me knight or servant, page or
boor. Whatever your mockery has done to me, you were given sin for
it when you rejected my service. If I were to enjoy your service,
mockery would bring regret to you, and if it never did me harm it
would still undermine your dignity."

The wounded man rode back to him and said: "Is that you,
Gawan? If you have ever lent me something, that is now paid back to
you in full. When your manly strength captured me in hard knightly
combat, and when you brought me to the house of your uncle Artus,
he did not forget me for four weeks: all that time I ate with the
dogs." Then Gawan asked: "Is that you, Urians? If you want to do
me harm now, I endure it without guilt: I earned you the king's favor.
A weak mind helped you and advised that you should be expelled
from the calling of the shield and that they should declare you bereft
of your rights, because a young lady lost her rights on account of
you, and her peace under the law of the land. King Artus would
gladly have avenged it with a rope if I had not spoken out on your
behalf." "Whatever happened there, you are now standing here. You
have heard it said before you in the past: whoever has helped another
to be cured has become the other's enemy afterwards. I do as do
those who are in their right mind. Crying is more seemly for a child
than for a bearded man. I want to have this horse for myself alone."
He applied the spurs and rode away from Gawan, fast. That meant
hardship to him.

*Gawan proceeds to tell Orgeluse the story of Urians. Urians was
caught after raping a young lady. He surrendered to Gawan. When
Artus and the Round Table wanted to condemn Urians to death
Gawan, who felt responsible for him since he had accepted his
surrender, pleaded with Ginover to intercede on Urians's behalf.
She did and Urians was spared, but on condition that he ate with
the dogs for four weeks. Orgeluse reacts to the story as follows:* She
said: "His judgment was wrong. I shall probably never grow fond of
you, but he received such reward for this before he parted from my

country, that he may speak of shame.[21] Since the king did not avenge there what happened to that lady, and it has fallen to me, I am now the guardian of you both, even if I do not know who you both are. He must be taken into combat for the lady's sake alone, and very little for your sake. People should avenge boorish behavior with blows and thrusts." Gawan went to the horse; he caught it there with a light jump. The squire had come behind them, to whom the lady spoke in the heathen tongue all that she wished to tell those in the castle. Now Gawan's grief comes near.

Malcreatiure went on foot then. My lord Gawan looked at the young man's horse: it was too weak for combat. The squire had taken it from a peasant before he had come down the hill. Gawan kept it for his horse: he had to accept the exchange. Orgeluse spoke to him—in hatred I think—"Tell me, do you want anything more?" Then spoke my lord Gawan: "My travels from here will be undertaken according to your advice." She said: "That will come late to you." "I am serving you for it now." "That is why you seem dumb to me if you do not want to avoid it: you must turn from joy toward sorrow; your cares will be all new." Then spoke he who desired love: "I am he who keeps offering you his service, whether I get joy or grief from it, since your love ordered me to be at your command, whether I ride or walk."

Gawan inspects the horse. It looks pitiful. Orgeluse mocks him again. The woman laughed much, who caused him much grief. He bound his shield on the horse. She said: "Are you carrying cloth for sale in my country? Who made it my lot to care for a physician and a merchant? Beware of tollgates on the way: some of my toll people will make you empty of joy." Her sharp salty words seemed so acceptable to him that he did not heed what she said: whenever he looked at her his pledge to sorrow was redeemed. She was the real time of May to him, a flowering beyond all sight, sweet the eyes and sour the heart. Since both losing and finding were part of her,[22] and since she could heal joy when it was ailing, he benefited from that at all times. He was free, Gawan, and very much a captive.

Many a master of mine says that Amor and Cupido, and Venus the mother of both, give people love like this,[23] with arrows and with fire.[24] That love is unseemly. Those who are close to heartfelt loyalty shall never become free of love, whether in joy or, sometimes, in sorrow. True love is real loyalty. Cupid, your arrow misses me each time, as does my lord Amor's javelin. You both may be masters of love, as is Venus with her hot torch, but I do not know about such cares. If I should speak of real love, that must come to me through loyalty. If my senses could help anyone at all where love is concerned, I am so fond of my lord Gawan that I would like to help him without reward. For he is without shame, even though he lies in the bonds of love, even though love touches him and destroys his strong defense.[25] And yet he was always so given to defense, so equal in defense to the worthy, that a woman would not conquer his worthy self.

Let your horse come closer, my lord Duress of Love. You pull so much joy out of the heart that the place of joy is left full of holes and the path of sorrow clears itself. So widens the trail of grief. If it led to a place other than the heart's high spirits, that would seem good for joy to me. If love is bold to mischief, it seems too old to me for that. Or does love pass it off as childishness when she causes pain in the heart? I would rather put down mischief to her youth than let her waste the virtue of her old age. Many things have been done by her: where shall I say they come from? If Love wants to confound her staid behavior with young resolve, she will soon be empty of praise. They should explain that better to her. I praise pure love, and all those who are wise, women or men, shall be my followers. When love answers love, pure and without tarnish, and when neither is shaken by the fact that love locks their hearts with a love from which wavering has fled forever, that love is exalted above all others. No matter how gladly I would take him from there, my lord Gawan may not escape from love unless she wants to weaken his joy. What help then is my attempt at freeing him from love, no matter what I may say about it? A worthy man should not defend himself against love, since love must help to heal him.

Gawan and Orgeluse come to a castle by a river. A knight rides toward them. Orgeluse the rich said with pride: "Your mouth will have to admit that I do not break my loyalty: I have told you so often before that you are looking for much hardship here. Now defend yourself if you are able to: nothing else will be able to heal you. A knight is coming here whose hand shall unseat you, so that your breeches will be split; that will leave you in shame before the women who are sitting up there and watching. What if they see your shame?"

The ship's master[26] came there in answer to Orgeluse's wish. From the land she went into the ship; that taught Gawan to weep. The rich wellborn lady shouted back at him in anger: "You shall not come in there to me: you must be a hostage[27] out there." He shouted back in sorrow: "My Lady, why are you in such haste to get away from me? Shall I ever see you again?" She said: "The honor of being allowed to see me may come to you again. I think the time of waiting for it will lengthen itself much." The lady parted from him like this. Here came Lischoys Gwelljus. If I were to tell you now that he flew, I would deceive you with these words.[28] He was in great haste anyway, so that his horse gained honor by it (for it showed speed) on that wide green meadow. Then my lord Gawan thought: "How shall I wait for this man? Which would be the wiser course: on foot or on this poor little horse? If he wants to ride straight at me, so that he cannot break off his charge, he shall ride me down. But what is his horse to expect there, except also to stumble over that poor horse of mine? If he will offer me combat then, when we are both on foot, I shall give him combat if he so desires, even though the greeting of her who assigned me this combat may never come to me again."

Both knights are unhorsed and proceed to fight on foot. After a while Gawan succeeds in bodily seizing his opponent and throwing him down under him. He then asks him to surrender, but to no avail: the other knight would rather die than forfeit his fame. Gawan does not want to kill him, though, and allows him to stand up. The other knight's horse turns out to be Gringuljet, the very horse Urians had stolen from Gawan. Here his saddened noble mood reverted to high spirits, except that sorrow compelled him, and loyalty in the service he bore for his lady who had offered him contempt enough. His thoughts chased after her. In the meantime the proud Lischoys jumped to where he saw his own sword lying, which Gawan the worthy hero had wrested out of his hands in combat. Many a lady saw their next combat. The shields were in such a state that each one left his lying, and they hastened to do combat as they were. Each of them came at the other in heartfelt manly defense. Above them sat a host of ladies in the windows of the high hall and they looked at the combat that was before them. There new anger arose at first. Each of the knights was of such high birth that his honor would suffer much if the other overcame him.

Helmets and swords came to grief: they were their shields against death. Whoever saw the combat of the heroes there, I think he spoke of it as great hardship for them.

Lischoys Gwelljus, the young sweet one fought like this: boldness and courageous acts followed the counsel of his high heart. He profited from many a swift blow; often he jumped away from Gawan and then again close toward him. Gawan kept a steady mind; he thought: "If I can grab you to me, I shall reward you more than enough." They saw sparks of fire there, and the swords often striking in valorous hands. They began to force each other to turn to the side, forward and backward. There was no need for their quarrel: they might have left it without combat. Then my lord Gawan grabbed him; he threw him under him with force. Such company should stay away from me with its embrace: I could not endure it.

Gawan asked for the assurance of surrender. Lischoys, who was lying under him, was just as unprepared to give it as he had been during the first combat. He said: "You are wasting your time without need: I give death for assurance. Let your worthy hand end whatever praise was once known about me. Before God I am cursed, He shall never again care for my honor. For love of Orgeluse, the noble duchess, many a worthy man had to leave his praise in my hands. You may earn much praise if you are able to make me die."

Then King Lot's son thought: "It is true I should not do this: I would lose honor's favor if I were to kill this bold hero undaunted without guilt. Love drove him to combat against me, the love that compels me too and brings me much grief: why do I not let him stay alive for her sake? If it should be that I have part of her, he cannot prevent that, if luck should send it to me. If our combat had been witnessed by her, I think she will have to admit that I can serve for love." Then my lord Gawan said: "I want to leave you alive for the duchess's sake."

The ferryman comes up to Gawan and asks him for the horse he won in combat, as is the custom there. Gawan refuses to give him his horse, but gives him the knight instead, much to the ferryman's delight:[29] with laughing mouth he spoke: "Such a rich gift I have never seen, if only it were fitting for a person to receive it. But, My Lord, if you want to be my guarantee for it, my desire is overpaid. In truth Lischoys Gwelljus's praise was always so brilliant that I would not gladly take five hundred horses strong and fast for him, for it would not be fitting to me. If you want to make me rich, do what a knight should: if you are that powerful, deliver him to my boat, that way you shall increase your honor. Then spoke king Lot's son: "I shall deliver him to you a captive, both into your boat and out of it, and inside your door." "Then you shall be well received," said the ferryman:[30] his great gratitude was not too weak to bow.

Then he spoke: "Dear lord of mine, if it pleases you also to stay with me tonight in comfort. Greater honor never happened to any ferryman, any peer of mine. Everybody will reckon it as great happiness if I hold such a worthy man in my house." Then my lord Gawan said: "I should ask what you desire. Great tiredness has overcome me, so that I have need of rest. She who assigned me to this discomfort, she can make sweet things sour and your heart's joy dear and yourself rich in grief. She rewards unevenly. Alas, you loss of what I wanted to find,[31] you lower one side of my breast for me, which once desired high things when God would confer joys on me. A heart lay under it; I think it has disappeared. Where shall I receive comfort now; must I err without help, in such sorrow for love? If she practices womanly loyalty she should heighten my joy for me, even though she is able to hurt me so."

The ferryman heard that Gawan was wrestling with sorrow and that love oppressed him. He said: "My Lord, such is life here, on the plain and in the forest and where Clinschor is lord, and no cowardice nor manly art can change it: today sad, tomorrow glad. It may be unknown to you, but this whole country is one adventure, by night and by day. Luck may bring help to manliness. The sun must be standing very low: My Lord, you should go to sleep." The ferryman asked that of him. Gawan led Lischoys away from there with him, on the water; they saw the hero follow him patiently, without any resistance. The ferryman pulled the horse behind.

They go to the ferryman's house. The ferryman's daughter disarms and bathes Gawan. His son makes the dining room ready for supper. The host came and they brought water there. When Gawan had washed himself he did not avoid one question: he asked the host for good company. "Let this young lady eat with me." "My Lord, it has never been thought of that she should eat with lords or sit so close to them: she would easily become too good for me. But we have had much profit from you. Daughter, do all that he desires: I shall endorse whatever follows."[32] The sweet one grew red for

shame, but she did what the host ordered: the lady Bene sat next to
Gawan. *The meal is described at some length, as is the eventual
making of Gawan's bed.* Gawan stayed there alone, they told me,
and the young lady with him. If he had desired anything from her, I
think she would have granted it to him. He should sleep now, if he
can: may God protect him. And so day came.

Book Eleven

Great tiredness pulled Gawan's eyes shut. So he slept until the early morning. Then the warrior woke up. The wall on one side of the room had many windows, with glass[1] in front of them. One of the windows was open to the orchard. He went to that one to look, to get air, and to listen to the birds' song. He did not sit there too long. He looked at the castle he had seen the night before, when the adventure had happened to him. There were many ladies in the high hall, and many among them were very beautiful. It seemed a great miracle to him that the women did not get weary of watching, that they did not sleep. And yet the day was not too light. He thought: "I will go back to sleep in their honor."

When he wakes up again Gawan asks Bene, the ferryman's daughter, about the castle. The young lady started with fright. She said: "My Lord, do not ask this now: I shall never tell you. I cannot tell you anything about them: even if I knew anything I should keep it unsaid. Do not be offended by me and ask for other things, I advise you, if you want to follow me." But Gawan spoke to her again with a question, following up the story of all the ladies he had seen sitting in the high hall there. The young lady was so loyal that she wept from her heart and showed great lamentation.

It was still very early, but in the meantime her father had come to them. He would have left things altogether without anger if the young lady fair of skin had been forced into anything and if there had been any wrestling there. She behaved as if there had been, the young lady rich in virtue, since she was sitting close to the bed. That left her father without hatred. He said: "Daughter, do not cry about it. What happens in jest like this is soon forgotten, even if it causes anger at first."² Gawan said: "Nothing did happen here, except what we want to speak about in front of you. I asked this young lady a few things: they seemed to spell my perdition to her and she asked me to leave off. If it does not offend you, let my service compel you to this, my host, that you would be pleased to tell me about the women above us here. I never heard in all lands that you could see so many fair women with such radiant headdresses." The host wrung his hands. Then he spoke: "Do not ask that by God, My Lord, there is grief beyond all grief." "Then I must lament their grief," said Gawan. "Mine host, you must tell me: why do my questions bring grief to you?" "My Lord, by your manliness: if you cannot give up questioning, you will probably want to know more. That will teach your heart hardship and make us empty of joy, me and all my children who have been born to your service." Gawan said: "You must tell me, but if you want to leave it altogether unsaid, so that your story passes me over, I shall still hear how things stand there."

The host spoke with loyalty: "My Lord, it must bring grief to me that you do not desist from questioning. I want to lend you a shield. Now arm yourself for combat. You are in *Terre marveile,* the Land of Wonders. *Lit marveile,* the Wondrous Bed is here. My Lord, the hardship in *Schastel marveile,* the castle of wonders, has never been endured.³ Your life wants to go into death. If adventure is known to you, whatever combat your hand fought until now was mere child's play: now sorrow's goal is coming closer to you." Gawan spoke: "I would regret it if my comfort would ride away from these ladies without investigating their lot more. I have also heard of them before. Since I have come so close now, it would not be good for me if I did not want to risk anything for them." The host lamented out of loyalty.⁴ He then told his guest: "All hardship is nothing to him to whom it falls to endure this adventure: it is harsh and unseemly, in truth and without lying. My Lord, I cannot deceive you."

Gawan renowned in praise did not turn to fear; he said: "Now give me advice for combat; if you agree to it I shall do a knight's deed here, if God allows it. I always gladly have your advice and your counsel. My lord Host, it would be wrong if I should part from here like this. Those who love me and those who hate me would call me a coward." At first the host began to lament, since such grief had never befallen him. He spoke to his guest: "If God shows us that you are not forfeit to death you shall become lord of this land. All the ladies who are hostages here, and many a squire and noble knight as well, were forced to come here by strong magic never yet conquered by a knight's honor. If your power sets these ladies free, your praise shall be exalted and God shall have honored you well: you shall be lord in joy over many a fair skinned lady from many lands."

The host continues to tell Gawan that he has acquired enough praise already by overcoming his opponent the day before. Gawan will not hear of it; he is armed by Bene. The host had been thinking; he stood before Gawan again. Then he spoke: "My Lord, I tell you what you should do against the danger to your life. You must carry my shield. It is neither pierced nor hacked to pieces since I rarely do combat: who could have damaged it then? My Lord, when you come to the castle, do one thing for the benefit of your horse. A merchant sits in front of the gate: leave the horse to him, in front of the castle. Buy something from him, it does not matter what: he shall keep your horse all the better if you leave it to him as a pledge.[5] If you are not harmed you will be glad to have the horse." Then spoke my lord Gawan: "Should I not ride in on my horse?" "No, My Lord, all the radiance of the women will be hidden from you. And so you will come closer to grief. You will find only the great hall, and no one who lives there, big or small. May God's grace rule you when you go into the chamber where Lit marveile stands. If that bed and its bedposts were put into the scales against the crown and all the riches of the Mahumellin[6] of Morocco, it would not be redeemed by those. On that bed such suffering will befall you as God intends for you. May he show it forth as joy in the end. Remember, My Lord, if you are worthy: never let this shield and your sword part from you. If you think your great grief has come to an end, that is when it will first be called to combat."

Gawan rides off, much to Bene's chagrin. He finds the merchant and asks to see some girdles and brooches. The merchant said: "I have in truth sat here many a year and not a man dared to look (nobody except worthy women) at what is lying in my booth. If your heart shows forth manliness you are lord of it all. It has been brought here from far away. If you have taken the prize to yourself (you must have come here on adventure), if success is yours, you may easily deal with me: whatever I have for sale will belong to you then.

Go, leave it to God. Did Plippalinot the ferryman show you the way here? Many a lady will praise your coming into this land if your hand sets her free. If you want to go in search of adventure let the horse stand quietly here: I shall guard it, if you want to leave it with me." Then spoke my lord Gawan: "I would gladly leave it with you if that agreed with your status. Now I am unsettled by your riches: my horse has never been in the care of such a rich groom, ever since I first sat on it." The merchant spoke without any hatred: "My Lord, I myself and all my possessions (why should I say more about them now?) are yours, if you prevail here. To whom could I belong with greater right?"

Gawan goes into the castle. He finds it empty. It was well decorated and well furbished inside. The columns in the windows were well worked, and high arches were placed above them. A wondrous array of beds stood here and there in the room, each bed on its own. Rich covers of many kinds lay on the beds. The ladies had been sitting there, and they had not forgotten, but gone away. They did not welcome the coming of their joy, the day of their salvation that rested in Gawan. If only they could have seen him, what might have happened to him? Not one of them was allowed to do that, even though he wanted to serve them.[7] They were innocent of this. Then my lord Gawan went both here and there. He examined the high hall. In one wall—I do not know on which side—he saw a door standing open wide. Beyond that door he would earn great praise, or die striving for it.

He walked into the hall. Its floor appeared clear and smooth, like glass. There was *Lit marveile,* the Wondrous Bed. Four wheels ran under it, round and made of shining rubies: even the wind was not as fast. The bedposts were welded to them. I have to praise its floor: it was made of jasper, of chrysolite, of sard, all as Clinschor, who had invented it, wanted it. From many lands his cunning knowledge had brought the materials that were put into this. The floor was so slippery that Gawan could hardly find a grip there to keep his footing. He went guided by luck, but the bed kept moving from the place where it had been standing before, each time he took a step.[8] It became difficult for Gawan to carry the heavy shield his host had entrusted to him. He thought: "How shall I come to you?[9] Do you want to swerve away from me like that? I shall let you know if I can jump into you." Then the bed stood before him; he prepared himself for the jump and jumped straight into the middle of it. No man shall ever know that speed again, how the bed hurtled itself here and there. It did not leave out any of the four walls: it flung itself against each one with great violence, so that the whole castle resounded.

So it rode many a great charge. The noise could not have been greater than whatever noise thunder makes combined with the sound produced by trumpeters, whether they are first or last to play. Gawan had to stay awake even though he was lying in the bed. What was the hero to do then? The noise had so overcome him that he pulled the shield over him: he lay, and left things in the power of Him who has help in His keeping and Who has never withheld help from whoever is able to ask Him for it in his grief. A wise man, steadfast of heart, will call on the Highest Hand when grief is known to him, for it bears rich help and aids him in a helpful way. That also happened to Gawan there. He now asked the mighty goodness of Him, Whom he had always called the cause of his praise, to protect him. Now the noise came to an end, so that the four walls were measured alike there, where the bed of wondrous build stood in the middle of the floor. Now greater fear was known to him: five hundred slings were ready to throw by the magic of things. The throw guided the stones to the bed where Gawan lay. The shield was so hard that he felt little of them. They were water pebbles, round and hard, and they bored through the shield here and there.

And so the stones had been thrown. Rarely had Gawan suffered such swift throws hurled at him. Now five hundred crossbows or more were primed for shooting.[10] They were all aimed at the bed where he lay. Whoever has suffered such hardship will know what arrows are. It took a little time until they had all whizzed past. Whoever wants to take his comfort should not come to such a bed: nobody gives him comfort there. Young people might turn gray with the kind of comfort Gawan found in that bed. And yet his heart and his hand, too, were free of cowardice. The arrows and the stones had not avoided him completely: he was bruised and cut through the chain mail. Then he had hope that there was an end to his misery, but he still had to win the prize with his hands. At the same time a door opened toward him. A strong oaflike man walked through it. He was built in a frightening manner. He was wearing a surcoat, a bonnet of fish skin, and two wide leggings of the same. He carried a club in his hands; its knob was thicker than a jug. He went up against Gawan. That was not what Gawan wanted at all, since the man's coming upset him. Gawan thought: "This man is without armor: his weapons are very weak against me."[11] He raised himself and sat, as if his limbs were not hurting in the least. The other man took one step back, as if he wanted to avoid him, and yet he spoke in anger: "You do not have to be frightened by me: I shall arrange it that something will happen to you for which you give your life as a pledge. You are still alive, through the power of the devil. Even if he has helped you here, you still have no defense against dying. I shall bring death to you as I leave you now." The boorish creature walked out the door again. Gawan cut the arrow shafts from his shield with his sword. The arrows had gone through all over, so that they clanked in his chain mail.

Then he heard a roar as if somebody had beat at least twenty drums to the dance. His firm courage entire, which true cowardice had never hurt nor cut, thought: "What will happen to me? I should be entitled to talk of hardship now: will my hardship increase? I shall turn to defense." Now he looked at the oaf-man's door. A strong lion jumped out of it: he was as high as a horse. Gawan, who always disliked to flee, took the shield by the straps. He did as defense required. He jumped on the floor. The strong big lion was fearful with hunger, but he profited little from it. He ran toward the man in anger. My lord Gawan defended himself. The lion had almost taken the shield away. His first attack had gone through the shield with all his claws. Such an attack by an animal rarely went through such hardness. Gawan defended himself against the lion's attack. He cut a leg off him. The lion jumped around on three legs. The fourth leg stuck to the shield. The lion gushed so much blood that Gawan could stand firm.[12] The battle now began to go back and forth. The lion often jumped at the stranger. With glittering teeth he gave many a snort through his nose. If they wanted to make him get used to eating good people, I would not gladly sit by him. Gawan regretted it too, who fought to the death with him there. He had wounded him so that the whole chamber was splashed with blood. The lion jumped there in anger and he wanted to pull Gawan under him. Gawan made a thrust through the lion's chest up to his hand,[13] and the lion's anger disappeared since he fell down dead.

Gawan had overcome this great hardship in combat. At the same time he thought: "What is good for me now? I do not sit gladly in this blood. I should also guard against sitting or lying on the bed if I am to show any wisdom, since it may run around with me."

Now his head had been so numbed from blows, and his wounds began to bleed so that his firm strength left him all alone without its company. He staggered about with dizziness. His head lay on the lion, the shield much lower under him. If he had ever gained strength or sense, those had both been taken away from him. He had been hard hit. All his senses left him. *One young lady has observed the combat. She reports to Queen Arnive, who sends two young ladies into the chamber to see if Gawan is still alive. They check to see if he is still breathing.*

Breath was found there. At the same time one lady told her companion to jump up quickly and bring pure water. Her companion with the fair skin brought it to her quickly. The young lady pushed her ring between Gawan's teeth. That was done with great decorum. Then she poured the water after it, softly, and then still more. But she did not pour much until he opened his eyes. He offered them his service and expressed his gratitude to the two sweet children. "That you should find me lying here in such an unseemly way. If you could pass that over in silence, I would take it as a sign of your good nature. May your good breeding prevent you from mentioning it." They said: "You were and are lying as one worthy of the highest praise. You have won the prize here, and because of it you shall grow old with joy: victory is yours today. Now comfort us poor people: may your wounds be such that we can be happy with you."[14] He spoke: "If you like to see me live you shall have to give me help." He asked the ladies: "Let someone look at my wounds who has knowledge of these things. If I am still to engage in combat, please untie my helmet and go away. I shall gladly fight for my life." They said: "You are now free of combat: My Lord, let us be with you, except that one of us should take the message that you are still alive to the four queens and earn the messenger's bread by doing so.[15] They should also prepare a bed for you and pure medicine, and faithfully take care of you with the proper salves that are a cure for bruises and wounds, and a helpful relief."

One of the ladies ran away from there so fast that she did not limp. She brought tidings to the court that Gawan was alive, "and so alive that he will make our joy rich with joy, if God wills it so. He has need of good help." They all said: "Praise be to God, *dieu merci.*" *Arnive, the old queen, takes charge. She has Gawan's armor removed and treats his wounds and bruises with her salves.*

She said: "I shall soon soothe your pain. Cundrie the sorceress is kind enough to see me often. She enables me to do well whatever may be done with medicine. Ever since Anfortas has come into such suffering through his grief that people have brought him help, this salve has helped him, so that he did not die. It came from Munsalvaesche." When Gawan had heard Munsalvaesche named he began to know joy: he thought he was close to it there. Then he who had always been free of falsehood, Gawan, spoke to the queen: "My Lady, you have won my senses that had run away from me back to my heart. My pain also soothes itself. Whatever strength or sense I have, that your servant owes to you alone." She spoke: "My Lord, we should all try to win your favor and do so with loyalty. Now follow my advice and do not speak much. I shall give you a root; it will make you sleep—it is good for you. You shall not be of a mind to eat and drink before the night. This way your strength shall come back to you. Then I shall come to you with food, so that you shall be well until the morning."

She put a root into his mouth; he fell asleep at the same moment.[16] She took good care of him with covers. And so he who was rich in honor and poor in harm slept the day away. He was bedded softly and he was warm. Sometimes he grew cold in his sleep, so that he hiccuped or sneezed, all because of the power of the salve. A large company of women went out and in. They had a fair, worthy appearance. Arnive the old queen ordered by her power that none of them should raise their voices while the hero was sleeping there. She also ordered the high hall closed: whatever knight there was, squire or burgher, none of them heard of these tidings before the next day. Then new lamentation came to the women.

So the hero slept until night. The queen was very considerate: she took the root out of his mouth. He woke up. Drinking seemed in order. Then the wise queen ordered them to carry drink to Gawan, and good food. He raised himself and sat; he ate with good joy. Many a lady stood before him. No worthier service was ever known to him. That service was done with good breeding. My lord Gawan looked closely at one lady, and then at another, and another still. He was back in the old longing for the fair Orgeluse, since in all his years no woman had come so close to him, whether he had received love or whether it had been withheld from him. Then spoke the hero undaunted to his guardian, the old queen: "My Lady, it offends my good breeding, and you may take it for boorishness that these ladies should stand before me. Order them to go sit, or tell them to eat with me." "There is no sitting here for any of them, except me. My Lord, they might be ashamed if they would not serve you as much as they can, since you are the summit of our joys. But, My Lord, what you command them they shall do, if we have any sense." The noble ladies of high lineage showed their good breeding in that they kept standing of their own will. Their sweet mouths asked him to allow them to stand there until he was done eating, and that not one of them should sit. When that happened they went away again. Gawan lay himself down to sleep.

Book Twelve

Whoever would take rest away from Gawan now, when rest befits him, would commit a sin, I think. According to the adventure he had strained himself and heightened and widened his praise with great hardship. *Wolfram proceeds to list a number of great feats accomplished by other knights of great renown, only to conclude that none can match what Gawan has just accomplished.* Orgeluse came into the thoughts of Gawan's heart, who was ever weak in cowardice and strong in true valor. How could such a great lady hide in such a small place? She came along a narrow path into Gawan's heart, so that all his pain disappeared because of these cares.[1] And yet they were low walls for such a great lady to sit inside. In his waking hours he never forgot her service in loyalty. Nobody should laugh about the fact that a lady can bring low such a warlike man.[2] Alas, alas, what can that be? Lady Love shows her anger at him who has earned praise. Yet she found him warlike and undaunted. She should abandon violence against his ailing wounds. It should count to his advantage that she conquered him once before, against his will, when he was in good health.[3]

Lady Love, if you want to earn praise you should allow yourself to be told that this combat is without honor for you. Gawan has always spent his life's time as your favor commanded him, as did his father Lot. His whole lineage on his mother's side did stand fast in your service. *Wolfram proceeds to give examples.* Many a man did sing of love whom love never oppressed like this.[4] I should probably be silent now.[5] Lovers should lament what happened to the man of

Norway[6] after he had recovered from the adventure when love's storms struck him too bitterly and he was without help.

He spoke: "Alas, that I ever saw these restless beds. One has hurt me and the other has increased my thoughts of love. Orgeluse the duchess must give me her favor if I am to remain in joy." He tossed with impatience so that some of his wounds' bandages broke. He lay in much discomfort. Now look, the day shone on him. He had waited for it in his distress. Before this he had often endured many a hard combat with swords, and yet each of them had been softer than this time of rest. Whatever hardship wants to count itself equal to Gawan's, whatever lover wants to claim such hardship for himself, let him first be healed after he has been wounded so with arrows: that may very likely hurt him as much as his love's grief ever did. *Gawan gets out of bed, puts on the fresh clothes that have been left for him, and wanders about the castle. In the high hall he sees a pillar, a marvel of craftsmanship.* My lord Gawan went up alone into the guard's house, which contained many an expensive stone, to look more closely. There he found such great wonders that seeing them did not displease him. It seemed to him that all lands were known to him inside the great pillar, that they went round and that the big mountains ran into each other with a violent shock. Inside the pillar he found people riding and walking, this one running, that one standing.[7] He went to sit in a window: he wanted to examine the marvel more.

Then came old Arnive with her daughter Sangive and her daughter's two daughters: all four of them went up to him. Gawan jumped up when he saw them. Queen Arnive spoke: "My Lord, you should be asleep still. Have you given up rest? You are too sorely wounded to be exposed to more discomfort." Then he spoke: "My lady and guardian, your help has given me such strength and sense that I shall serve you if I am to stay alive." The queen said: "If I am to understand that you, My Lord, said to me that I am your guardian, you must kiss these women, all three. You will be protected against shame if you do so:[8] they were born of a king's lineage." He was happy with that request. He kissed the fair women then, Sangive and Itonje, and the sweet Cundrie. Gawan himself sat down as the fifth. Then he looked at the bodies of the fair young ladies, now one and then the other. And yet a woman ruled him, who lay in his heart. These young ladies' looks were a day of fog compared to Orgeluse.

She seemed to him of such fair skin, the duchess of Logrois: his heart hunted for her.

Well, Gawan had been received by the three ladies. They showed themselves of such fair skin that a heart could easily have been cut that had not suffered grief before.[9] He spoke to his guardian about the pillar he had seen there: she should tell him its story. What was it made of?" She said: "My Lord, since it was first known to me this stone has shone by day and every night six miles around in the land. Whatever happens within those limits people see in that pillar, be it on water or in the fields: of that it is the true messenger. Birds or beasts, foreigners or foresters, strangers and acquaintances, people have found them in there. Its radiance shines for more than six miles. The pillar is so strong and entire that neither a hammer nor a smith could overcome it. It was stolen in Thabronit, from Queen Secundille, against her will, I think."

At that time Gawan was allowed to see a knight and a lady riding in the pillar. It seemed to him that the lady was fair, the man and the horse heavily armed, and the man's helmet adorned. They came riding hastily to the plain, along the paths. Their travels led them toward it. They came on the paths through the marsh, just as Lischoys the proud rode, whom Gawan brought low. The lady guided the knight with the reins: jousting was his desire. Gawan turned himself away; his cares increased. It seemed to him the pillar had deceived him: but he had in truth seen Orgeluse de Logrois and a knight *courtois* on the meadow by the jetty. As hellebore is swift and strong in the nose,[10] the duchess entered the narrow dwelling of his heart through his eyes above.

A man helpless against love is my lord Gawan, alas. He spoke to his guardian when he saw the knight coming: "My Lady, a knight is coming here with his spear raised high: he does not want to leave off searching, and his searching should find its goal too. Since he desires deeds of knighthood, I shall give him combat. Tell me, who might the lady be?" She said: "That is the duchess of Logrois, the fair. Who is she riding with there, in falsehood? The Turkoit has come with her, whose heart has often been called undaunted. He has earned praise with his spear: three countries could be furbished with it.[11] You should avoid combat now against his warlike hand. Combat is much too soon for you: you are too sorely wounded for it. Even if you were altogether healthy, you should still leave off

fighting against him." Then spoke my lord Gawan: "You say I
should be lord here. So, if anyone seeks deeds of knighthood so near
to my honor, My Lady, I must have my armor if he cares for
combat."[12] Because of this, great weeping was done by the ladies, all
four. They said: "If you want to enrich your happiness and your
praise, do not do combat in any way. If you were to lie there before
him, dead, our grief would grow. But if you recover from combat
with him your earlier wounds will take your life if you want to be in
armor; and so we are given to death."

Gawan was wrestling with grief: you may hear what oppressed
him. He had taken the coming of the worthy Turkoit as a shame
upon himself. His sore wounds oppressed him too, and love much
more, and the sorrow of the four ladies, since he saw loyalty in them.
He asked them to give up weeping. Moreover, his mouth began to
desire armor, horse and sword. The ladies fair and worthy guided
Gawan back. He asked them to go before him, down to where the
other ladies were, sweet and fair. *Gawan is armed and rides away
from the castle in secret. The ferryman gives him a spear. Before the
joust begins the ferryman makes it clear that he is entitled to the
loser's horse. Gawan thrusts his spear through his opponent's visor
and rides off with his helmet. The Turkoit falls down in the grass.*
Gawan came riding over him until he promised him assurance. The
ferryman bespoke the horse. That was his right, who denies it? "You
would be glad to rejoice, if you knew why," said Orgeluse the fair,
with evil mind toward Gawan, "since the strong lion's paw in your
shield must follow you, you think praise has befallen you because
these ladies have seen your joust done. We must leave you in joy, if
you are happy with it. Even though the Wondrous Bed took such
small revenge on you, still your shield is broken as if you had known
real combat. You may also be too sorely wounded for the strain of
battle: that would hurt you over and above the fact that I called you a
goose. Yet you may like that shield full of holes, like a sieve, that so
many an arrow pierced, because you may want to boast of it. You
would dearly like to flee from the discomfort of these times. Ride
back to the ladies and let them set your finger.[13] Would you dare to
look on the combat I would have to require if your heart wanted to
serve me as love demands?" Gawan spoke to the duchess: "My Lady,
if I have wounds, they have found help here. If you would think it
worthy of your help to care to accept my service, no hardship has

ever been thought so dire that I would not be called upon to suffer it in your service." She said: "I shall let you ride with me to do combat for more praise in my company." Because of this the proud, worthy Gawan became rich with joy. He then sent the Turkoit away with his host Plippalinot. To the castle he sent word that all the ladies of fair skin should take care of him[14] with honor.

Gawan's spear had remained whole, even though both horses had been driven with spurs to the shock of the joust. In his hand he carried it away from the bright meadow. Many a lady wept over his riding away from them. Queen Arnive spoke: "Our comforter has chosen for himself what is soft to his eyes, but a thorn in his heart. Alas he now follows Orgeluse the duchess to *Li gweiz prelljus*, the perilous ford. That will not be a good thing for his wounds." Four hundred ladies were in lamentation. Gawan rode away from them in search of praise. Whatever grief came to him from his wounds, the radiance of Orgeluse's skin had transfigured it altogether. She said: "You shall get me a wreath from the branch of a tree. I shall praise your deed, and if you will give it to me you may desire my love." He said: "My Lady, wherever that branch is, I shall break it off if death lets me. It may earn me such high praise and happiness that I may lament my grief[15] for you, My Lady, to gain your favor."

Whatever bright flowers stood there, they were nothing compared to the color of Orgeluse's skin. Gawan thought of her and his former discomfort did not speak of any sorrow to him. So she rode with her guest about a journey's stage away from the castle, on a road wide and straight, toward a fair forest. The trees had to be tamarisk and redwood. That was Clinschor's forest.[16] Gawan, the hero bold, spoke: "My Lady, where shall I break the wreath that shall make my pockmarked joy whole?" He should have pushed her down, as has often happened since to many a fair lady.[17] She spoke: "I shall let you see where you may have praise." Across the fields they rode so close to a ravine that they saw the tree with the wreath. Then she said: "My Lord, he who took my joy away guards that tree. If you bring me a branch from it, no knight ever earned such high praise with service for love." So spoke the duchess. "Here I want to interrupt my journey. May God guard you. If you want to travel farther you must not wait long: you must jump on your horse across *Li gweiz prelljus* with courage."

She held still on the plain. On rode my lord Gawan. He heard a swift waterfall that had dug out a valley wide, deep, unpassable. Gawan, the man rich in courage, took to the horse with the spurs. The hero wellborn drove it so hard that it stepped across on the other side with two feet. The jump had to end with a fall. The duchess wept over this. The current was swift and strong. Gawan took advantage of his strength but he wore the burden of armor. A tree's branch had grown into the water's flow there. The strong man grabbed it, since he had a great desire to live, after all. His spear floated next to him there. The warrior seized it. He climbed up on the shore. *Next Gawan rescues his horse Gringuljet.*

When Gawan had broken the branch and the wreath had become his helmet's roof, a fair knight rode up to him. The years of his time had been neither too short nor too long for him. Out of arrogance his mind compelled him never to do combat with one man, no matter how much harm that man might do to him, but only with two or more. His noble heart was so exalted that whatever one man did to him he would let pass without combat. The son of King Irot bade Gawan good morning: he was King Gramovlanz. He said: "My Lord, I have not given up my claim to this wreath. My greeting would have remained unspoken altogether if there had been two of you who would not have shied away from taking such a branch from my tree to earn high praise. They would have been given combat, but combat now would disgrace me."

Gawan would also rather not do combat since the king is unarmed. The king gathers that Gawan has overcome the Wondrous Bed. He wanted to do the same, but Clinschor the magician advised him against it. The king goes on to say that he killed Cidegast, Orgeluse's husband. "Orgeluse I led away then; I offered her the crown and all my land. Whatever service my hand offered her, she turned her heart's malice against it. I held her for a year with constant supplication. I could not earn her love. I must lament to you from my heart. I know well that she offered love to you since you intend my death here. If two of you had come you might have taken my life away, or you would both have died. My heart goes out to another love, and you can do me the favor of your help, since you have become lord of *Terre marveile.* Your combat has earned that praise for you. If you want to do a good deed now, help me with a young lady for whom my heart laments its sorrow. She is King Lot's child. All who are on earth have never had such power over me. I

have her keepsake here. Now promise my service to the young lady
fair of skin there, too. Also, I trust that she is fond of me since I have
suffered hardship for her sake. Since Orgeluse the rich denied her
love to me with heartfelt words, it has been the worthy Itonje's doing
if I earned praise since, or if good things happened to me, or bad. I
have unfortunately not seen her.[18] If your comfort will promise me
help, bring this ring to the fair sweet lady of mine. You are altogether free of combat here, unless you would happen to be part of
a larger group, two or more. Who would speak of me with honor if I
killed you or forced you to give me assurance? My hand has always
avoided that kind of combat."

Then said my lord Gawan: "I am a warlike man. If you do not
want to earn praise from the fact that I have been slain by your hand
I, too, shall have no praise for having broken this branch. Who
would speak of me with great honor if I killed you, unarmed? I shall
be your messenger: give me the ring and let me profess your service
and not hide your sorrow." The king thanked him much for that.
Gawan asked him more: "Since you spurn combat against me, My
Lord, tell me who you are."[19] "You should not reckon it as my
shame," said the king: "My name is not hidden. My father was
called Irot. King Lot killed him. I am king Gramovlanz. My high
heart has always been so valiant that I shall never fight at any time
over what one man might do to me, except against one, who is
called Gawan. I have heard such praise of him that I would gladly go
up against him in combat for my grief. His father broke faith: he
killed my father while still greeting him. I have enough to lament
about that. Now Lot has died and Gawan has earned such praise
beyond all of us that no one of the Round Table may be likened to
him in praise. I live for the day of my combat against him."

Then spoke the worthy son of Lot: "If you want to speak such
false mischief of her father for the love of your lady love—if that she
is—and if you would like to kill her brother as well, she should be an
evil young lady indeed if she did not lament such behavior on your
part. If she were a true daughter and a true sister, she would be both
their protector against you, so that you would abandon this hatred.
How would it befit your father-in-law to have broken faith? Have you
not avenged the very fact that you have accused him, who is dead, of
falsehood? His son shall not be slow to do this; it will not be grief to
him if he cannot profit from the love of his sister fair of skin. He gives

himself as a pledge. My Lord, my name is Gawan. What my father has done to you, avenge it on me. He is dead. If I have lived a worthy life I should give it as a pledge in combat for him, for the hardship done to him by slander."

The king and Gawan agree to meet in combat before Artus on the plain of Joflanze, sixteen days later. So my lord Gawan parted from that worthy man. With joy he galloped. The wreath adorned him. He did not want to keep the horse back. With his spurs he drove it to the ravine. Gringuljet took off on time and jumped so wide that Gawan avoided falling altogether. The duchess rode toward him where the hero had dismounted from the horse on the grass to tighten the saddle girth. The rich duchess quickly dismounted before him. She offered herself to him at his feet. Then she spoke: "My Lord, such hardship as I have desired for you was not worthy of my honor. In truth your hardship gives me that pain in my heart a loyal[20] woman should receive on account of her beloved friend."

He said: "My Lady, if it is true that you greet me without deceit you are coming closer to praise. I am that wise after all: if the shield shall have its due, you have done wrong to it. The calling of the shield is so exalted that he who does the deeds of knighthood well always extracts himself from mockery. My Lady, may I just say: whoever has seen me in this will have to admit that deeds of knighthood are mine. You once said otherwise, since you saw me for the first time.[21] I leave that be: take the wreath. You shall never offer such dishonor to any knight again through the radiance of your skin. If your mockery were aimed at me I would rather be without love." The fair and rich one spoke from her heart, crying: "My Lord, if I were to tell you my grief, what of it I carry in my heart, you would give me the prize of distress. The one against whom my senses are addled should forgive me because of his breeding. I shall never lose more joys than I lost with Cidegast the chosen one.

"My fair sweet *beas amis*, my handsome friend, so illustrious was his praise in the pursuit of true worth that this one or that one whom a mother ever bore had to speak well of his worth, which no other praise ever overcame in the years of his time on earth. He was a living source of virtue, and his youth bore so much of it, guarded from false obligations. Out of darkness he made himself visible against the light, and he pegged his praise so high that nobody

could reach it. His praise could grow tall out of the seeds of his
heart, so that others were under it. How does swift Saturn run his
course above all the other stars? He was a unicorn[22] in loyalty, the
man I wished for myself,[23] since I am now able to speak the truth.
Maidens should lament for that animal:[24] it is slain by purity. I was
his heart, he was my body. Him I lost, a woman destined for
bereavement. King Gramovlanz killed him, from whom you took
this wreath.

"My lord, if I wished you harm I did so for this reason: I wanted
to find out whether I should offer you love on account of your honor.
I know well I wished you harm, My Lord: I wanted to test you. You
should take revenge by losing your anger and forgiving me altogether. You are the one rich in courage. I would compare you with
gold they temper in the fire: your mind has been tempered altogether. The man I brought you here to harm, as I planned and still
plan, has brought pain to my heart."

Then my lord Gawan said: "My Lady, unless death turns me away
I shall teach the king such hardship that it will wound his pride. I
have pledged my loyalty to ride in combat against him in a short
while. There we shall show manliness. My Lady, I have forgiven you.
If you would not allow yourself to spurn my boorish counsel because of your good breeding, I shall now counsel you in keeping
with your honor as a lady and the precepts of true worth:[25] there is
nobody here but us, so, My Lady, grant me your favor." She spoke:
"I have rarely grown warm in an arm encased in iron. I do not want
to fight against it if you want to earn this reward from me some
other time. I shall lament your hardship until you grow all well
again wherever you are wounded, until the harm is healed. I shall go
with you to *Schastel marveile*." "You want to increase my joy," said
the man who desired love. He lifted the well-shaped lady to him on
the horse, and pressed her against him. She did not think he was
worthy of this before when he saw her by the spring and she spoke
such cross words.

Gawan then rode in joy; yet her weeping was not avoided and he
lamented with her. He asked her to tell him what she was crying
about, and that she should leave off, in God's name. She spoke: "My
Lord, I must lament to you about him who has slain the worthy
Cidegast. For this grief has groped its way into my heart, where joy
used to lie when I had Cidegast's love. I am not so utterly lost that I

have not since contrived to harm the king at any cost, and many a rough joust have I fostered against his life. If help were to come from you it would make me rich and avenge me on the grief that whets my heart.

"To bring about Gramovlanz's death I accepted the service a king offered me who was lord of all he desired. My Lord, he was called Anfortas. For love I accepted from his hand the merchant's booth from Thabronit that still stands before your gate, where great riches go toward it.[26] The king earned in my service what spoiled all my joy. When I was about to grant him love I had to earn new hardship. In my service he earned pain. Anfortas's wound gave me the same grief, or more, than Cidegast could give. Now tell me: how should I, poor woman, keep my senses in such distress, since I am loyal by nature? Sometimes my senses sicken because he is lying there so helpless whom I chose after Cidegast to compensate and avenge me. My Lord, now hear me tell how Clinschor came by the rich booth before your gate.

"When the fair Anfortas, who sent me that gift, was bereft of love and joy I did fear shame. Clinschor is highly renowned in the art of necromancy, so that he can prevail on both woman and man with magic. Whatever worthy people he sees, he does not leave them without sorrow. For the sake of peace I gave Clinschor my booth plied with riches. Once the adventure had been endured, I was to seek love from him who had conquered the prize. If he did not care for me the booth would be mine again. It shall be both of ours now. That they swore who were present. I wanted to lure Gramovlanz with this ruse, which has unfortunately not yet achieved its goal. If he had taken up the adventure he would have suffered death.

"Clinschor is courtly and wise. To do himself honor he allowed my renowned retinue to do deeds of knighthood all over his land, with many a thrust and stroke. All the weeks, all their days, all the weeks in the year I have special patrols on the road, some by day and others by night. At great cost I plotted harm to high-minded Gramovlanz. He does many a combat with them. What keeps protecting him? I was well able to threaten his life. As to those who were too rich for my pay: if none of them grew fond of me otherwise, I allowed many to serve for love but I did not grant them the reward for it.[27]

No man ever saw my body whose service I could not have, except for one, who wore red armor. He brought my retainers to grief. He came riding before Logrois where he destroyed them: his hand strewed them about in such a way that I enjoyed it very little. Five of my knights followed him between Logrois and your jetty. He brought them low on the plain and gave the horses to the ferryman. When he had overcome my people, I myself rode up to the hero. I offered him the land and my body; he said he had a more beautiful wife and one that was dearer to him. That speech was heavy to me. I asked who that might be. 'The one of radiant skin is called the queen of Pelrapeire. I myself am called Parzival. I do not want your love: the grail gives me other grief.' So spoke the hero in anger. The chosen one rode away. If I have done wrong there—will you let me know that—when I offered love to the worthy knight out of the distress of my heart, my love is weakened by that." Gawan spoke to the duchess: "My Lady, I know him for a worthy man, the one of whom you desired love. If he had chosen you for love, your praise would not have been lost on him."

Gawan the courtly one and the duchess of Logrois looked at each other long. Then they had come riding so close that they were spotted from the castle where the adventure had happened to Gawan. He said: "My Lady, please do as I shall ask of you: leave my name unrecognized, by which the knight has named me who rode Gringuljet away from me. Do what I have asked you to. If anyone wants to ask you about it, just say: 'My companion is unknown to me; he was never named to me.' " She said: "I shall very gladly hide it from them since you do not wish me to tell them." *Knights come riding out of the castle. At first Gawan thinks they might attack them, but Orgeluse says they are Clinschor's men, come to meet them. The ferryman has come to ferry them across. His daughter disarms Gawan and provides both him and his lady with food.*

For the first time the duchess saw his face where they sat next to each other. Gawan and the duchess could take water themselves if they thought washing was needed. They both did. He was counseled by joy that he should eat with her, through whom he wanted to experience both joy and hardship. When she offered him the flask her mouth had touched new joy was revealed to him in that he should drink after her. His sorrow began to limp away, and his high spirits rose fast. Her sweet mouth, her radiant skin drove him so far away from care that he did not lament any of his wounds.

Gawan promises to pay the ferryman a ransom for both of his opponents, so that they will be set free. The ladies in the castle are overjoyed to see Gawan again, and he and Orgeluse are well received. What more can I say? Except that the worthy Gawan and the well-shaped duchess were received by the ladies of *Schastel marveile* in such a way that they both had reason to be happy. You may count it as his luck that this happiness should ever have come to him. Then Arnive led him to his room, and those skilled in the art took care of his wounds.

Gawan said to Arnive: "My Lady, I want a messenger." A young lady was sent. She brought a squire, manly, wise in good breeding, an honor to squiredom. The squire swore an oath that he would not tell anyone anything, there or elsewhere, except where he had to tell it, whether that would bring him joy or sorrow. Gawan asked that they should fetch him ink and parchment. Gawan, the son of King Lot, wrote skillfully in his own hand. He sent word to the land of Löver,[28] to Artus and his wife, of the service of his person, with unbreakable loyalty. And if he had gained praise in harsh combat, that would be dead to honor unless they would help him in his distress, be mindful of loyalty, and bring their retinue with a host of ladies to Joflanze. He himself would come to them there, to do combat for his honor. He also told them more: the combat had been agreed to in such terms that the king had to come in state. Then my lord Gawan also sent word to the whole retinue, be they woman or man, that they should keep faith with him and that they should advise the king to come. That would enhance their honor. To all the worthy he sent word of his service and the hardship of his combat.

The letter bore no seal: he wrote it in such a way that it would be recognized well enough, with distinctive marks that would not lie. "Now you should not delay any longer," said Gawan to his squire. "The king and the queen are at Bems by the Korca. You should speak to the queen there early one morning. Whatever she advises you to do, do it. And let one piece of wisdom stay with you: do not tell them that I am lord here, and do not tell them that you belong to the household here." The squire went away from there in haste. Arnive softly stole behind him. She asked him where he wanted to go and what he had to say. He said: "My Lady, I am not telling you, if my oath is to be kept. May God protect you, I want to go from here." He rode off toward a host of worthy people.

Book Thirteen

Arnive had become angry because the squire did not tell her where he was sent. She asked the man who took care of the gates: "When the squire rides back, be it night or day, make him wait for me until I have spoken with him; use your skill." And yet she showed hatred toward the squire. She went in again to ask more of the duchess. The duchess also used her senses so that her mouth did not mention which name Gawan bore. His request had been well served by her: she did not divulge his name or his lineage. The sound of trumpets and other sounds rang out in the high hall, announcing joyful things. Many a tapestry was hung in the hall. There was no walking there except on carpets well made. It would have scared a poor host.[1] All around and to all sides many a seat[2] was put down there with soft down cushions, on which they spread rich covers.

After his hardship Gawan stayed asleep in the middle of the day. His wounds had been bound up with great skill, so that if a lady love had been lying by him and he had made love, it would have been soft and good. He also had a better mind to sleep than that night when the duchess gave him gain of discomfort. He woke up about vesper time. Yet in his sleep he had fought love's combat with the duchess once more. *Gawan dresses in new clothes, as do the knights he overcame before: Lischoys and the Turkoit. They go to the high hall.* Gawan saw four queens standing by the duchess. He asked the two knights to go closer, in his courteous manner. He ordered the three younger ladies to kiss these two. The lady Bene had also gone there with Gawan; she was well received there.

The host did not want to stand any longer: he asked the two knights to go sit with the ladies where they wanted. That request did not cause them pain, since that was what they had to do. "Which lady is Itonje?" asked the worthy Gawan:[3] "she should let me sit with her." He asked it quietly of Bene. Since that was his will, Bene showed him the fair young lady: "The one who has the red mouth there, the brown hair, and the shining eyes. If you want to speak to her in secret, do so with good grace," said the lady Bene, rich in good breeding. She knew of Itonje's grief in love and that the worthy King Gramovlanz had offered his service to her heart with a knight's full loyalty.

Gawan sat down by the young lady (I am telling you what I was told). He began his speech with good grace, because he was able to do so. She, too, knew how to behave: from such short years as Itonje had borne her youth, she had gathered enough good breeding. Gawan had moved toward her with the question whether she was already able to submit to love. The young lady said with good sense: "My Lord, whom should I love? Since my first day appeared to me there has not been a single knight to whom I have ever spoken a word, except as you have heard today." "But stories may have come to you in which you have heard of manly behavior, of prizes won with deeds of knighthood, and of who is able to offer service for love with the power of his heart."[4] To this the fair young lady replied: "Service for love has remained unspoken for me, since many a courteous knight serves the duchess of Logrois, both for love and for pay. Many a one has ridden in jousting where we could see it. None of them have come so close as you have come to us. Your combat exalts your praise." He spoke to the young lady fair of skin: "Where does the duchess's host fight, so many a chosen knight? Who has lost her favor?" "King Gramovlanz, who bears the wreath of worth, as people say of him. My Lord, I know nothing else of this."

Then said my lord Gawan: "You shall have more knowledge of him, since he is coming closer to praise and hastens toward it of his own will. From his mouth I have heard that he has come wholeheartedly with service, if it pleases you, to seek help through the comfort of your love. It is just that a king should receive hardship from a queen. My lady, if your father's name was Lot, you are the one he means, for whom his heart weeps; and if your name is Itonje you cause him pain in his heart. If you can bear loyalty you should turn his lament away from him. I want to be the messenger for both sides. My Lady, take this ring: the fair one sent it to you. I shall also act without fear: My Lady, leave all that boldly to me." She began to color all red: the color of her mouth showed all over her face. After that she quickly turned another color. She took the ring very shyly there; it was soon recognized: she accepted it in her fair hand.

Then she said: "If I may say so in front of you, My Lord, I can see you rode away from him my heart desires. If you give good breeding its due now, My Lord, it will teach discretion to your mind. This gift has been sent to me before by the worthy king's hand. This ring truly speaks of him: he received it from my hands. Whatever sorrow he may have earned, I am altogether innocent of it, since I have granted his body in thought what he desires of me.[5] He would have heard this earlier if I could ever have gone beyond this castle. I did kiss Orgeluse who is capable of contriving his death. That was a kiss like Judas gave, and they still speak of it.[6] All loyalty vanished from me when I had to kiss the Turkoit Florant and the duke of Gowerzin. I shall never accept complete reconciliation with those who are able to keep showing their hatred for King Gramovlanz. You shall hide this from my mother, and from my sister Cundrie." That Itonje asked of Gawan.

"My Lord, you asked me that I should receive their kiss, still unforgiven, on my mouth. Of that my heart is ill. If joy shall ever be known to us both, that help stands in your hand. In truth the king loves my body before all women. I want to let him enjoy it: I am fond of him before all men. May God teach you help and advice so that you leave us with joy." Then said he: "My Lady, teach me how. He has you there, you have him here, and yet you are separated. If I could give you both such advice in good faith that would profit your worthy life, I would do so: for that I would leave nothing undone." She spoke: "You shall have power over the worthy king and over me. Your help and God's blessing must look after our love, so that I, a stranger, may avert this sorrow from him. Since all his joy stands rooted in me, and since I am devoid of disloyalty, it is always my heart's desire that I grant him my love."

Gawan heard from the young lady's speech that she wanted to be in love; also her hatred against the duchess had not faded. So she showed love and hatred. He also brought more sin on himself toward the simple young lady who had lamented her cares for him, since he did not also tell her that one mother had borne him and her, and that Lot had been father to them both. He offered his help to the young lady; she bowed to him stealthily because he had not denied comfort to her.

A banquet is held, at which the knights and ladies of the castle meet. They could well speak of hospitality there. It had never happened before to the ladies and the knights since Clinschor's power had overcome them with his ruses. They were unknown to each other, and yet the same gate had locked them in, but they could never speak to each other, the ladies and the men. My lord Gawan let these people see each other; much pleasure came to them from this. Pleasure had also come to Gawan, yet he had to look stealthily at the fair duchess who ruled the feelings of his heart.

Now the day began to stumble, so that its shine had almost fallen and they could see through the clouds those they called the messenger of the night: many stars that ran fast because they found lodging for the night.[7] Behind these banners Night herself soon came. Many an expensive crownlike chandelier was artfully hung all around the high hall that was suddenly well provided with candles. They carried candles separately to each table, a wondrous thing. In addition the adventure tells us that the duchess was so radiant that it would not have been night around her, even if not one candle had been brought: her looks alone could bring the day. That is what I heard said about the sweet one. Unless they want to speak wrong of Gawan, you have never seen a host so rich in joy before. And so with joyful desire the knights there, the ladies here often looked at each other. Those who were shy because they were strangers became better acquainted by and by; that I shall allow them without hatred.

Unless there was a glutton among them, they have eaten enough there now, if you approve.[8] They carried all the tables away then. Next my lord Gawan asked about good fiddlers, if none of them were there. There were many worthy squires well taught in string music. Yet nobody's art was so consummate that they did not have to strike up an old dance. Of new dances little was heard there, many of which have come to us from Düringen.[9] Now say your thanks to the host: he did not disturb them in their joy. Many a lady fair of skin went to dance before him there. Their dance was well ordered and the knights were mixed in well among the host of ladies; they came to defend themselves against sorrow. You could also see many a fair knight walking there between two ladies: you could sense joy coming from them. Whatever knight had the sense to offer his service for love, that request was allowable. Poor in cares and rich in joy they whiled away the time with words spoken to many a sweet mouth.

Gawan, Sangive, and Queen Arnive sat quiet by the group of dancers. The duchess fair of skin went over to sit next to Gawan. He received her hand in his; they spoke of this and that. He was happy about her coming to him. His sorrow became narrow there, his joy wide; and so his grief vanished from him. If the joy of others was great in dancing, Gawan had even less sorrow here. Queen Arnive spoke: "My Lord, now think of your rest. You should rest at this hour because of your wounds. If the duchess has decided that she wants to see to it that you are well covered tonight, as the companion of your sleep, she is rich in help and advice." Gawan said: "Ask her about it. I am here at both of your commands." The duchess spoke as follows: "He shall be in my care. Let these people go to sleep. I shall treat him so well tonight that no lady love ever treated him better. Leave Floran of Itolac and the duke of Gowerzin in the care of the knights."

After that the dancing soon came to an end. Young ladies with radiant color sat here and there; the knights were sitting among them. Whoever spoke there out of worthy love, his joy took revenge on sorrow when he found sweet answer. The host made it known that they should bring his night drink to him. Those who were wooing had reason to lament this. The host wooed along with the guests: love also knew how to weigh on him. Their sitting seemed far too long to him: worthy love also ruled his heart. The drinking gave them their leave.[10] Squires carried many a cluster of candles before the knights. Then my lord Gawan commended his two guests, Lischoys and Florant, to all who were there. That was sure to please them well. They went to sleep at once. The duchess was very considerate: she said she wished them a good night. Then the whole host of women also went where they took care of their rest. They began their bowing with the breeding they were well able to show. Sangive and Itonje went away then, as did Cundrie too.

Bene and Arnive then saw to it that the host was assured of his comfort. The duchess was also close at hand with her help. These three led Gawan with them for his comfort. He saw two beds standing separately in a chamber. It will be kept from you altogether how they were adorned:[11] other tidings are coming near.[12] Arnive spoke to the duchess: "Now you must give good comfort to the knight you brought here. If he desires help from you, your help shall bring you honor. I am not telling you any more now, except that his wounds have been dressed with such art that he might well bear arms now.[13] Yet you must lament his cares: if you soften them for him, that is good. If you teach him high spirits we shall all profit from that: let this not trouble you now." Queen Arnive went when she was allowed to take her leave. Bene carried a light in front of her. My lord Gawan locked the door. Now the two of them are able to steal love, I cannot easily hide that. I could tell you very easily what happened there, except that they always accuse him who spreads hidden tidings of bad taste. It is still distasteful to the courtly person, and whoever does it makes himself unhappy. Let good breeding be the lock on love's ways.

Stern love and the fair duchess now saw to it that Gawan's joy was consumed. He would never have stayed alive if he had been without a lover. The philosophers and all who ever sat where they measured strong magic, Kancor and Thebit, and Trebuchet the smith who chiseled Frimulet's sword from which strong wonder took its course, together with the skill of all physicians—even if they had all shown him great favor with a mixture of healing roots, he would have had to bring his sharp distress to bitter death without a woman's company.[14]

I want to make the story short: he found the right root that helped him so that he healed, and there was no more hardship for him. That root was white and brown. A Briton on his mother's side, Gawan the son of King Lot gave himself up to sweet softness instead of bitter grief, with worthy help that was given to him until day came. That help was such that it was kept from all the people. Since then he took charge of the joy of all the knights and ladies, so that their sorrow almost vanished. Now hear also how the squire did whom Gawan had sent to the land of Löver, to Bems on the Korca. King Artus was there and his wife the queen and many a bright radiance and a flood of worthy retinue. Now listen how the squire did.

It was early one morning. He took charge of his message. The queen was to chapel; during her devotions she read the Psalter. The squire knelt before her and offered her joy's reward: a letter she took from his hand, in which she found written a handwriting she recognized before the squire she saw kneeling there had named his lord. The queen spoke to the letter: "Hail the hand that wrote you! I never remained without sorrow since the day when I saw the hand by which this writing was done." She wept and yet was happy. To the squire she said: "You are Gawan's servant." "Yes, My Lady, he offers you what is his duty: loyalty in service without any wavering, and with it his sickly joy, unless you want to make joy grow tall for him. Things never stood this pitiful with his honor. My Lady, he sends you word also that he would live in worthy joy if he were to receive the gift of your comfort. You can see all that in the letter, better than I could tell you."

She said: "I have in truth understood why you were sent to me. I shall give worthy service to him there, with a host of lovely ladies who, in truth, have won the battle for praise in my time. Except for Parzival's wife, and Orgeluse's body I do not recognize any of such worth on earth, who have been baptized. Since Gawan rode away from Artus sorrow and grief have worked their zeal on me with a heavy blow. Meljacanz of Liz told me he had seen him since at Parbigoel. Alas," she said, "Plimizoel, that my eyes ever saw you! What suffering befell me there! Cunneware de Lalant was never known to me again, my sweet worthy friend. Many of the Round Table had their birthright broken there with words. Five and a half years and six weeks it is since the worthy Parzival rode toward the grail from Plimizoel. Then also did Gawan turn toward Ascalun, that worthy man. Jeschute and Ecuba parted from me there. Great longing for those worthy people has parted me from steadfast joy since."

The queen spoke much of her sorrow. Then she spoke to the squire as follows: "Now follow my advice: turn away from me in secret until the day raises itself high and people are likely to be at court: knights, squires, the whole household. Gallop boldly toward the court, do not allow anyone to hold your horse. You should boldly go from it to where the worthy knights are standing. They shall ask you about adventure. Behave with words and with gestures as if you were running from a fire in great haste. They will hardly be able to wait for the tidings you bring. What does it matter to you as long as you push yourself through the crowd to the true host who shall not avoid greeting you? Give him this letter into his hand, by which he shall soon have recognized your tidings and your lord's desire. He shall grant it in what follows. I want to teach you more: you should speak openly to me, where I and other ladies can hear you and see you. Appeal to us there as you are well able to, if you do not begrudge your lord good things. And tell me, where is Gawan?" The squire said: "That will be left undone: I shall not tell you where my lord is. If you will it so, he shall remain with joy." The squire was happy with her counsel. He parted from the queen as you have heard, and came as he should.

The squire does exactly as the queen told him. When Artus reads the message he exclaims: "Hail this sweet day, in whose light I have heard true tidings that have come to me of my sister's worthy son. If I can do manly service for kin and companionship, if loyalty ever gained power over me, I shall do what Gawan has asked of me, if I can." He said to the squire: "Now tell me, is Gawan happy?" "Yes, My Lord, if you wish it he shall become a companion to joy." So spoke the wise squire: "He would be altogether parted from praise if you abandoned him now. Who could devote himself to happiness in that case? Your comfort will lift up his joy until it chases the worry that you might forsake him out of his heart, through the gate of grief. His heart also offered his service to the queen; it is his desire, too, that the Round Table should take up his service, that they should be mindful of loyalty and not sicken his joy, so that they may advise you to go to him." All the worthy ones there asked the king to do so.

Artus spoke: "Dear friend in truth, carry this letter to the queen, let her read it and say why we should rejoice and why we should lament. That King Gramovlanz can marshal such arrogance and such evil against my kin! He must think my nephew Gawan is Cidegast, whom he killed. Enough sorrow comes to him for that. I shall increase his sorrow and teach him a new way to behave." The squire came walking to where he was well received. He gave the queen the letter. Because of it many a sweet eye overflowed when her sweet mouth read all that was written in it: Gawan's lament and his request. The squire did not allow the occasion to be wasted: he pleaded with all the ladies; his skill did not weaken.

Gawan's kinsman, the rich Artus, pleaded from his heart with his household to undertake these travels. Ginover the courteous also guarded herself from delay; she pleaded with the ladies to go on that proud journey. Keie said in his anger: "If I dared to hold the belief that ever a man was born as worthy as Gawan of Norway, then pull him closer, get him there! If you don't he may soon be elsewhere. If he wants to scurry about like a squirrel you may well soon lose him."[15] *The squire goes back to Gawan. Arnive wants to find out where he has been, but the squire refuses to answer. He goes on to report to Gawan, who is overjoyed to hear that Artus, his knights, and his ladies will be at Joflanze even before the appointed time.* Gawan was happy at all times. One morning it so happened that many a knight and lady were in the rich high hall. He took a spot for himself alone, in a window overlooking the river, where he and Arnive sat, who did not forget strange tales. Gawan spoke to the queen: "Alas, my dear lady, may it not sit heavy on you that I have to ask you about tales done that have been kept from me! Only through the gift of your help do I live now in such worthy joy. If my heart ever bore manly sentiment, the noble duchess has locked it in her power. I owe it to you that my grief has been softened. I would be dead of love and wounds if your helpful comfort had not freed me from those bonds. Now tell me, lady that brings me blessings, about the marvel that was here, and is, and by which strong magic the wise Clinschor invented it. Except for you, I would have lost my life."

The wise of heart (never did youth come into old age with such womanly praise) said: "My Lord, his works of marvel here are small against the great marvel he has wrought in many lands. Whoever counts that as our shame earns nothing but sin. My Lord, I shall tell you about his behavior: it has turned sour on many people. His land is called *Terra de Labor*.[16] He is born from the lineage of him who has also worked many a work of wonder: Virgilius[17] of Naples. Clinschor, his kinsman, lived as follows: Caps was his capital. He walked such a high path to praise that he was never devoid of it. Women and men spoke of Clinschor the duke until he came to shame as follows: Sicily had a worthy king, he was called Ibert. His wife was called Iblis. She had the loveliest body that was ever taken from a mother's breasts. Clinschor had come into her service and she rewarded him with love; for that the king dishonored him.

"If I have to tell you about his secret, I should have your leave first, and yet that tale is unseemly for me to tell: of how he came to live in a sorcerer's way. Clinschor was made into a capon with one cut." Gawan laughed much about this. She told him more: "In Kalot enbolot he earned the world's mockery: Kalot enbolot is a castle well-known as a fortress. The king found him with his wife: Clinschor slept in her arms. If he had lain warm there, he had to give this pledge for it: he was made smooth between the legs by the king's hands. It seemed to the host that was his right. He cut Clinschor into the body so that he could never bring shame again to any woman. For that many people have come to grief. It is not in the country of Persia that the first magic was invented, but in a city called Persida. He traveled there, and from there he brought this knowledge: he can achieve whatever he wants through his skill in the arts of magic. Because of the shame done to his body he was never again prepared to show goodwill to either man or woman, I mean among those who show valor. Whatever joy he can take away from them, that pleases him in his heart.

"There was a king called Irot, of Rosche Salines, who was afraid of that same distress. He offered to give Clinschor what he wanted of his, so that he should have peace. Clinschor received from his hand this mountain known for a fortress, and at the same time the land eight miles around it. Clinschor then wrought on this mountain this strange work you can see. There are great wonders here, of all kinds of the wealth of this world. If they wanted to besiege the castle, there would be food for thirty years here, in abundance. Clinschor also has power over all those, evil or good, *mal* and *bea schent,* all the spirits that live between the firmament and the limits of the earth, except for those God wants to protect.

"My lord, since your great grief has turned from you without death, Clinschor's gift stands in your hand. He shall never again return to this castle and the land measured with it. You shall also have peace from him. He said this in public (he is true with words): that his gift would be left to him who endured this adventure. What he saw of worthy people on Christian earth, be they maiden, wife, or man, those are subject to you here. Many a heathen man and woman also had to stay here with us. Now let these people go home, where lament may well be heard for us. Exile brings a chill to my heart. He Who has counted the stars must teach you help and turn us toward joy. A mother bears a fruit; that fruit becomes its mother. From water comes ice; that does not prevent in any way that water should come from it again. If I take the thought into my mind that I was born in joy, and if joy is seen in me again, there one fruit gives fruit to the other. That is what you should do, if you have good breeding.

"It is a long time since joy fell away from me. The keel goes fast because of the sail. The man who walks on it is faster still. If you understand this example your praise will grow high and fast. You could make joy for us, so bright that we might bring joy to many a land where sorrow is known on our account. I was a woman who bore a crown; my daughter also wore a crown, as was fitting, before the princes of her land. We both had dignity. My lord, I never advised harm to any man; I was able to deal with both man and woman according to their rights. They may see me and recognize me for a real lady of the people, if it please God, since I never did any man wrong. Now every happy woman should deal well with all good people if she wants to show her honor. She may very easily come to the grief of sorrow where a weak boy may give wide space to her narrow joy.[18] My lord, I have waited here long: the one who would recognize me and turn my sorrow away from me has not come here yet, riding or on foot."

Gawan promises to set all people inside the castle free. Artus's army then sets out for Joflanze, but on the way it is attacked by Orgeluse's knights. Gawan, who knows Artus is an ally, does not tell anyone.[19] Then my lord Gawan ordered the outer gates to be shut. Old and young listened to what he asked them with good breeding. "A great army is camping there on the bank on the other side of the river. Neither on land nor on sea did I see an army traveling with such powerful troops. If they want to besiege us here in strength, help me, and I shall give them battle fit for a knight."

That they promised all alike. They asked the rich duchess if the army was hers. She said: "You must believe me, I know neither shield nor man there. He who has done me harm before may have ridden into my land and done battle before Logrois. I think he found it well defended. They would have fought this army from ramparts and battlements. If the angry King Gramovlanz did deeds of knighthood there, he was seeking restitution for his wreath; but whoever they are, they must see spears raised in the desire for the joust." Her mouth lied little in this. Artus suffered many losses before he came to Logrois. There many a Briton was unseated in a fair joust. Artus's host also paid back the market wares they offered them there.[20] They came to grief on both sides. *The prisoners taken on both sides are listed.* My lord Gawan should have told the duchess that a helper of his was in her land. Then the battle would not have taken place. But he did not want to tell her or anyone else before she herself could see it. He did as he saw fit and planned his travels to Artus the Briton with expensive tents. Nobody there was neglected because he was unknown to him. Generous Gawan's hand began to give them so much of his own will, as if he did not want to live any longer. Foot soldiers, knights, ladies had to receive and observe his gifts so great that they all said alike true help had come to them. Joy was also heard among them there. The worthy hero ordered strong packhorses brought, beautiful horses for the ladies, and armor for all the knights. A great force of foot soldiers in coats of mail was prepared there. Then he could do what he did: my lord Gawan took four worthy knights apart, so that one became his chamberlain, the second his cupbearer, the third his steward, and the fourth should not forget he was his marshal. This Gawan did. The four did as he wished.

Finally, the two armies meet on friendly terms. Artus said to his nephew: "Who are these companions of yours?" Gawan said: "I would like to see My Lady kiss them. It would be harsh to keep that from them: they are both of noble lineage." The Turkoit Florant was kissed there at once by Ginover the queen, as was the duke of Gowerzin. They went back into the tent. It seemed to many that the wide field was full of ladies. Artus did not act like one dejected. He jumped on a Castilian. He rode around the ring of all those well-shaped ladies and all the knights by their sides. With good breeding Artus's mouth welcomed all of them at the same time. It was Gawan's will that they would all hold still until he rode from there with them; it was a courteous custom.

Artus dismounted and went into the tent. He sat next to his nephew. He implored him to tell him who the five ladies were. My lord Gawan spoke first with the noblest one. He spoke to the Briton as follows: "If you knew Utepandragun, this is Arnive his wife: from those two comes your body.[21] This lady is my mother, the queen of Norway, and these two are my sisters; now look what pretty young ladies they are." New kissing was done there. All who wanted to see it saw joy and sorrow; they endured it for love. Their mouths could show full well both laughing and weeping. That happened because of great love. Artus spoke to Gawan: "Nephew, I am still free of the tale of who the fair fifth lady could be."

Then spoke Gawan the courteous: "It is the duchess of Logrois; I am here at her mercy. I have been told that you were looking for her. Whatever profit you have gained from that, show it to me without delay. You might do well as a widow."[22] Artus said: "She has your sister's son Gaherjet there, and Garel, who did the deeds of knighthood in many a charge. The fearless one was taken from me, right at my side. One of our charges had come crashing as far as their bulwark. My God, what deeds were done there by the worthy Meljacanz of Liz! Under a white banner he was captured and taken into the castle. That banner has received a black arrow of sable for a coat of arms, painted with the heart's blood, looking like man's sorrow. 'Lirivoyn,' shouted the whole throng that rode to battle under it: they have earned praise for the castle. My nephew Jofreit was also captured up there: I am sorry about that. The rearguard was mine to lead yesterday: that gave me this pain."

The king spoke much about his losses. The duchess spoke with good breeding: "My Lord, I absolve you of dishonor: you would not have had my greeting otherwise. You may have done me harm that I did not deserve. Since you went looking for me,[23] may God advise you how to compensate me. When he to whose help you have ridden did combat with me, I was recognized to be without defense and attacked on my unprotected side. If he wants to do more combat, it will be finished without swords."[24] Gawan then said to Artus: "What do you advise? Should we cover this plain more with knights, since we are well able to do so? I can well ask the duchess that your men should go free and that her knights should come from there with many a new spear." "I follow you in that," said Artus. The duchess then sent to her castle for the worthy men. I think there was never a more beautiful gathering on earth. Gawan asked for leave to begin his journey toward his lodging. The king granted him that. Those they had seen coming with him, went with him to their rest. His rich lodging was erected in such a knightly manner that it was valuable and empty of poverty.

To his lodging rode many who were sorry in their hearts for his long absence. Now Keie had also been healed after his joust at the Plimizoel. He examined Gawan's wealth and said: "Never did any grief come to us from my lord's brother-in-law Lot: he never tried to outdo us and he had no separate encampments."[25] Then he thought of another thing: that Gawan had not avenged him when his right arm was broken. "God does wonders with people. Who gave Gawan this pack of women?" So spoke Keie in his mockery. That was unfitting behavior toward a friend. The loyal man is happy when a friend is honored. The disloyal one shouts hell and damnation when good things happen to his friend and he sees that.[26] Gawan displayed happiness and honor. If anyone desires more, where does he want to take his thoughts? Those addled in their mind are full of jealousy and hatred. It does the worthy man good when his friend's praise stands so fast that shame goes fleeing from him. Gawan never forgot manly loyalty without false deceit. He did not owe the happiness they saw him in to any injustice.

How did the man of Norway take care of his people, his knights and his ladies? Artus and his followers were able to observe the wealth of the worthy son of Lot. They should also sleep after they have eaten. I am not jealous at all of their rest. In the morning, before the day, people of warlike behavior came riding there, the duchess's knights all. Artus and his people could see their ornaments by the light of the moon, where they lay. They moved through Artus's army until they reached the other side where Gawan lay with his wide ring. Whoever raises such help with his valorous hand may be recognized as worthy of praise. Gawan asked his marshal to show the newcomers a place of lodging. As the duchess's marshal advised, the worthy people of Logrois pitched many a ring of tents away from the others. It was well into the middle of the morning before they were lodged. New cares are approaching here.

Artus well-known in praise sent his messengers to Rosche Sabbins in the city. He asked King Gramovlanz: "If it should now be unavoidable that he will not give up his combat against my nephew, my nephew shall grant him this. Ask him to ride soon against us, since his power is known to be such that he does not want to avoid combat. It would be too much for another man." Artus's messengers left then. My lord Gawan took Lischoys and Florant aside; he asked them to show him without delay the soldiers of love from many lands who were so fond of the duchess and stayed in her service for high reward. He rode toward them and welcomed them in such a way that they said all together that the worthy Gawan was a manly, courteous man.[27]

With that he turned back from them. He then did things in secret. He went into his chamber; at the same time he covered his body with armor, to see if his wounds had been healed enough, so that the scars would not weigh him down. He wanted to exercise his body since so many men and women would see his combat, where the experienced knights might judge whether his undaunted hand would be recognized for praise that day. He had asked a page to bring him Gringuljet. He soon gave it free rein: he wanted action, so that he and the horse would be prepared. No ride of his ever brought such sorrow to me: alone rides my lord Gawan, away from the host, far on the plain. May luck take care of all! He saw a knight halt by the waters of the Sabbins whom we might well call a rock of manly strength. He was a hailstorm in deeds of knighthood. Falsehood never conquered his heart. He was so sensitive in his person to what they call lack of praise that he did not suffer it in any way, neither half a finger's length nor the breadth of a hand. You may well have heard of that worthy man before: this story has come to its true mainstay.

Book Fourteen

I f the worthy Gawan now rides a warlike joust, I have never feared
for his honor so much in any combat. I should also have fear for
the other one, but I want to leave that out of my worries. He was a
one-man army in combat. His gleaming armor had been brought
from heathen lands far across the sea.[1] Redder still than a ruby were
his gambeson and his horse's trappings. The hero was riding for
adventure: his shield was pierced through and through. He had also
broken a shining wreath from the tree Gramovlanz guarded, and
Gawan recognized the branch. Then he feared the shame: was the
king waiting for him there? If he had ridden against him for combat,
combat would have to be done there, even if not a single lady should
see it.

From Munsalvaesche they were, both horses that galloped closer
to each other in a violent charge; they were urged on by spurs. All
green clover (not dusty sand) stood there, bedewed, where the joust
took place. Both their discomfort hurts me. They rode their charge
right: both were born from a lineage of jousters. Whoever wins the
prize there has gained little and lost much: he shall always regret it,
if he is wise.[2] Steadfast was their loyalty to each other, which never
received holes or scratches. Now listen how the joust went:

With a clash, and yet such that both of them had reason to be sad.
Well-known kin and high companionship had come together there
with hateful force in sharp combat. No matter who took the prize,
his joy was pledged to sorrow. Each one's hand guided the joust in
such a way that the kinsmen and companions had to fell each other
with horse and all. And afterwards they fought like this: they slashed

and hacked with swords. Shards of shields and the green grass were
one and the same mixture since they had begun to fight. They had to
wait to be parted far too long:[3] they started early in the morning.
But nobody there seized the chance of parting them.

*In the meantime Artus's messengers reach King Gramovlanz. A
description of Gramovlanz's army follows.* Artus's messengers had
arrived; they spoke these words to him who showed forth the
fullness of pride. "My Lord, Artus has sent us here, who used to be
known for having shown honor until now. He also has enough
dignity. You want to spoil that for him. How can you think of
wanting to bring such shame to his sister's son? If the worthy Gawan
has caused you great pain in your heart, he would still find help from
each of the Knights of the Round Table, since all those who desire to
sit around it grant him their companionship."

The king spoke: "My undaunted hand shall fight the promised
combat in such a way that I shall be able to say today that Gawan has
earned praise, or that he is in distress. I have learned in truth that
Artus has come with his host, and his wife the queen. She will be
welcome. If the fierce duchess's advice to Artus is lack of love for me,
you pages should stand in between. Nothing else may come to pass
there, except that I want to do combat. I have so many knights that I
am not upset by violence. What is done to me by one hand, that
hardship shall I endure. If I should now avoid what I have sworn
myself to I would leave off service for love. To its mercy I have given
all my joy and my life; God knows well how Gawan profits from
that, since it has always displeased me to do combat against one
man, except that the worthy Gawan has pledged his life to it; I shall
be happy to do combat with him. In this way my manhood lowers
itself: such an easy fight I have never fought. They say of me that I
have fought (ask them about it if you want to) against people who
say about my hand that it is known for praise. I have never stood
against a man alone. The ladies will not praise me if I gain victory
today. I have been told that she has been freed of her bonds,[4] for
whom the combat will not be done,[5] and that brings joy to my
heart. Artus the far renowned, so many a strange land, *terre,* is said
to be under his command; maybe she has come here with him, to
whom I shall bring joy and grief in service to her command until my
death. What greater good might befall me than that I shall have the
good fortune that she will be pleased to see my service?"

Bene sat within reach of the king's arms. She felt no dislike for the combat. She had seen the king's manliness so often where he did battle that she wanted to leave it out of her worries. But if she had known that Gawan was her lady's brother, and that these harsh words referred to her master, she would have been cheated of joy. She had brought the king a ring Itonje the young queen had sent him out of love, and which her brother well-known for his honor had fetched across the Sabbins. Bene had come on the Poynzaclins in a small boat. These tidings she did not leave unsaid: "My lady has gone away from *Schastel marveile* together with a host of ladies." She urged him to loyalty and honor for her lady's sake, more than a child[6] ever sent word to a man, and that he should be mindful of her distress, since all her gain was but to offer service for his love. That put the king in high spirits. And yet he did injustice to Gawan. If I had to suffer like this for my sister's sake I would rather be without a sister.

King Gramovlanz arms himself and rides away to battle. Artus's messengers ride back to their camp. On their way they happen to witness the last stage of the battle between Gawan and Parzival. It had almost come to the point that Gawan's companion in combat had taken victory. His power over Gawan was so great that Gawan the worthy hero would have lost the victory if the pages who recognized him had not named him in their lament. He who had been warlike in combat before then lost his desire to fight against Gawan. Far out of his hand he threw the sword: "Unhappy and unworthy am I," said the weeping stranger. "I am deprived of all happiness, since my dishonored hand was known to do this combat. That was too much shame. I want to give myself up for guilty. My unhappiness stepped forth here and parted me from choicest happiness. That old coat of arms of mine has shown itself over and over again.[7] That I should have done combat here against the worthy Gawan! I have fought too much against myself and unhappiness has caught up with me here. When the combat was begun, happiness had run away from me."

Gawan heard and saw the lament. He spoke to his companion in combat: "Alas, My Lord, who are you? You speak kindly to me. If only that speech had been made while I could still speak of my strength! I would not have strayed from praise then. You have taken the prize here. I would gladly have tidings from you as to where I could find my honor again, if I went to look for it.[8] As long as it pleased my happiness I always fought well against one foe." "Nephew, I shall make myself known to you, at your service now and at all times. I am your nephew Parzival." Gawan spoke: "So it was right: crooked stupidity has become straight here.[9] Here two simple hearts have tested their power with hatred. Your hand has overcome both of us, now let that bring sorrow to you and to both of us. You have vanquished yourself if your heart knows loyalty."[10]

When this speech was done, my lord Gawan could no longer stand for lack of strength. He began to walk giddily because his head was numbed with sound. He stumbled down on the grass. One of Artus's pages jumped toward him and held up his head. Then that sweet page untied his helmet and fanned the air under his eyes with a hat with white peacock feathers. That page's zeal taught Gawan new strength. *In the meantime Gramovlanz sees to it that the lists are made ready for the combat. He then rides in search of Gawan.*

When that combat was done on the flower-colored plain, King Gramovlanz came: he also wanted to avenge his wreath. He understood well that a combat had happened there, and that fiercer fight with swords had never been seen. Those who fought against each other had done so without any guilt. Gramovlanz rode away from his followers to those weary of battle, and lamented their distress from his heart. Gawan had jumped up, his limbs were still strained. Here stood these two. Now my lady Bene had also ridden with the king into the lists where the combat had been endured. She saw Gawan without strength, whom she had chosen above all the world for the crown of her highest joy. With a scream expressing her heart's grief she quickly jumped from her horse. She embraced him tight with her arms. She said: "Cursed be the hand that has made this grief known to your fair body. Your fair skin was a manly mirror for all men, that is true." She put him down on the grass. Her crying was little hidden. Then the sweet young lady wiped blood and sweat from Gawan's eyes. He was hot in his armor. King Gramovlanz then spoke: "Gawan, I am sorry about your discomfort, it was not done by my hand. If you want to come to the plain again tomorrow to fight against me, I shall gladly wait for that. I would rather stand against a woman now than against your powerless body. What praise would I gain from you until I hear it said you are in better strength? Now rest tonight! You will need it if you want to take King Lot's place."

The strong Parzival showed neither weary limbs nor signs of growing pale. When the worthy king saw him he had untied his helmet. Parzival spoke to him with good breeding: "My Lord, whatever my nephew Gawan has done against your favor, let me stand pledged for it. I still show a warlike hand: if you want to turn your anger against him, I shall prevent you from doing so with the sword." The host from Rosche Sabbins spoke: "My Lord, he shall give me interest tomorrow; that will be paid for my wreath. Its praise shall become high and whole, or it shall chase me away to the place where I step on the road of dishonor. You may well be a hero elsewhere, but this battle has not been chosen for you." Then Bene's sweet mouth said to the king: "You faithless dog! Your heart lies in his hands, and that is where your heart shows its hatred. Where did you give yourself up for love? She must live by his mercy. You pronounce yourself without victory. Love has lost its right with you: if you ever showed love, you did so with false feelings."

There was much anger there, and the king spoke apart to Bene. He asked her: "My Lady, do not be angry that the combat is taking place on my account. Stay here with your lord. Tell Itonje his sister I am her servant in truth, and I want to serve her when I can." When Bene had heard with true words that her lord, who was to fight there on the grass, was her lady's brother, the oars of sorrow drew a furrow of grief deeply felt in her heart, since that heart showed loyalty. She spoke: "Go away, cursed man, you never won any loyalty."

The king rode then, and all who were his. Artus's young pages caught the horses for the two knights. The combat also showed itself on every horse. Gawan and Parzival and Bene of fair skin rode away toward their host. Parzival had won the prize with manlike fighting. Those who saw him coming there all spoke high praise of him. I shall tell you more if I can. The experienced men in both armies spoke only of this one man who had taken the prize there, in that they began to praise his deed of knighthood. If you want to say his name too, it is Parzival. He was of such fair skin, never was a knight better shaped: all women and men said that, where Gawan brought him. Gawan was so considerate that he ordered clothes brought for him. They then brought both of them similar garments made at great expense. With these tidings it became known that Parzival had come there. It had been heard often that he hunted for high praise. Many a man said this, in truth.

Gawan said: "If you want to see four ladies of your kin and other ladies of fair skin, I shall gladly go there with you." Gahmuret's son said: "If there are worthy women here, you should not importune them with my presence. No lady likes to see me, who has heard false words about me by the Plimizoel. God guard their womanly honor! I always want to speak good of women and I am so ashamed; I do not gladly turn toward them." "Yet it must be," said Gawan. He then led Parzival where four queens kissed him. It pained the duchess that she had to kiss him who had not wanted her greeting before, when she had offered him love and her land (shame brought her to grief there for that reason), when he had fought before Logrois and she had ridden so far after him. They talked without fear in the presence of Parzival the fair, so that all shame was led out of his heart then. He became happy without delay.

For good reasons Gawan commanded the lady Bene on pain of forfeiting his favor that her sweet mouth should not tell Itonje "that King Gramovlanz hates me because of his wreath and that we shall give each other combat tomorrow at the time appointed for fighting. You should not tell my sister that, and you should hide your weeping altogether." She spoke: "I should be allowed to weep and to make lament always, for whichever one of you shall be left lying there, my lady shall show sorrow for him. She is slain on both sides. I must lament my lady's fate and mine. What help is it that you are her brother? You want to do combat with her heart."

Gawan, Parzival, and the ladies sit down to eat. Itonje did not overlook this: she saw in Bene's eyes that they concealed weeping. Then she, too, began to look sad. Her sweet mouth avoided eating altogether. She thought: "What is Bene doing here? I had sent her to him who holds my heart that hurts me so much here. What revenge is taken on me?[11] Has the king refused my service and my love? His loyal manly heart may earn no more than that my poor body, which I show here, must die for him with heartfelt lamentation." When they stopped eating it was already beyond the middle of the day. Artus and his wife, the lady Ginover the queen, rode with a host of knights and ladies where the one fair of skin sat with a group of worthy ladies. Parzival was greeted as follows: he had to see himself kissed by many fair ladies. Artus did him honor and thanked him much because his high dignity was so long and so wide that he should have praise above all men for good reason.

The man of Waleis spoke to Artus: "My Lord, when I last saw you, a charge[12] was ridden against my honor. I gave such a high pledge for praise that I almost went astray from it. Now, My Lord, I have heard from you, if you tell me so without deceit, that praise has some right to me, at least. No matter how hard it is for me to admit this, I would gladly believe you if other people, from whom I parted then in such shame, would believe it too."[13] Those who sat there said of his hand that it had won the prize in many a land with such high praise that his honor was unspoilt.

Orgeluse's knights arrive and join the company. They all sing Parzival's praises. Gahmuret's son rose. He said: "Let all those who are here sit still and help me to earn what I lack so grievously. A mysterious wonder parted me from the Round Table. Those who gave companionship to me when seated around it, let them help me through the power of their companionship to be seated there again." What he desired Artus courteously granted him. He made another request there (he stepped aside with a few knights): that Gawan would give him the combat he was to fight in the morning at the time appointed for battle. "I will gladly wait for him there, who is called King Gramovlanz. From his tree I broke a wreath early this morning, so that he would give me combat. I came into his land to do combat, with no one else than with his hand. Nephew, little could I expect you to be there; such true sorrow has never come to me before. I thought it was the king who did not keep combat from me. Nephew, let me stand against him yet. Should dishonor come to him, my hand shall do him such harm that it will be abundant indeed. My rights have been restored to me here: I am allowed to live in company, dear nephew, with you too. Remember me as one of your known kin and let the combat be mine. I shall show manly courage there." Then said my lord Gawan: "I have here many kinsmen and brothers with the king of Britain; I shall allow none of them to do combat for me. I am sure that is my right; should luck will it, I shall be allowed to win the prize. God reward you for offering combat: it is not time for me to accept that yet."[14]

Both Parzival and Gramovlanz arm themselves early in the

morning. Gramovlanz rides out to do combat and becomes angry when he does not see Gawan anywhere. Now Parzival also had stolen away in great secrecy. He took a strong spear from Angram from a set of spears. He was also wearing his whole armor. The hero rode alone then to the posts smooth as mirrors[15] where the combat was to be. He saw the king standing there. Before either had spoken a word to the other, they say, each of them pierced the other's shield through the rim so that the splinters twisted up in the air from their hands. They were both able to joust, and also to do other combat. Along the width of the meadow the dew was scattered and helmets touched with sharp blades that cut well. The meadow was trampled down and the dew stamped on in many a place. I am sorry for the red flowers and more for the heroes who suffered hardship there without cowardice. *In the meantime, Gawan also prepares for combat: he arms himself, hears mass and* the host rode out all over, where they heard the sound of swords and saw fire leaping from helmets and blows offered with strength. King Gramovlanz had always observed this principle: he was very irritated by the thought of fighting against one man. It seemed to him now that six took part in this combat. And yet it was Parzival all alone who showed warlike deeds to him. He taught him the kind of breeding people still praise today. Since then King Gramovlanz never again claimed the honor for himself that he would offer combat to two men only: one man gave him too much to do here.

The armies had come from both sides to the wide green meadow, both to their appointed place. They observed the battle game. The valorous heroes' horses had been left standing. The worthy ones fought on foot on the ground, a hard combat known to be fierce. The heroes often threw their swords up high from their hands: they turned the blades around. And so King Gramovlanz received sour interest for his wreath. His beloved lady's kin also endured small pleasure from him. So the worthy Parzival won suffering for Itonje the fair of skin, instead of the joy he would have won if right had come to right.[16] These two well-traveled men had to pay for praise with combat: one fought for his friend's need and Love ordered the other to fight, since he was subject to love. My lord Gawan also came there when it had very nearly come to pass that the proud, brave man of Waleis would have gained victory. Brandelidelin of Punturtoys, and Bernous de Riviers, and Affinamus de Clitiers, these three rode closer to the combat, bareheaded. Artus and Gawan rode out on the plain from the other side, toward the battle-weary men. The five agreed that they wanted to separate the combatants. Gramovlanz thought the time was right to end the combat. He spoke to bespeak victory to him they had seen fighting against himself there. More people had to admit that too. Then King Lot's son said: "My lord King, I will do for you what you did for me yesterday, when you offered me rest. Rest tonight: you are in need of it. He who offered you this combat would recognize your strength as too weak against my warlike hand. I could well stand against you alone now, but you never fight unless against two. I want to chance it on my own tomorrow. May God show it as is right." The king rode from there to his men. Before doing so he gave his pledge that he would come to the plain in the morning, to do combat against Gawan.

Artus said to Parzival: "Nephew, it so happened that you asked for the combat, and acted like a man, and Gawan said no to you, so that your mouth lamented much. Now you have fought this combat after all, against him who was waiting there for Gawan, whether that brought sorrow to us or joy. You stole away from us like a thief; otherwise we would have turned your hand away from this combat. Now Gawan should not be angry that they give praise to you for it." Gawan said: "I do not regret my nephew's high honor. But tomorrow is much too early for me if I have to take part in combat. If the king would release me from it I would speak well of his sense of good measure."

Gramovlanz sends messengers to Artus to ask him to make sure only Gawan will do combat the next day. Gramovlanz also gives his messengers the following instructions: The king said: "You must look for her you would praise among all those fair ladies. You must also look particularly at the lady Bene is sitting with. Commit to your mind what mood she is in. You must observe in secret whether joy dwells with her, or sorrow. You can see in her eyes if she harbors grief for a friend. See that you do not leave this undone: give the letter and this ring to Bene, my friend, she knows well to whom they should go afterwards. Do this as it should be done and you shall do well."

Now it had come to pass on the other side that Itonje had heard that her brother and the most beloved man a maiden ever enclosed in her heart had to fight each other and would not leave off. Then grief burst through shame. Whoever takes pleasure in her grief does so without my advice since she did not deserve it. Both her mother and her grandmother led the young lady away from there, into a small tent of silk. Arnive blamed her for that pain and reprimanded her for her bad behavior. But there was no other counsel there: she said there openly what she had long hidden from them. The young lady known for her honor said: "Shall my brother's hand now cut down the love of my heart? He would gladly avoid that."

Arnive spoke to a young page: "Tell my son that he should speak with me soon, and that he should be alone." The page brought Artus. Arnive had planned to let Artus hear for whom the fair Itonje was in such pain. Maybe he could annul the combat then. King Gramovlanz's pages had come to Artus. They dismounted in the field. One of them saw Bene sitting before a small tent, next to her who was speaking to Artus. "Does the duchess[17] count that as praise, if my brother kills my lover for her, on her frivolous advice? He would speak of that as an outrage. What has the king done to him? He should let him enjoy me.[18] If my brother is sensible he knows about our love, so pure without darkness. If he is loyal, that should bring him grief. If his hand were to gain a bitter death for me after the king has died,[19] My Lord, that is my lament before you," said the sweet young lady to Artus. "Now remember that you are my uncle: end this combat through your loyalty."

At that time Artus spoke with his wise mouth: "Alas, my dear niece, that your youth should show such high love! That must be bitter for you. Your sister Surdamur had such love for the emperor of the Greeks. Sweet and gentle young lady, I would like to end this combat if I knew from both of you that your heart and his are brought together. Gramovlanz, Irot's son, walks in such a manly manner that combat will be done, unless your love prevents it. Has he ever seen your fair skin to his joy, and your sweet red mouth?" She said: "That has not happened: we love each other without seeing. He has sent many of his keepsakes to me through the power of love and through true companionship; he has also received from my hand what belongs to true love and destroyed both our doubts. The king is loyal to me, without the counsel of a false heart."

Then the lady Bene recognized the two pages, King Gramovlanz's messengers, who had come to Artus. She said: "No one should be

192 · Wolfram von Eschenbach

standing here. If you want me to, I shall order these people to move on, beyond the tent ropes. If my lady wants to stir up such lamentation about her lover, the story shall soon come among the people." My lady Bene was sent outside. One of the pages slid the letter and the ring into her hand. They had also heard full well their lady's high grief, and they said they had come and wanted to speak with Artus, if it would please her to arrange that. She said: "Stand over there, far away, until I summon you to come to me." Bene the sweet young lady said in the tent that Gramovlanz's messengers were there and asked where Artus, the king was. "It did not seem fitting to me to show them to this conversation; I have had no cause to avenge myself on my lady by letting them see her crying here."

Bene gives the letter to Artus. Itonje urges him to read it, since it will convince him of the seriousness of her love for Gramovlanz. Artus reads. "I greet the one I should greet, where I earn greeting with service. My young lady, I mean you, since you comfort me with comfort. Our loves keep each other good company. That is the root of the strength of my joy. Your comfort weighs more than other comforts since your heart shows loyalty to me. You are the lock on my faith and the loss of my heart's sorrow. Your love gives me help and counsel so that no wrongdoing of any kind was ever seen in me. I may well speak of your goodness, steadfast without wavering as the *polus artanticus*, the South Pole, stands against the *tremuntane*, the North Star, neither of which leave their place. Our loves should stand fast in faith and not move away from each other. Now think of me, worthy maiden, of the sorrow I have lamented before you, and be not slow with your help for me. If ever a man wanted to part you from me out of hatred, remember love will reward us both well. You should follow Lady Honor and let me be your servant: I want to serve you however I can."

Artus spoke: "Niece, you are right, the king greets you without deceit. This letter gives me tidings of such a wondrous find of love I have never seen measured before. You shall turn his discomfort away from him, and he yours from you. Both of you should leave this to me: I want to prevent the combat. In the meantime you should avoid weeping. But you were a prisoner; tell me, how did it happen that you became fond of each other? You should share the reward of your love with him; he shall serve you for it." Itonje, Artus's niece, said: "She is here who arranged it. Neither of us ever spoke about it. If you want it, she will arrange for me to see him, to whom I give my heart." Artus said: "Show her to me. If I can, I shall see to it that your will be done, for his sake and yours, and both your joy shall be complete." Itonje said: "It is Bene. There are also two of his pages here. If my life is of concern to you, will you undertake that the king, on whom my joy depends, will see me?"

Artus, the wise courteous man, went out to the pages soon: he greeted them when he saw them. One of the pages spoke to him: "My Lord, King Gramovlanz asks you that you will honor the pledge that has been agreed on between him and Gawan, for your own honor's sake. My Lord, he also asks you that no other man will bring combat to him. Your army is so great that it would not be right if he had to overcome them all. You should let Gawan come, since the combat was arranged against him." The king said to the pages: "I want to free us from this. Never did greater sorrow happen to my nephew when he himself did not fight there. He who fought with your lord comes from a lineage well used to victory: he is Gahmuret's son. All those who are in the armies that have come from all sides never heard of a hero so manly in combat: his deeds are altogether equal to his praise. He is my nephew Parzival. You shall see him, fair of skin. I shall do what the king told me, so that Gawan's faith may not come to grief."

Artus, Bene, and the two pages rode here and there. Artus let the pages observe the shining radiance of many ladies. They could also observe many rustling crests on the helmets. It would do little harm to a man of true riches if he acted so companionably. They did not get off their horses. Artus let the pages see the worthy men in the whole army where they could see the most exalted knights, maidens, and ladies, many a beautiful body. There were three divisions of the army, and two empty spaces in between. Artus then rode with the pages far from the army, out to the plain. He said: "Bene, my sweet young lady, you must have heard what Itonje, my sister's child, has lamented before me: she cannot leave off weeping. If they want to, my companions who are standing here will believe that Gramovlanz has almost extinguished Itonje's bright radiance. Now help me, you two, and you also, my friend Bene, that the king may ride here to me and do combat tomorrow. I shall bring my nephew Gawan against him on the plain. If the king rides to my army today, he shall be better armed tomorrow. Love offers him a shield here that will be too much for his companion in combat: I mean the high spirits inspired by love that do harm to the enemy. He should bring courteous people.[20] I want to mediate between him and the duchess here. Do this with skill, companions of my trust: you shall have honor of it. I should lament more before you: what have I, unhappy man, done to King Gramovlanz, that he should treat my kin, which probably does not ride high in his scales, with great love and great lack of love? Any other king, my peer, would gladly spare me. He now wants to reward with hatred the brother of her who loves him; if he will think again he shall see that his heart becomes unfaithful to love when it teaches him those thoughts."

One of the pages said to the king: "My Lord, if my lord wants true courtesy he should let be what you speak of as discomfort. You know about the old hatred: it suits my lord better to stay away than to ride toward you here. The duchess still behaves as if she has denied him her favor and she has complained about him to many a good man." "He should come with few people," said Artus. "Meanwhile I shall have won peace for that anger from the wellborn duchess. I shall give him good escort: Beakurs, my sister's son, shall take care of him at the halfway point. He shall travel in the care of my escort: he dare not speak of that as shame. I shall let him see worthy people." *The pages ride away. Gramovlanz is overjoyed and agrees to come. He meets Beakurs and his escort.*

Beakurs showed bright radiance; the king did not delay to ask, and Bene told him who that fair knight was. "He is Beakurs, son of Lot." Then Gramovlanz thought: "My heart, now find her who looks like him who rides here with such loveliness. She is in truth his sister. She who sent me the hat made in Sinzester, together with a sparrow hawk, if she shows me greater favor I shall take her alone, no matter how many riches there are on earth. She must mean to be loyal. I came here at her mercy: she has comforted me so before. I trust her well that she will do to me what shall make my spirits rise even more." Her fair brother's hand took his hand: it was also recognized as fair.

Now it had come to pass in the army that Artus had won peace from the duchess. Gain of recompense had come to her after Cidegast whom she had lamented so steadfastly. Her anger was almost buried, since many an embrace from Gawan had awoken her to new life: that was why her anger was so weak. *Gramovlanz and Artus come face to face.*

Artus said to Gramovlanz: "Before you begin to sit, see if you do not love one of these ladies and kiss her. Let that be allowed to you both here." The letter he had read in the field had told Gramovlanz who his lady friend was: I mean that he had seen her brother, the spokesman of the worthy love she bore for him in secret, and not for the whole world. Gramovlanz's eyes recognized her who bore love for him. His joy was great indeed. Since Artus had allowed them both to show their greeting of welcome to each other without hatred, he kissed Itonje on the mouth.

King Brandelidelin sat with Ginover the queen. King Gramovlanz also sat next to her who had watered her bright radiance with weeping.[21] That was the profit she had had from him. If he did not want to take revenge on one not guilty, he had to speak to her and offer his service for love. She also knew how to treat him, in that she thanked him for his coming. Their speech was not heard by anybody: they gladly looked at each other. If I should learn that language I shall find out what they said there: no or yes.[22]

Artus said to Brandelidelin: "You have now told enough of your tale to my wife."[23] He led the undaunted hero to a smaller tent, a short way across the plain. Gramovlanz sat quietly (that was Artus's will) with his other companions. Women showed their fair looks there, so that little pained the knights. Their pleasure was so great that a man who wanted to grasp joy after sorrow would gladly endure it again.

They then brought the drinks before the queen. Since they drank enough, both knights and ladies, their color kept improving. They also brought drinks to Artus and Brandelidelin. The cupbearer went away again. Artus began his speech as follows: "My lord King, let them do it: let the king, your sister's son, kill my sister's son; if he then wanted to show love for my niece, the young lady who lamented her sorrow for him where we left them sitting, and if she conducted herself with good sense, she would never become fond of him, but give him such reward of hatred that it would cause great discomfort to the king if he wanted to profit of her at all. When hatred subverts love it turns joy away from the steadfast heart."

Then the king of Punturtoys said to Artus the Briton: "My Lord, they are our sisters' children who are in hatred against each other: we shall prevent the combat. Nothing else may come to pass than that they love each other with heartfelt sentiments. Your niece Itonje should order my nephew first to leave off the combat for her, since he desires her love. So the combat with its warlike customs shall in truth be avoided altogether. And that shall also help my nephew to the duchess's favor." Artus said: "That I shall do. Gawan, my sister's son, must have such power over her that she will abandon her claim to him and me, in good breeding. And you settle the dispute on your side." "I shall," said Brandelidelin. They both went in again.

Reconciliation takes place as planned. Itonje is given to Gramovlanz in marriage, Cundrie to Lischoys, and Sangive to the Turkoit Florant.[24] The duchess said that Gawan had served her love with praise highly renowned, so that he was by right lord of her body and her land. That speech seemed heavy to her soldiers, who had broken many a spear before out of their desire for her love.

Gawan and his companions, Arnive and the duchess, and many a lady of fair skin, and also the worthy Parzival, Sangive, and Cundrie took their leave; Itonje stayed with Artus there. Now nobody dare say where a more beautiful wedding took place. Ginover received in her care Itonje and her lover, her *amis* the worthy king, who had often won many a prize before with deeds of knighthood. Love for Itonje had forced him to this. Many a man there rode to his lodgings whom high love had given sorrow. We may well forget the story of their meal at night. Whoever had shown true love there wished it was night rather than day.[25]

King Gramovlanz sent word (his pride's need forced him to) to Rosche Sabbins, to his men, that they should work hard to break up camp by the sea and come with his army before the day, and that his marshal should occupy a place that would fit the army well. "Prepare high things for myself, and for every prince his own ring of tents." He thought of this because of the high cost. The messengers rode. Then it was night. They saw there many a sad man, whom woman had taught this: when a man's service fades for him and he does not find reward, he must hasten to sorrow, except if a woman's help overtakes him.

But now Parzival thought of his wife with the fair skin and her sweet, flawless nature. What if he greeted another, offered her service for love and taught himself disloyalty? He spares himself such love.

Great loyalty has protected his manly heart and his body so that in truth no other woman ever had power over his love except the queen Condwiramurs, the beautiful flower, *bea flurs,* in blossom. He thought: "What has love done to me since I was capable of loving? I was born out of love, how did I lose love this way? If I want to strive for the grail, the chaste embrace of her I parted from too long ago must always rule me. If I am to see joy with my eyes and speak of sorrow in my heart, those labors stand uneven. Nobody grows rich in high spirits off such a life. May luck tell me what is best for me in this." His armor lay close to him.

He thought: "Since I am lacking what the happy have (I mean love that makes many a poor mind happy with the help of joy), since I have no share in that, I do not care what happens to me now. God does not want me to have joy. If our love, mine and that of her[26] who forces me to long for love, was such that absence was part of it and doubt destroyed us, I might well come to another love, but now her love has taken from me any other love and the comfort that shows forth joy. I am unredeemed of grieving. Luck should grant joy to those who honestly desire it. May God give joy to this whole host: I want to go away from these joys." He seized his armor where it lay, which he often used to do alone, and had soon armed himself with it. Now he wants to gain new pain. When the man who flees from joy had his whole armor on he saddled the horse with his hand. Shield and spear he found prepared. They heard his journey lamented in the morning. Day began to break when he rode away.

Book Fifteen

Many people have been annoyed because this story was kept from them; many were unable to hear it. I will not keep it from you any longer now, I shall tell it to you true to the plot, since I carry the lock of this adventure in my mouth: how the sweet and noble Anfortas became healthy and well. The adventure tells us how the queen of Pelrapeire guarded her flawless womanly heart until she reached the place of her reward, where she stepped into high happiness. That was Parzival's doing, if my art is not spoiled.[1] I shall first tell you of his distress. Whatever combat his hand had fought, had been fought with children up till now. If I could change this story I would not gladly put him at risk;[2] I would also dislike it myself. Now I commend his good fortune to his heart, that partakes of God's blessing, where courage lay next to flawlessness, since it never showed cowardice. That should give him steadfastness so that he may keep his life now, since on his undaunted travels he was impelled toward him who stood a master of all combat. That same courteous person was a heathen man who had never acquired the knowledge that comes with baptism.

Parzival soon rode toward a rich stranger in a wide clearing in a big forest. It will be a marvel indeed if a poor man like me could tell you about the rich finery the heathen wore. If I told you more than enough about it I could still tell you more, if I would not be silent about his wealth. *The stranger is described at some length. We are also told that he has brought an immense army with him.* And yet there he rode in search of adventure, away from his army, this one man, to take exercise in the forest. Since they take this right for themselves, I let the kings ride and fight for praise alone. Parzival was not riding alone: his self and his high spirits kept him company; they offer such a manly defense that women should praise them unless they want to gabble away through lack of truthfulness. Here two men wanted to ride against each other who were lambs in flawlessness and lions in courage. Alas, since the earth is so wide, that they did not avoid each other, those who fought there without guilt! I would worry about the one I brought there, if I did not think of the consolation that the grail's power would sustain him. Love shall defend him too. He was a servant to them both, with the strength of service, without wavering.

My art does not give me the knowledge to tell of this combat in detail, how it went. Each man's eye received a spark when he saw the other coming; each man's heart spoke of joy, but sorrow stood close by. These pure men, free of corruption, each bore the other's heart: their strangeness was intimate enough. I may not separate this heathen from the baptized man now, if they want to show hatred. That should bend down the joy of those who are known as good women. Each of them was offering his flesh to hardship for his lady love. May good fortune separate them without death.

His mother gives birth to the lion dead, and he comes to life through his father's roar. These two were born out of the roar of battle, the choicest praise that came from many a joust. They also knew the art of jousting and the expense of wasting many spears. Leaving their horses free rein at first, they tightened the reins and looked around them, so they would not miss when they charged. They did so without forgetting to sit firm in the saddle, to prepare for the joust, and to prick the horses with spurs. Here the joust was ridden in such a way that both gorgets were cut with strong spears that did not bend: the splinters flew from that joust. It was a hateful thing for the heathen that the man before him was still sitting, since nobody he had moved against in combat had ever done so before. Did they carry swords where they came up against each other? They were sharp and all prepared. Their skill and their manliness were soon shown there. The horses grew hot with weariness; the knights tried many new lists.[3] They both jumped off their horses; the swords sounded first.

The heathen caused the baptized man pain. His cry was "Thasme," and when he cried "Thabronit," he took a step forward. The baptized man was warlike; many a quick lunge they took toward each other. Their combat had come to the point that I may no longer keep this speech silent: I must lament it in good faith since one flesh and one blood show so little mercy to each other. They were both children of the same man, the very basis of refined loyalty. Love never disturbed the heathen, and therefore his heart was strong in combat. He bore a will to fame on account of queen Secundille, who had given him the country of Tribalibot: she was his shield in need. The heathen gained in combat; what do I do to the baptized man now? Unless he wants to think of love he cannot escape: this combat must win death for him by the heathen's hand. Avert this, virtuous grail, and you, Condwiramurs fair of skin: here stands both your servant in the direst need he ever encountered. The heathen swung his sword on high. Many a blow of his was dealt in such a way that Parzival sank to his knees. You may say: "They fought like this," if you want to call them both "two." They were both nothing but one. My brother and I are one body, as are a good man and a good wife.[4]

The heathen's shield is described. He appears to be gaining the upper hand because he is thinking of his wife, Queen Secundille, while he is fighting.[5] They swung their arms with skill: sparks of fire jumped out of the helmets, and from their swords came a bitter wind. May God sustain Gahmuret's son there. That wish should be fulfilled for them both, the baptized man and the heathen: I just named both as one.[6] They would also begin to think so if they had been better known to each other, and they would not have set such a high pledge. Their combat did not risk more than joy, happiness, and honor. Whoever wins the prize there, if he loves loyally he has lost worldly joy and always chosen sorrow for his heart.

Why do you hesitate, Parzival, that you do not think of the flawless one with the fair skin (I mean your wife), if you want to keep your life here? The heathen kept companionship with two, and therein lay his greatest strength. One: that he showed love that lay in his heart with loyalty. Two: the precious stones[7] that taught him high spirits with their pure, noble nature, and increased his strength. It disturbs me that the baptized one grows so weary in combat, in lunging, and in strong blows. If neither Condwiramurs nor the grail would help him now, the warlike Parzival, he should have one comfort still, so that the fair, sweet boys should not be orphaned so soon, Kardeiz and Loherangrin, whom his wife both brought to live birth when he last embraced her body. Children sired in true chastity are a man's salvation, I think.

The baptized man increased in strength. He thought (and not too soon) of his wife the queen and her worthy love he had won from Clamide before Pelrapeire with the play of the sword, where a fire of blows had jumped out of helmets. Countercries were weighed here against Thabronit and Thasme. Parzival began also to get into the habit of crying "Pelrapeire." At a distance of four kingdoms Condwiramurs took care of him in time with love's power.[8] Then shards jumped from the heathen's shield, I think, and they were worth many a hundred marks. Gahaviez's strong sword broke with one blow on the heathen's helmet, so that the bold rich stranger stumbled down to his knees, as if he was seeking prayer. It no longer pleased God that booty taken from the dead would thrive in Parzival's hand: he had taken the sword from Ither in his stupidity.[9] The heathen who had never before sunk beneath the power of the sword jumped up quickly. The combat is still undecided: it stands to judgment for them both before the Hand of the Highest. May His Hand turn death away from them!

The heathen was rich in nobility. He then spoke courteously in French, which he could speak, from a heathen mouth: "I can see well, warlike man, that your combat will have to be done without a sword. What praise would I win off you then? Stand still, and tell me who you are, warlike hero. In truth you would have conquered my honor that had been granted to me for a long time,[10] if your sword had not broken on you. Now let there be peace from both of us until our limbs are better rested." They sat down on the grass. Manliness and good breeding was in both, and both their years were such that they were neither too old for combat, nor too young. The heathen spoke to the baptized man: "Now believe me, hero, that I have never seen a man in my days who would have been more entitled to the prize one should win in combat. May it please you now, hero, to tell me both your name and your lineage; in that case my travels here have been well guided." Then spoke Herzeloyde's son: "If I should do so through fear, nobody should desire that of me, except if I were to grant it under duress."[11] The heathen from Thasme said: "I shall name myself first, and let the shame be mine. I am Feirefiz Anschevin, so rich that many a country serves my hand with tribute."

When that speech was done Parzival spoke to the heathen: "How are you an Anschevin? Anschouwe belongs to my inheritance, castles, land, and cities. My Lord, you shall choose another name at my request.[12] If I should have lost my land and the worthy city Bealzenan, you would have done me injustice. If any of us is an Anschevin, I should be of that lineage. Yet it has been told to me as the truth that a hero undaunted lives in heathen lands. He has earned love and praise through the power of knighthood, so that he rules over both. He has been named my brother; they have recognized him there as worthy of praise." Again Parzival said: "My Lord, if I could see the color of your face I could soon tell you if it is as I have been told. My Lord, if you want to leave it up to me, uncover your head. If you will believe me, my hand will avoid combat against you altogether until your head is armed again."

Then spoke the heathen: "I have little fear of your fighting. If I stood altogether unarmed,[13] you would have come to shame as long as I had my sword, since your sword is broken. All your warlike skill will not save you from death unless I want to spare you anyway. Before you would begin to fight I would let my sword sound both through iron and through skin." The heathen strong and swift showed manly virtue: "This sword should be both of ours." The bold hero threw it far away from him in the forest. He said: "Should combat come to pass here now, the chances should stand even." Then spoke the rich Feirefiz: "Hero, by the observance of your good breeding, since you might have a brother tell me, how is he built? Make his face known to me, how his color has been described to you." Then spoke Herzeloyde's son: "Like a parchment written on, black-and-white here and there. So Eckuba described it to me." The heathen said: "That am I." They both then little delayed: each of them quickly freed his head of helmet and coif of mail at the same time. Parzival found a high find, and the dearest one he ever found. The heathen was quickly recognized because he bore the mark of the magpie. Feirefiz and Parzival ended their hatred with kisses. Anyway, friendship was more fitting to them both than jealousy in the heart against each other. Loyalty and love put an end to their combat.

The heathen spoke with joy: "Oh happy am I that I ever saw the worthy Gahmuret's son: all my gods are honored in this. My goddess Juno may well be happy with this honor. My powerful god

Jupiter has granted me this happiness. God and goddess I shall always love your power. Praised be the shining of the planets in which my travels for adventure were undertaken toward you, awesome and sweet man, and almost stolen from me by your own hand. Praised be the air and the dew that fell on me this morning. My courteous key to love! Oh happy the women who shall see you! What happiness has come to them!" "You speak well; I would speak better if I could, without any hatred. But I am unfortunately not so gifted that your worthy praise might be heightened with words. Still, God knows my intention. Whatever skill heart and eyes have in me, they both do not slacken: your praise speaks first; they follow. Greater hardship never came to me from any knight's hand than from you, that I know as the truth," spoke the man from Kanvoleiz. Then spoke the rich Feirefiz: "Jupiter has expended all his art on you, worthy hero; you should no longer address me formally: we both had the same father, after all." With brotherly loyalty he asked that he be spared formal address and that Parzival would address him informally. Parzival regretted that speech. He said: "My brother, your wealth compares itself well to that of the Baruc, and you are also older than I am. My youth and my poverty should guard against the levity of my addressing you informally as long as I care about good breeding."

Parzival informs Feirefiz that he, too, never knew their father. They eulogize him, but Feirefiz also blames him for his mother's death. "Alas, the irredeemable grief!" spoke the heathen, "is my father dead? I may well speak of loss of joy and yet look at joy found, in truth. In these hours I have lost joy and found joy. If I can grasp the truth, my father and you and I, we were all one, but the one showed itself in three parts. When you see a wise man, he does not count anything as kinship, except between a father and his son, if he wants to find the truth. You have done combat here against yourself. I came riding into combat against myself; I would have gladly killed myself, but you could not refrain from defending my own body against me. Jupiter, write down this wonder: your power revealed your help to us so that our death was averted." He laughed and wept in secret. His heathen eyes began to shed tears altogether befitting the ways of baptism.[14] Baptism should teach faith, since our new faith was named for Christ: in Christ is faith recognized.

Feirefiz invites Parzival to come with him to his army, but Par-

zival prevails on him to visit the armies of Artus and Gramovlanz. After Parzival's disappearance had been discovered, Artus decided to wait for him on the same spot for eight days. Parzival and Feirefiz ride into Artus's camp, where they become Gawan's guests. He has his squires disarm them. His armor was taken from him.[15] Then they looked at this man of many colors; all those who were able to speak of wonder could see it there in truth: Feirefiz bore strange marks. Gawan spoke to Parzival: "Nephew, inform me about your companion: he has such a wondrous appearance, I have never seen the like of it." Parzival said to his host: "If I am your kinsman, so is he: Gahmuret shall be your guarantee of it. This is the king of Zazamanc. My father won Belakane there with honor, and she bore this knight." Gawan then kissed the heathen much; the rich Feirefiz was both black and white all over his skin, except that half of his mouth showed red. They brought velvet garments known for their high cost to both of them. They carried them out of Gawan's room there. Then came ladies light of skin. The duchess let Cundrie and Sangive kiss first; she herself and Arnive kissed Feirefiz later. He was happy to see such fair women; I think he derived pleasure from it.

Gawan spoke to Parzival: "Nephew, your helmet and your shield tell me of your new discomfort. Combat has played with both of you, you and your brother. Against whom did you gain this pain?" "No fiercer combat was ever known," said Parzival. "My brother's hand forced me into defense in great need. Defense is the best charm against death. My strong sword broke in a blow on that familiar stranger. Then he gave evidence of small fear: he threw his sword far out of his hand. He feared he would commit a sin against me, even before we had reckoned our kinship. Now I have his favor indeed, which I shall gladly earn with service." Gawan spoke: "I was told of an undaunted combat. In *Schahstel marveile* they see what happens within six miles of the castle in the pillar in the guardhouse. My uncle Artus said that the one fighting there at that time was you, nephew from Kingrivals. You have brought us the true tidings, but the combat was already thought of as yours. Now believe me when I tell you we have been waiting for you for eight days with great, rich festivity. Both your combat grieves me: you shall rest from it with me. But since you two have done combat you must know each other all the better. Now choose friendship instead of hatred."

Gawan offers a banquet to his guests. It is described at some length, as are the participants. Feirefiz the rich spoke to Parzival his brother: "Jupiter has thought of my travels for my salvation, since his help has brought me here, where I see my worthy kinsman. By rights I give praise to my father, whom I have lost: he was born from true honor." The man from Waleis said: "You shall see other people still, and you will have to speak in their praise: many a knight of manly shape around Artus, the leader. This meal is passing quickly and it will not be long until you see the worthy come, of whom much praise is heard. Only three knights sit here of those who represent the power of the Round Table: the host and Jofreit, although I too have won the honor that they desired me to sit at it, which I granted them."

They took the tablecloths away then before all the ladies and before the men. It was time for this when they had eaten.[16] Gawan the host did not sit for long: he began to ask and urge the duchess and also his grandmother that they would take Sangive and the sweet Cundrie and go where the heathen of many colored skin sat, and that they would take care of him. Feirefiz Anschevin saw these ladies walking toward him. He began to stand up for them, as did his brother Parzival. The duchess of radiant skin took Feirefiz by the hand, and she asked whatever knights and ladies she found standing there to sit down, all of them. Then Artus rode up there with his people, to the sound of music. You heard trumpets blowing there, the beating of the drums, the playing of flutes and shawms. The son of Arnive rode up with great clamor. The heathen spoke of this merry business as a worthy thing. So Artus rode up to Gawan's ring with his wife and many fair people, with knights and with ladies. The heathen was able to see that there were also people young with such years that they showed radiant color. There was King Gramovlanz, still in Artus's care; and on the same road there also rode Itonje his beloved, the sweet one free of falsehood.

Then the group of the Round Table dismounted, with many women of fair color. Ginover let Itonje kiss her nephew the heathen first; she herself then went closer there. Feirefiz greeted her with a kiss. Artus and Gramovlanz received this heathen with love altogether loyal. They both did him honor and offered their service, and many more of his kinsmen showed him their goodwill. Feirefiz Anschevin had come to good friends there: he had soon gathered that from their behavior. Down sat woman and man and many a maiden well shaped. If he wanted to apply himself to it, many a knight could find sweet words there from sweet mouths, if he knew how to woo for love. That request left many a fair woman who sat there altogether without dislike. You never see a good woman in anger when a worthy man bespeaks her help: she has "deny" and "allow" before her eyes.[17] If you grant joy anything that brings tribute, true love must pay the interest. I have always seen the worthy ones live like this. There sat service and reward. Hearing a lady love's speech is a helpful sound that may stand friends in good stead.

Artus sat next to Feirefiz. Then neither of them forgot to give questions their due, and sweet straight answers too.[18] Artus said: "Now I praise God that he sent us the honor of seeing you here. From heathen lands there never came a man to the countries that observe baptism to whom I would rather grant service with serving hands if your will desires it so." Feirefiz spoke to Artus: "All my misfortune broke when the goddess Juno arranged the weather for my sailing toward these western realms. You act much like a man whose worth has been spread far with tales; if you are called Artus, your name is known afar."

Artus said: "He did honor to himself, whoever praised me to you and other people. His own breeding gave him that advice, more than I deserved it: he has done it out of courtesy. I am called Artus and I would gladly know how you came into this land. If a lady you love has sent you on your way she must be very lovely since you have gone so far for adventure's sake. If she has not withheld her reward that exalts a woman's service even more. Every woman should receive hatred from her servants if you went unrewarded."[19] "The tale I have to tell is different," said the heathen. "Now listen to the story of my coming. I lead such a powerful army that the Trojans defending their land, and those who besieged them, would have to get out of my way. If they were still alive on both sides and if they strove for combat against me they would not be able to gain victory; they would have to suffer shameful defeat by me and mine. In great hardship have I pursued with deeds of knighthood the lady who now grants her favor to me: the queen Secundille. What she desires is my will. She has disposed my life for me:[20] she ordered me to give generously and to take good knights with me. That should be fitting for me, for her sake. All this came to pass as follows: many a knight of known worth is named among my household, armed with his shield. In return her love is my reward. Whenever I have come to distress since then, her love has brought help as soon as I thought of her. She has been a warrant of better comfort than my god Jupiter."21

Artus spoke: "These far travels in the service of a lady fully fit the nature you inherited from your father. I want to let you know about service greater than what has never been given on earth to any woman's lovely person. I mean the duchess who is sitting here. For her love many a forest has been wasted; her love has pledged joy to many a good knight and turned his high spirits awry." He spoke of the fighting for her, and also of Clinschor's army, which sat there on all sides, and of the two combats Parzival his brother had fought at Joflanze on the wide meadow. "And he himself should inform you of whatever else he has experienced, since he was never able to spare his person. He seeks a high find: he strives for the grail."

Artus asks both Feirefiz and Parzival to tell him about the people and the countries they have come to know on their travels. They both oblige at some length. In the meantime Gawan has Feirefiz's armor brought in. It is much admired by all. Gramovlanz, Artus, Parzival, and Gawan then proceed to plan a banquet for the next day, to honor the Round Table.

It has rarely become night without the sun always bringing the next day, as is its nature.22 The same also happened there: day shone on them sweet, pure, and fair. Many a knight smoothed his hair and put a wreath of flowers on it. Many an unpainted lady's skin you could see there, with many a red mouth, if Kyot has told the truth. Knights and ladies wore garments not cut in one country: wide headdresses, low, high, as it went according to the ways of their land. There was a group gathered from far away; that was why their customs were different. Whatever lady was without an *amis* did not dare to come to the Round Table in any way. If she had accepted service for her reward and if she had given assurance of reward she rode to the ring of the Round Table. The others had to leave it be: they sat in their lodgings.

When Artus had heard mass you could see Gramovlanz coming, and the duke of Gowerzin, and Florant his companion. The three each desired the calling of the Round Table. Artus granted it to them soon. If a woman or a man were to ask you who showed the richest hand of those who ever sat at the Round Table, from any country, you cannot do better than tell them that it was Feirefiz Anschevin. With that let those words be. They moved toward the circle in worthy order. Many ladies were pushed about;[23] if their horses had not been well girthed they would have quickly fallen. Many a rich banner you could see coming from all sides. Bohourts[24] were ridden in a wide circle around the Round Table's ring. It was a matter of courtesy that not one of the knights would have ridden inside the ring. The field was so wide on the outside that they could bring the horses to a gallop and meet with a clash, and also ride with such skill that the ladies were glad to see it. They also came and sat where the worthy ones were eating. Chamberlains, stewards, cupbearers had to think how they would serve there with good breeding. I think they gave them enough there. Every woman had won praise, who sat there with her *amis*. Many had been served with a high feat on the advice of a longing heart. Feirefiz and Parzival had the sweet choice to observe one set of ladies and another. You never saw so many of lighter skin nor redder mouth at any hour in field or meadow, as you could find by that ring. That was joy revealed to the heathen.

Hail the coming day! Honored be the story of its sweet tidings as it was heard from her mouth. *A young lady is seen approaching. She wears the emblem of the grail, many small turtledoves, and she rides straight toward Artus.* In French was her speech. She asked that revenge would be taken on her and that they would listen to her tale. She asked the king and the queen for help and to support her words. She turned away from them at once, to where she found Parzival sitting close to Artus. She hastily began her jump from the horse on the grass. She fell before Parzival's feet with the breeding that was in her; she begged for his greeting in tears, so that he lost his anger against her and forgave her without a kiss. Artus and Feirefiz were eager in support of her request. Parzival bore hatred toward her; his friends' request made him forget it in good faith, without deceit. The worthy lady, though not fair, jumped up again fast; she bowed to him and expressed her gratitude to those who had helped her to favor after great guilt.

With her hands she undid her headdress: whether veil or fastening, she threw it away from her in the ring. Cundrie *la surziere* was soon known there,[25] and the grail's arms she wore were much looked at. She still showed the same body, which so many men and women had seen coming to the Plimizoel. You have heard about her face: her eyes still stood as they had, yellow as a topaz; her teeth were long; her mouth looked like a violet painted with woad.[26] If she was not of a mind to earn praise she had worn her expensive hat on the plain of the Plimizoel without any need: the sun would have done nothing to her. It could not have darkened her skin with its dangerous radiance through all her body hair. She stood with good breeding and pronounced what they spoke of as exalted tidings. She began her speech like this: "Hail to you, Gahmuret's son! God now wants to show mercy to you. I mean the one Herzeloyde bore. Feirefiz of many colors must be welcome to me on account of Secundille my lady and of much high worth that has earned his praise from childhood and youth."

To Parzival she said: "Now be faultless and happy too, hail to you for your high calling, you crown of man's salvation! The inscription has been read: you shall be lord of the grail. Condwiramurs your wife and your son Loherangrin are both named there with you. When you left the land of Brobarz she bore two sons there, who lived. Kardeiz has enough there. If no more happiness were ever revealed to you, except that your true mouth shall now greet the worthy and the sweet with speech, that the question from your mouth shall now sustain king Anfortas and turn away from him the great grief of many sighs, where would your peer in happiness be?"[27]

Seven stars she named there in the heathen tongue. The rich and worthy Feirefiz recognized those names as he sat before her, black and white. She said: "Observe now, Parzival, the highest planet Zval, and the fast Almustri, Almaret, and the radiant Samsi show happiness to you. The fifth is called Alligafir, and the sixth Alkiter, and closest to us Alkamer.[28] I do not say this because I dreamed it: they are the reins of the firmament, they must moderate its speed. Their opposition has always fought against its progress. Sorrow is now an orphan where you are concerned. Wherever the journey of the planets runs, and whatever their shine covers, that is set for you as your goal, to reach and to achieve. Your grief must perish. Only of excess will they not let you partake, the grail and the grail's power: they forbid false companionship. You fostered sorrow when you were young; the joy that is coming has taken it from you. You have overcome the grief of the soul and waited in sorrow for the joy of the body."

Parzival was not saddened by her tale. For love water flowed from his eyes, the mainspring of the heart. Then he said: "My Lady, such things as you have named here—if I am known before God so that my sinful self and my son, if I have one, and my wife, too, shall have this duty, then God has done well by me. You show your good faith by offering me this compensation. And yet if I had not done wrong you would have spared me your anger before. But then it was not time for my salvation yet; now you are giving me such an exalted share that my sorrow has an end because of it.[29] Your clothes tell me the truth. When I was at Munsalvaesche with the grieving Anfortas—whatever shields I found hanging there were all marked as your garment is: you are wearing many turtledoves here. Now tell me when or how should I travel toward my joy and do not let me delay it long." Then she said: "My dear lord, a man should be your companion. Choose him. Count on me for guidance. Do not delay long, for the sake of assistance."

In the whole ring it was heard that Cundrie *la surziere* had come, and what her tidings meant. Orgeluse wept for love because Parzival's question would turn Anfortas's torment away. Artus desirous of praise spoke to Cundrie with good breeding: "My Lady, ride to your comfort, let yourself be attended, tell us yourself how." She spoke: "Is Arnive here? Whatever room she gives me, there do I want to live for the time being until my lord rides away from here. If she has been freed from prison, allow me then to see her and the other ladies on whom Clinschor had imposed his torment for many a year now." Two knights lifted her on her horse; the worthy maiden rode to Arnive.

Now it was time for eating. Parzival sat next to his brother. He asked him for company. Feirefiz was all prepared to ride with him to Munsalvaesche. At the same time people stood up all over the ring. Feirefiz thought of exalted things: he asked King Gramovlanz if the love between him and his niece was flawless, and to show him proof if it was. "Help her and Gawan, so that the kings and the princes we have here, the barons and also the knights, not one should ride away from here before they see my presents. Dishonor would have been done to me here if I had gone away free of giving.[30] Whatever traveling artists may be here, they may all count on a gift from me. Artus, I want to ask you now: make haste to press this request on the highly placed, so that they do not hold it in contempt, and be my warrant to them against dishonor: they have never yet seen such a rich hand. Give me messengers to send to my harbor, from where the presents shall come." Then they promised the heathen they would not remove themselves from the field for four days. The heathen was happy, so I heard it said. Artus gave him experienced messengers to send to his harbor. Feirefiz, Gahmuret's son, took ink and parchment. His handwriting was not devoid of identification marks; I doubt if ever a letter asked for so much.

The messengers rode away dutifully then. Parzival began his speech as follows. In French he told all of them what Trevrizent had said before, that nobody could conquer the grail at any time, except him who has been called there by God. This news spread to all countries: no fighting could win the grail. Many people then left off trying to win it, which is why it is still hidden.[31] Parzival and Feirefiz taught the ladies intensity of grief. They would not gladly have avoided it. They rode to the four parts of the army; they took their leave of all the people. Each of them went away with joy, well armed against the hardship of combat. On the third day gifts were brought to Joflanze from the heathen army, so great that they baffled the imagination. Whichever king received his gift there profited his country forever. Never had such expensive gifts been shown to every man according to his status. All the ladies were given rich presents from Triande and from Nourient. I do not know how the army left there, but Cundrie and these two, they rode away.

Book Sixteen

Anfortas and his people still suffered pain through hardship. Their loyalty left him in distress. He often asked them for death. Death would soon have come to him if they had not often let him see the grail and its power. He spoke to his group of knights: "I know well that you would take pity on my grief if you were loyal. How long shall this go on with me? If you desire what is yours by right, you must answer for me before God. I was always gladly at your command, ever since I first bore arms. I have atoned enough for all the dishonor that ever happened to me and that none of you have seen. If you have been spared disloyalty, set me free in the manner of the helmet and by the order of the shield.[1] You have often observed, if you did not spurn to do so, that I brought both[2] undaunted to the task of knighthood. I have wandered through valley and mountain with many a joust and played the sword so that it brought hardship to my enemies, no matter how little I profited from it for your benefit.[3] I, exiled from joy, shall accuse you at the last judgment, one and all. Therefore your fall approaches unless you let me go from you. You should be sorry for my distress. You have seen and heard how this misfortune has come to me. What good am I as a lord to you now? It will happen all too soon that your souls will be lost on my account. What kind of behavior have you chosen for yourselves?"

They would have set him free of his misery except for the reassuring comfort Trevrizent had spoken of before, as he had seen it written on the grail. They were waiting again for the man whose joy had run away from him there, and for the hour of help, the question from his mouth. The king used to keep his eyes closed, sometimes for almost four days. Then he was carried to the grail, whether that was joy to him or sorrow. And then his illness forced him to lift up his eyes, and so, against his will, he had to live and not to die. This is how they could tend to him until the day when Parzival and many-colored Feirefiz rode toward Munsalvaesche with joy. Now time had waited until Mars and Jupiter had come back in their orbit all in anger (when Anfortas was lost) to the point they had started from before. That caused pain in Anfortas's wound; he suffered so that maidens and knights often heard the sound of his screams and saw the looks of distress he made known to them with his eyes. He was wounded beyond help; they were unable to help him. Yet the adventure says true help was coming to him now.

Wolfram briefly sketches how Anfortas's wound is tended, with the help of herbs and diamonds. But now joy is heard about him. To *Terre de salvaesche* has come who rode away from Joflanz, whose cares had abandoned him: Parzival, with his brother and a maiden. I was not told for true how far it was between the two places. They would have had sharp challenges to combat if Cundrie, their guide, had not kept them away from distress. They rode toward a lookout tower. Many a Templar, well mounted and fully armed, hastened toward them there with great haste. They were very courteous. Looking at the guide they saw that joy should be coming to them. When he saw many turtledoves shining on Cundrie's clothes the leader of the group said: "Our cares have an end. With the grail's insignia comes whom we always longed for since the bonds of sorrow were tied around us. Hold still: great joy is coming toward us."

Feirefiz Anschevin urged his brother on and hastened to combat at the same time. Cundrie caught him by the reins so that his joust did not take place. Then the maiden of unsightly color said quickly to her lord Parzival: "You should soon recognize the shields and the banners. You have nothing there but a group that belongs to the grail; they are very much at your service." The worthy heathen said: "Let combat be avoided then." Parzival asked Cundrie to ride toward them on the path. She rode and told them the tidings of the joy that had come to them. Whatever Templars were there, they dismounted on the grass. At the same time many a helmet was untied. They welcomed Parzival on foot; his greeting seemed a blessing to them. They also welcomed Feirefiz, the black and white. To Munsalvaesche they rode, weeping, and yet in joy.

They found people uncounted, many a charming old knight and noble page, many squires, the whole household that had reason to be happy with their coming. Feirefiz Anschevin and Parzival were both well received on the stairs in front of the high hall. They went into the high hall. There lay a hundred carpets round and broad, as was their custom, with a down cushion on each of them and a long cover of samite. If the two kept their wits about them they could find many a place to sit until the squires took their armor from them. A chamberlain walked up to them; he brought them rich clothes, the same for both of them. Whatever knights were there sat down. They brought many a precious goblet to them, of gold (it was not glass). Feirefiz and Parzival drank and then went to Anfortas, the sad one.

You have heard before that he used to lean and rarely sit, and how his bed was furnished. Anfortas received both of them with joy, and yet in sorrow. He said: "I have hardly been able to wait, but if anyone shall make me happy, it will be you. You parted from me before in such a way that people see you in sorrow for it, if you believe in helpful loyalty.[4] If ever praise was spoken of you, ask the knights and the maidens who are here to give me death, and let my misery come to an end.[5] If you are named Parzival prevent me from seeing the grail for seven nights and eight days: with that all my lament shall be turned away. I do not dare to suggest anything else; hail to you if they say of you that you bring help. Your companion is a stranger here; I do not allow him to stand before me. Why do you not let him go to his rest?"

Weeping, Parzival said: "Tell me where the grail lies; if God's goodness has conquered me, all these people will see it." He fell to his knees there in the end, three times, in honor of the Trinity. He prayed that help should be given for the pain in the sad man's heart. He stood up, and asked: "Uncle, what ails you?" He Who ordered a bull to walk away from death alive for Saint Sylvester's sake and asked Lazarus to rise,[6] the Same One helped Anfortas to grow healthy and to be healed. What the French call *flori*, flowery, that glow came over his skin. Parzival's beauty was now a mere breath of air, as was Absalom's, David's son, and Vergulath's of Ascalon, and all those to whom beauty came by birth, and the beauty they ascribed to Gahmuret when they saw him ride into Kanvoleiz, so handsome; none of their beauty was equal to that which Anfortas showed after his sickness. God is able to work more wonders still.

No other election took place there than of him whom the writing on the grail had named lord over them: Parzival was soon recognized as king and lord. I think nobody could find anywhere else two men as rich as Parzival and Feirefiz, if I know anything about wealth. They offered much eager service to the host and his guest. I do not know how many stages Condwiramurs had ridden toward Munsalvaesche in joy. She had heard the truth before: a message had come to her that her misery and lamentation were turned away from her. Duke Kyot and many another worthy man had led her to Terre de salvaesche in the forest where Segramors was felled in the joust and where the snow had likened itself to her before, with blood. There Parzival should fetch her; that journey he would gladly suffer.

These tidings a Templar told him: "Many a courteous knight has brought the queen with good breeding." Parzival was very thoughtful: he took part of the grail's group with him and rode to Trevrizent. The hermit's heart grew happy with the tidings that things stood so with Anfortas that he did not die from the joust and that the question had brought rest to him. Then he spoke: "God has many secrets. Who ever sat on his council, or who knows the end of his power? All the angels with their companionship will never find its limit. God is man and his father's word; God is father and son, his spirit can bring great help."

Trevrizent said to Parzival: "Greater wonder never happened, since you railed against God in anger, than that his infinite Trinity grew ready to grant your will. I cunningly lied about how things stood with the grail to keep you away from it. Grant me forgiveness for that sin: I shall be obedient to you now, my sister's son and my lord. You learned from my tale that the spirits who had been driven out dwelled around the grail with God's help, and that they waited for His mercy there. But God is so steadfast that he always fights against those I told you were in his favor. Whoever wants to earn the least part of God's reward must forswear them.[7] They are lost forever; that loss they themselves have chosen. I am sorry about your hardship: it had always been uncommon that anyone could win the grail by fighting at any time. I would gladly have taken you away from that pursuit. Now it has come to pass differently for you: your gain has been increased. Now turn your senses to humility."

Parzival spoke to his uncle: "I want to see them, whom I never saw in five years. When we were together she was dear to me, as she still is now. I want to have your advice while death does not part us; you advised me once in dire need. I want to go to my wife: I have heard of her coming toward me, to a place by the Plimizoel." Parzival then asked Trevrizent to give him leave. The good man commended him to God. Parzival rode away that night. The forest was well-known to his companions; when day broke he found a dear find: many a tent pitched. Many banners were raised there from the land of Brobarz, as I heard them say; many a shield had traveled behind them. The princes of his land lay there. Parzival asked where the queen herself lay, if she had a separate ring of tents. They showed him where she lay and that she had a well-furbished ring encompassed by tents. Now Duke Kyot of Catalonia had risen early that morning; they rode toward him.

The day's look was still gray. Yet Kyot recognized the grail's arms in the group: they all carried turtledoves. Then his old body sighed because Schoysiane his chaste wife had given him joy at Munsalvaesche—she died at Sigune's birth. Kyot went up to Parzival; he received him and his people well. He sent a page to the queen's marshal and asked him to give good comfort to all the knights he saw still on their horses there. He himself guided him by the hand to where he found the queen's chamber, near a small tent of buckram. His armor they took from him altogether there. The queen did not know of this yet. Parzival found Loherangrin and Kardeiz lying by her (then joy had to overcome him) in a tent high and wide, where a group of fair ladies lay on all sides. Kyot slapped the sheets: he asked the queen to wake up and laugh for joy. She looked up and saw her man. She had on nothing but a shirt; she swung the sheet around her and jumped on the carpet in front of the bed, Condwiramurs of light color. She embraced Parzival. They told me they kissed each other. She said: "Good fortune has sent you to me, joy of my heart." She bade him welcome: "I should be angry now, but I may not. Honored be the time and the day that brought me this embrace, from which my sadness grows ill. I have now what my heart desires: sorrow is utterly powerless against me."

Now the children woke up too, Kardeiz and Loherangrin; they were lying on the bed all naked. That did not annoy Parzival; he kissed them lovingly. Kyot rich in good breeding asked that they be carried away. He also began to tell all the women that they should go out of the tent. They did so after they had welcomed their lord after his long journey. Kyot the courteous commended her husband to the queen; he then led away all the young ladies. It was very early yet; chamberlains closed the tent sides.

If blood and snow had once torn Parzival away from the company of his wits (he had found them lying on the same meadow), Condwiramurs now gave him recompense: she had it in her power. His body never received love's help for love's need elsewhere, even though many a worthy lady had offered him love. I think he devoted himself to pleasure until the middle of the day's morning. The army rode from everywhere to see; they observed the Templars, who were well dressed, and their shields well shattered, much pierced with jousts and cut with swords. Each of them wore a gambeson of pfeffel-silk or samite. They still had their iron leggings on; the rest of their armor had been taken away from them.

No more sleeping was to be done. The king and the queen rose. A priest said mass. Great jostling arose in the ring on the part of the valorous host that had once been at war with Clamide. When the benediction had been done, his vassals welcomed Parzival in good faith and honor, many a knight rich in courage. They took away the sides of the tent. The king spoke: "Where is the boy who shall be king over your land?" To all the princes he made known there: "Walis and Norgals, Kanvoleiz and Kingrivals he shall have by right, Anschouwe and Bealzenan, if he ever comes to a man's strength. Keep him company there. Gahmuret was my father's name, who left it to me in rightful inheritance. With happiness I have inherited the grail; at this time you shall receive your fiefs from my son, if I find loyalty among you." With goodwill that came to pass; they saw many banners brought forward there. Two small hands bestowed many an expanse of wide lands there. Kardeiz was crowned there. Since then he conquered Kanvoleiz and much that had been Gahmuret's. Seats were put out on the grass by the Plimizoel, and a wide circle cleared where the people could come to their bread. Breakfast was eaten quickly there. The host turned toward the journey home: they took down all the tents. They rode back with the young king.

Many a young lady parted from the queen, as did her other companions; they all showed forth lamentation. Then the Templars took Loherangrin and his well shaped mother and soon they rode toward Munsalvaesche. "At one time," said Parzival, "I saw a hermit's dwelling standing in this forest; a swift, clear spring did quickly run through it. If you know of it, show me the way to it." His companions told him they knew of one: "A maiden lives there, always lamenting on her friend's coffin; she is an ark of true goodness. Our journey passes close by her; one hardly finds her free of grief." The king spoke: "We shall see her." They agreed with him on this. They rode swiftly on ahead and late that evening they found Sigune dead in her devotions. There did the queen see the misery of need. They broke in. Parzival asked them to lift up the coffin's stone for his niece's sake. Schianatulander appeared, undecayed, beautiful with the color of embalming. They laid her close to him there, who had given him her maiden love when she lived, and closed the grave. Condwiramurs began to lament her uncle's daughter, I heard say, and was left without much joy, because Schoysiane, the mother of the dead maiden, who was Parzival's aunt (if the Provençal[8] read it right) had raised her as a child; therefore joy fled from her.

Duke Kyot, King Kardeiz's preceptor, knew little about his daughter's death. It is not bent now, the bow, this story is true and straight.[9] They paid the journey its due and rode into Munsalvaesche by night. There Feirefiz had been waiting for them, pleasantly whiling away the time. Many candles they lit, as if the whole forest was on fire. A Templar from Patrigalt rode armed next to the queen. The courtyard was broad and wide; on it stood many separate groups. They welcomed the queen, and the host, and his son. Then they carried Loherangrin to his uncle Feirefiz. The boy did not want to kiss him because he was black and white. It still happens that good children are afraid.

The heathen laughed. They began to part from each other in the courtyard, after the queen had dismounted. Gain had come to them with the coming of the joy she brought with her. They led her where a worthy group of many fair ladies was. With good breeding Feirefiz and Anfortas both stood with the ladies on the steps. Repanse de Schoye, Garschiloye from Greenland, and Florie de Lunel showed bright eyes, light skin, and maidenly praise. Slender as a reed there also stood who was not lacking in beauty and goodness and who was spoken of as the daughter of Jernise of Ryl: the maiden called Anpflise. There stood Clarischanze from Tenabroc, I was told, a sweet maiden, of bright skin altogether unblemished, with a waist like an ant's.

Feirefiz stepped toward the hostess; the queen asked him to kiss her. She kissed Anfortas too and was happy with his deliverance. Feirefiz led her by the hand where she found Repanse de Schoye standing, the host's mother's sister. Many kisses had to be exchanged. For this their mouths had always been so red; they now endured[10] the hardship of kissing. It grieves me and I am sorry that I cannot do the same for the queen, since she had come to them tired.[11] Young ladies led their lady away. The knights stayed in the high hall well furnished with candles that burnt very bright. There, with good breeding, preparations were begun to receive the grail. They always carried it before the people, not to show it, but only for the high holy days. When they had been without joy, that evening,[12] because of the bleeding spear, the grail had been carried before them out of a desire for help; Parzival had left them in sorrow since. It is now carried before them with joy; their sorrow is altogether overthrown.

When the queen had taken off her traveling clothes and put on her headdress, she came as well befitted her; Feirefiz she welcomed at the door. It is now without dispute that never at any time a man heard of, or spoke of such a beautiful woman. She wore on her body pfeffel-silk an experienced hand had woven in Sarant, with the great skill invented earlier in the city of Thasme. Feirefiz Anschevin brought her in, and she showed forth radiance. In the middle of the high hall three big fires had been lit, and the fires smelled of *lign aloe*.[13] Forty carpets lay there, and more seats than at the time when Parzival, too, had seen the grail carried before him. One seat had been adorned above all others, where Feirefiz and Anfortas were to sit with the host. They kept their wits about them with good breeding, whoever wanted to serve there when the grail was to come.

The grail procession is very briefly described. Feirefiz has noticed Repanse de Schoye's beauty and he feels attracted to her. The heathen asked for knowledge: what made the empty golden vessels before the table grow full? Observing the miracle made him happy. Then spoke the fair Anfortas who had been given to him as a companion: "My Lord, do you see the grail lying before you?" The many colored heathen said: "I see nothing except an *achmardi*.[14] My young lady brought that to us, who stands there before us, wearing a crown. Her looks go into my heart. I thought my body was so strong that no maiden or woman would ever take the strength of joy away from me. If ever I received worthy love, it has become hateful to me. Ill breeding would undermine my good breeding if I made my need known to you, since I never offered my service to you. What help is all my wealth, and what I have ever won for a woman's sake, and whatever my hand has given, if I have to live in such pain? My powerful god Jupiter, why did you will me to come here to such discomfort?" The power of love and the weakness of joy made him pale in his white spots. Condwiramurs known for her fair skin very nearly found rivalry in the look of the fair maiden's skin. Then Feirefiz the worthy guest bound himself with the bonds of her love. His first love was broken because of his will to forget. What help was her love to Secundille, or her country of Tribalibot? A maiden gave him such dire distress that Clauditte and Olimpia, Secundille and where else in the wide world women had rewarded his service and furthered his praise—all their love now seemed weak to Gahmuret's son from Zazamanc.

Then the fair Anfortas saw that his companion was in pain. His white spots even turned pale, so that high spirits abandoned him. Anfortas said: "My Lord, my sister—I am sorry if she teaches you pain—which no man has yet suffered on her account.[15] No knight has ever ridden in her service, and so nobody ever took reward of her. She was with me in great misery. They have so rarely seen her happy; that has also dulled her color in part. Your brother is her sister's son; he should be able to give you help." "If that maiden is your sister," spoke Feirefiz Anschevin, "who wears the crown there on her uncovered hair, give me advice on loving her. All my heart's desire is for her. If ever I gained praise with the spear, why could it not have been done on her account, and why could she not have pledged her reward to me! Tournaments may include five kinds of handling the spear; my hand has done all five.[16] *Feirefiz proceeds with a technical analysis of the five kinds of handling the spear, and ends with renewed protestations of his love.*

The father of these two was called Frimutel. Anfortas and his sister had the same face and the same skin. The heathen often looked at her, and then again often at Anfortas. No matter how many men carried food back and forth, his mouth did not eat of it; yet he sat there like one eating. Anfortas spoke to Parzival: "My Lord, your brother has not seen the grail yet, I think." Feirefiz began to say to the host that he did not see the grail. That seemed strange to all the knights. Titurel, the old bedridden cripple, also heard these tidings. He said: "If it is a heathen man he should not want his eyes to reach such understanding that they can see the grail without the power of baptism. A barrier has been built against it." These words he sent to the high hall. There the host and Anfortas said that Feirefiz should observe what all those people lived on; any heathen would have been prevented from seeing that. They urged him to accept baptism and acquire endless gain.

"If I come to baptism on your account, is baptism to my advantage?" asked the heathen, Gahmuret's son. "Whatever combat or love forced me to do until now, it was a breath of air. Whether it was a short while or long since the shield first covered me, I have never been given such grief since. In good breeding I should hide love, but now my heart cannot conceal it from her." "Who do you mean?" said Parzival. "That one maiden marked with radiant brightness, my companion's sister here. If you want to help me with her I shall make riches known to her so that lands flung wide will serve her." "If you want to allow baptism to be granted to you," said the host, "you may then desire her love. I may now speak to you informally: our wealth is almost alike, through the grail's power on my side." "Help me to friendship," spoke Feirefiz Anschevin, "brother, for your aunt's sake. If people can earn baptism by combat, take me there at once and let me serve for her reward. I always liked to hear that sound where splinters flew from the joust and swords rang on helmets."

The host laughed much about this, and Anfortas even more. "Can you receive baptism like that?" asked the host. "I shall bring her close to your power by means of true baptism. You must lose Jupiter your god for her sake, and forswear Secundille. Early tomorrow I shall give you advice that will be fitting for your endeavor." *The banquet comes to an end and the ladies withdraw, much to Feirefiz's disappointment. The next morning Parzival and Anfortas lead Feirefiz to the baptismal font in the castle. Parzival reminds Feirefiz that he will have to renounce all his gods.* "Whatever I have to do to get the maiden," spoke the heathen, "shall be done and it shall be shown that I have done so with loyalty."[17] The baptismal font was tilted a little toward the grail. Suddenly it was full of water, neither too warm nor too cold. There stood a gray priest, old, who had immersed many a little child from heathen lands in it. He said: "You must rob the devil of your soul and believe in the Highest God alone, whose Trinity is common to all and yields good to all alike. God is man and his Father's word.[18] Since He is Father and Son, Who are honored alike, and Spirit exalted to the same height, may this water defend you against heathendom through the full power of these three, the power of the Trinity. In water He went to baptism from whom Adam received His features.[19] By water trees are given their sap. Water makes fruitful all created things man speaks of as creatures. Through water man can see. Water gives many a soul such radiance that the angels could not be brighter."

Feirefiz spoke to the priest: "If it is good for my discomfort I shall believe what you command. If her love rewards me I shall gladly do his bidding. Brother, if your aunt has a God I believe in Him and in her[20] (I have never been given such great grief). All my gods are forsworn. Secundille will also have lost whatever she desired for me. Command me to be baptized by your aunt's God."[21] They began to treat him in a Christian manner and spoke the blessing of baptism over him. When the heathen had received baptism and the robing with the baptismal robes for which he could hardly wait had come to pass, they made the maiden ready for him: they gave him Frimutel's child. He was blind to the sight of the grail before baptism covered him; since then the grail was revealed to him, to his sight. After the events of the baptism they found written on the grail that any Templar whom God's hand gave as their lord to foreign peoples should forbid questions about his name or his lineage, and that he should help them to their rights. If such a question is asked of him they may no longer have his help. Because the sweet Anfortas had been in bitter pain for so long, and because the question had avoided him for so long, questioning is hateful to them now, and forever. All companions of the grail's care do not want questions about them.

Feirefiz invites Anfortas, twice, and Loherangrin to accompany him to his kingdom. Anfortas declines and Parzival declines in his son's name: both must devote their lives to the grail. Twelve days later Feirefiz leaves. On the way back to his army he is received with great hospitality by the burgrave of Carcobra, who is in turn handsomely rewarded. When Feirefiz and Repanse de Schoye finally reach their army's camp, they hear that Secundille has died.

Then Repanse de Schoye could feel happy about her journey for the first time.[22] Since then she bore a son in India, whose name was Johan. They called him Prester John;[23] ever since they have let the kings there keep that name. Feirefiz ordered writings to be sent over all the land of India as to how the Christian life was lived. It was not so strong there before. We call it India here; there it is called Tribalibot. Through Cundrie Feirefiz sent word back to his brother in Munsalvaesche how things had gone with him since, and that Secundille had passed away. Anfortas was happy then that his sister was now undisputed queen over so many wide flung lands.

The true tale has come to you of Frimutel's five children, that they strove after goodness and how two of them died. One was Schoysiane, without falsehood before God; the other was called Herzeloyde, who pushed falsehood out of her heart. Trevrizent gave up his sword and his life as a knight for the love of God and for gain without end. The worthy fair Anfortas was manly with flawless heart. Following the rules of his order he rode many a joust; for the grail he fought, not for a lady. Loherangrin grew manly, strong; cowardice hid itself from him. When he understood the deeds of knighthood he gained praise in the service of the grail.[24]

Do you want to hear more now?[25] A long time later there sat a lady, guarded against all falsehood. Wealth and high lineage had both come down to her as her inheritance. She could behave in such a manner that she acted with true faultlessness: all human desire had perished in her. Many worthy people wooed her, of whom many wore a crown, and many a prince, her peer; her humility was so great that she did not turn to them. Many counts of her country began to hate her for t'is: why did she want to delay in taking a man who would be suitable for their lord? She had trusted in God altogether, no matter what was done to her in anger. Many abused her for her innocence. She called a court for the lords of her land. Many a messenger from a faraway land traveled to her. She forswore all those men, except the one God would show her, whose love she would gladly accept as her prize.

She was a duchess in Brabant. From Munsalvaesche was sent he whom the swan brought and whom God had in mind for her. In Antwerp he was taken ashore. She was altogether treated without deceit by him. He knew how to behave well: in all the realms where they ever gained knowledge of him they had to admit that he was fair and manly. Courteous, wise in breeding, a man truly generous without a heartbeat's hesitation was he, bare of wrongdoing. The lady of the land received him well. Now listen how his words were spoken. Rich and poor heard them, who stood there on all sides. Then he spoke: "My lady Duchess, if I shall be lord of this land, I must give up what is worth as much.[26] Now hear what I shall ask of you: let it never be asked who I am, then I shall be able to stay with you. If I am the target of your question you shall have lost my love. If you do not let yourself be warned by this, God shall warn me, he knows whereof." She pledged a wife's assurance, in which she wavered since, because of love, that she would stand by his command and never go beyond what he ordered her to do, if God left her in her senses.

That night his body experienced her love. Then he became lord in Brabant. The wedding took place in a rich manner: many a lord received his fief from Loherangrin's hand, the fief that was rightfully his. The same man became a good judge; he also engaged in deeds of knighthood often, so that he earned praise with his strength. They had beautiful children together. There are many people in Brabant still who remember them well: how she welcomed him and how he parted from her, how her question chased him away and how long he stayed there. He left against his will. But now his friend the swan brought him a small smart ship.[27] He left his keepsakes there: a sword, a horn, a ring. Away went Loherangrin. If we want to do justice to the story he was Parzival's son. He traveled over water and over land until he was back in the service of the grail. Why did the good woman lose the lovely person of her worthy friend? He had forbidden her to ask earlier, when he had come before her from the sea. This is the place where Ereck should speak: he knew how to punish with words.[28]

If Master Cristjan of Troys[29] has done this tale wrong, that may well anger Kyot who brought word to us of the right tale. At the end the Provençal says that Herzeloyde's son gained the grail, as it had been ordained for him when Anfortas had forfeited it. From Provenz the right tale was sent to us in German lands, and the outer limit of the adventure. No more shall I tell of it now, I, Wolfram von Eschenbach, than the master told there.[30] I have named Parzival's children for you, and his high lineage, as is fitting, and I have brought him where salvation devised his going, in spite of all.[31] If a man's life ends in such a way that God is not cheated of his soul through his body's fault, and if he can yet keep the world's favor with honor, that is gainful work indeed. If good women have sense, and even if only one of them does not begrudge me good things, I must be more valuable to them now, since I have told this tale to the end. If it has been done for a woman, she shall have to speak sweet words to me.[32]

Translated by André Lefevere

Notes

Book One

1. Much has been written about Wolfram's cryptic prologue to *Parzival*. He seems to use it to sound the major theme of the work: the praise of loyalty, which is the glue that holds all human relationships together, on the personal and the social level. He also uses it to foreshadow details that will surface again later. The image of a man's courage "checkered" with its opposite is an analogue of the color of Feirefiz's skin. Parzival's half brother, born from the marriage of Gahmuret, their father, and Belakane, a black heathen queen, is checkered black-and-white all over. Doubt, the first concept introduced, functions as a foil to loyalty. Even if people are not perfect, Wolfram suggests, they may, or even will be saved if they set out a course of action for themselves that is inspired by loyalty and if they loyally try to pursue it, even if they do not always succeed.

2 It is obvious from the text that Wolfram knew what he was doing, i.e, that he did not indulge in gratuitous obscurity. Rather, he gives an "example" of his style, much in the way preachers of his time taught religion by means of *exempla*, exemplary stories and anecdotes. Unlike the preachers, however, Wolfram does not reveal the "moral" of his *exemplum*. The listeners/readers have to find that out for themselves. Wolfram makes it clear that this will not be an easy task, especially not for the "stupid" listeners/readers weaned on the "wrong" exempla, represented by the work of Hartmann von Aue and Gottfried von Strassburg. Wolfram adds insult to injury by comparing the "stupid" listeners to rabbits, precisely the kind of comparison listeners (and poets) well disposed toward the Hartmann/Gottfried school would have abhorred.

3. A circumlocution for a mirror, which consisted of glass coated with tin on the back. The "stupid" are stupid because they do not reflect things, because they are not open to what happens around them.

4. The implied meaning seems to be something like: those who attack me there must know me very well indeed, so that they can attack me most efficiently. This makes all the more sense if we accept that the prologue was composed after parts of the work had already been circulated, recited/read, and attacked by "members" of the opposite school. Wolfram imagines one such attack here, and reacts to it.

5. It is natural to be afraid when you are attacked at such close (even intimate) quarters. There is no shame in it; it does not make you a coward.

6. In other words: am I setting an impossible task for myself? Or maybe two impossible tasks: is it as impossible to find loyalty as it is to compose this type of literary work about the finding of loyalty?

7. Wolfram appears to suggest that people who use their common sense (and are not waylaid by the fashion, or fashions of the day) will have no real trouble understanding both the "wisdom" contained in his work, and its style.

8. At a time when a good harvest usually meant the difference between subsistence and starvation, a hailstorm flattening the wheat in the fields was a catastrophe indeed.

9. Wolfram probably thinks of a cow bitten by gadflies. Its tail is too short to keep them away.

10. Women also have to choose between loyalty and lack of it, in their personal and social life. It is remarkable that Wolfram so pointedly refers to them in an epic poem. They were usually relegated to lyrical poetry in his time. But since Wolfram's epic is designed to represent a blueprint for a better world, that better world should also be inhabited by better women.

11. Like the rabbit above, another instance of Wolfram's "realistic" style, or rather of the tension he manages to build up between what pertains to the plot line and the comparisons, which are usually taken from another kind of discourse altogether.

12. Wolfram may well be alluding to Gottfried von Strassburg here, and telling his audience what he thinks of Gottfried's style: Gottfried is more style than substance.

13. Wolfram draws attention to the fact that he is retelling the story of "Perceval," first told by Chrestien de Troyes. This kind of statement was expected from him. Writers had to reveal whose authority backed their work. In fact, Wolfram was attacked by his critics because he deviated from his source to some—sometimes comsiderable—extent. It seems very likely that Wolfram may have been given Chrestien's *Li contes del Graal* only after he had already composed the first two books of *Parzival* as we know it. Because he did not want to let his own work go to waste, he ran his own two books together with Chrestien's story, which ends with book 13 of Wolfram's *Parzival*. Once he had been "freed" of Chrestien Wolfram goes back to the material he used in books 1 and 2 and uses it again in the composition of books 14, 15, and 16.

14. The audience does not really need Wolfram to inform it of the implications of the right of primogeniture.

15. The emphasis may be taken to suggest that Wolfram does not approve of the custom, which brought real hardship to younger brothers, effectively marginalizing them in society and turning them into potential threats to the social order. Many of them became mercenaries or even robber barons. In Wolfram's time, which was also the time of the crusades, many went to the Middle East, to carve out a kingdom for themselves, as Gahmuret does.

16. Wolfram links his first hero with the house of "Anschouwe," or Anjou. He may have done so because he may have chosen Richard the Lion-Hearted, king of

England and count of Anjou as a partial model for Gahmuret. In the person of Eleanor of Aquitaine, queen first of France and then of England, the house of Anjou also acted as the patron of the emerging epic poetry centered around King Arthur, or Artus, as he is called in Wolfram's work, after the French version of the name.

17. I shall meet a lady worth meeting and offer her my "service," i.e., be at her disposal for all kinds of knightly pursuits. That service usually, eventually brought with it some kind of "reward" of a sexual nature.

18. Gahmuret's brother was able to enter into the service of a lady without Gahmuret's knowing.

19. Baghdad. The spelling is indicative of Wolfram's somewhat shaky knowledge of the Orient, which hardly matches his fascination with it. Wolfram probably had the caliphs in mind.

20. *Baruch* indeed means "The Blessed One," but in Hebrew, not Arabic.

21. It should be clear that most knights simply had to do so, since they were disinherited at their father's death.

22. Because it was the customary farewell drink that signaled the end of the visit.

23. A somewhat roundabout way of saying that her castle was well lit. This, in turn, means that she is rich indeed.

24. It was indeed the custom for servants to sleep in the same room as their lord.

25. The queen wants to take care of Gahmuret herself, for obvious reasons. That is why she shoos his squires away.

26. He is already planning his escape. Wolfram's audience would probably have reacted with sympathy to this. Gahmuret is a knight, after all, and that means he should go in search of adventure, since that is what knights do, and not sit idly in his castle. Add to this that he is married to a heathen, and that such a marriage cannot be legally binding on a Christian.

27. Wolfram does not think it necessary to slip in the merest word of apology for his hero's behavior.

28. I, Gahmuret (one partner in love) send love to you, Belakane (another partner in love).

29. Gahmuret gratefully, if not graciously, uses the legalistic excuse referred to above.

30. The supreme irony: she is perfectly willing to grant him his wish, i.e., to be baptized, but it is too late now. He has purposely not given her a chance to prove herself in this respect. Some commentators have interpreted this as showing some disapproval of Gahmuret's behavior on Wolfram's part.

31. In medieval French *vair* means "checkered." *Feirefiz* therefore means something like "son with the checkered skin."

32. It is unclear whether the brave Gahmuret is being dishonest here, or whether he plans, after all, to go back to Belakane at some later date. It is not rare for brave knights to be a little, or even seriously flawed: Anfortas, the grail king, is the most obvious case in point.

Book Two

1. The tournament must have been very dangerous and therefore it must have scared many cowards away.

2. This was by no means uncommon in the Middle Ages: in fact, it was often the only way in which a widow—as Herzeloyde turns out to be—could keep at least some of the power and possessions left to her by her late husband. Noble ladies are quite simply forced into manipulating men if they want to keep what men left them.

3. It is Isenbrant's old tent that Gahmuret has surreptitiously appropriated near the end of the previous book, when he has it stowed away on one of his ships.

4. Since Gahmuret is a "waster of spears," if not "forests," his squires always have to keep him supplied with new spears.

5. Herzeloyde's kingdom and her rank together are not valued at half the value of Gahmuret's tent.

6. The spasm in Gahmuret's leg betrays his emotion

7. A new plot line starts here, or, as we should call it, *adventure* in the parlance of the time. It becomes obvious later on that the queen of France has been in love with Gahmuret for quite a while. Now that her husband is dead she feels free to pursue this love interest openly.

8. Again a somewhat abrupt change, back to the tournament. These sudden twists back and forth in the plot line are characteristic of Wolfram's style. They are probably linked to the oral recitation of the text, during which the reciter could easily indicate the beginning or—provisional—end of a plot line to his audience, by using his hands, e.g., or other body language, or simply by raising or lowering his voice.

9. Wolfram probably alludes to knights who were professional jousters: they would go from tournament to tournament and exact ransom from the opponents they vanquished. A fair number of knights succeeded in making a fairly decent living that way.

10. Namely that the vanquished knight will do what the victor orders him to do, since the victor technically holds the life of the vanquished in his hands.

11. The queen of France.

12. I.e., from Gahmuret, some time in the past. It is obvious that there must have been an *adventure* involving Gahmuret and the queen of France. It is alluded to here, off and on. Those in the audience who were familiar with it must have enjoyed Wolfram's *ars combinatoria* in weaving it into his second book, without ever really telling the *adventure* in its entirety.

13. The helmet he has received at the end of book 1, when his ship "miraculously" met the ship taking helmet and armor to Belakane. Since the helmet consists of a huge hollowed out diamond it is very hard indeed, and wards off all blows to the head.

14. The tournament gets out of hand, as was often the case. Instead of negotiating with the vanquished, the victors just keep the spoils.

15. It becomes obvious that Gahmuret is not very good at choosing between the ladies who lay claim to his heart. For a while it appears as if he wants to give

preference to the queen of France, for old time's sake. But it is important that he should marry Herzeloyde, because she is still a virgin and Parzival will be conceived in their union.

16. I.e., the queen of Waleis. It is sometimes very difficult to figure out who is meant, at least on the basis of the written text. Obviously the reciter had other means at his disposal to identify either the speakers or those spoken of. That is why Wolfram is not more "careful" in identifying who is who.

17. Gahmuret is under no obligation; all he needs to do is to accept the love offered by the queen of France.

18. Gahmuret is now referring to Belakane. The fact that he is longing for her at this precise moment does not augur well for his ability to choose between the queen of Waleis and the queen of France.

19. A sign that his brother has died.

20. After he lands in Seville Gahmuret visits his cousin Kaylet, the king of Spain. Kaylet is the Spaniard referred to here.

21. Gahmuret is referring to his coat of arms.

22. It should be remembered that she herself pronounced Gahmuret the victor. Under the terms of the tournament he is now obliged to accept "her body and her lands."

23. Again, Herzeloyde could definitely count on the sympathy of Wolfram's listeners: a Christian's marriage to a heathen had no legal value whatsoever.

24. A good example of Wolfram's syntax, which can be rightly called "convoluted" only if it is restricted to the written text on the page. If the sentence is read aloud it makes much more immediate sense.

25. A diplomatic way of disappointing the queen of France. Her people will have none of it, however.

26. They have done their level best, and so has she.

27. That means the foetus begins to stir in the womb. In the Middle Ages the first stirrings of the foetus were interpreted as the beginning of life.

28. Self-irony, but probably also a way of pointing out that he considers himself a knight first and foremost, albeit a knight who is able to "sing a little" indeed.

29. Speculation about the identity of this woman, though sometimes highly creative, remains inconclusive to this day.

30. Probably an allusion to the exaggerated praise composers of love lyrics tended to heap on the object of their love. Wolfram may well be referring to a particular poem, but it has not come down to us.

31. Presumably since Wolfram did neither compose, nor publish it as a book. Rather, he composed parts of it, which were written down, circulated, and recited. It is a sobering thought that nobody in the Middle Ages probably heard the whole of *Parzival*, since it could not possibly have been recited at one, two, or even three sittings. Moreover, since the recitation often took place during a banquet, it is not altogether unlikely that a fair part of the audience was more than mildly inebriated. Maybe Wolfram thought that a knight who composed poetry should do just that, and that the writing down should be left to scribes who were not knights.

32. Endless debates have been, and are still waged as to whether this is an ironic statement or not. It may mean that Wolfram alludes to the Latin *literatura*, which could be rendered by the Middle High German equivalent of "letter." In that case the statement might be taken to mean something like: "Since I know no Latin, I am considered illiterate," or "I do not know the letter of stories," which kills, as opposed to their spirit, which allows the composer to run creative variations on his source.

33. The allusion is to the medieval equivalent of a sauna. Wolfram uses his brush of twigs to conceal a certain part of his anatomy strategically.

Book Three

1. In other words: Herzeloyde does not move to some kind of "summer retreat"; rather, she withdraws from the world altogether and becomes a recluse.

2. Herzeloyde surrounds herself with peasants. She is trying to construct a world without knights. Wolfram's point is, of course, that such a world cannot last long, and would not be worth living in if it did.

3. A most uncommon habit in the Middle Ages.

4. To attract animals, so he can kill them with his javelin.

5. No wonder Parzival wants Artus (King Arthur), the most accomplished of knights, to make him a knight. He does not yet understand that there is another world over and beyond Artus's world of knights, and that his true destiny lies with the grail. But he cannot reach the world of the grail without first partaking fully in Artus's world.

6. Orilus, a contraction of the French *orgueilleux*, is the first in a fairly long row of characters who torment others with their arrogance.

7. The young lady did not think that the partridges would end up being eaten by Parzival.

8. How could he, since he has not been introduced to the etiquette of courtly banquets?

9. Jeschute becomes conscious of the implications of the situation: if Parzival is really "severed from his wits," there is no telling what he could do to her.

10. People immediately assume that Parzival is good and virtuous precisely because he is "well shaped" and "fair." The Middle Ages strongly believed that the body was the mirror of the soul. People with beautiful bodies therefore had to have beautiful souls.

11. Parzival is traditionally associated with Wales. By having Herzeloyde marry Gahmuret, Wolfram linked his own narrative with that of Chrestien, but not to everybody's liking: he was attacked for turning Chrestien's work into a more unwieldy amalgam.

12. Parzival is unwittingly cast as a villain by the code of chivalry: since he is Sigune's lover's lord, he should have defended him. Parzival can therefore technically be said to have sinned, even though he never intended to. The notion of sin and guilt is further elaborated on mainly in books 5 and 9.

13. A spaniel's leash caused his death. Schianatulander tried to bring Sigune a spaniel's leash while he was trying to reconquer Parzival's lost lands. The deadpan

style here may well point to a certain irony on Wolfram's part. True knighthood and true love are his ideals, but he may well have thought that Sigune's "true love" was altogether too much of a good thing.

14. Sigune has obviously waited too long to give her knight his "reward."

15. Wolfram has little sympathy for the lower classes, since they do not, in his opinion, "know their place" anymore. Their dealings in money, rather than land, must also have been repugnant to him. Yet the future was on their side, not his.

16. Obviously the fisherman lives by a code that could be termed the perfect antithesis of the code of chivalry.

17. This is Wolfram throwing down the gauntlet to Hartmann von Aue, whose *Erec* and *Iwein* had made him the uncontested master of the German Arthurian romance. Wolfram demands recognition for his own brand of Arthurian writing; if he does not get it, he will let one of Hartmann's major characters, Erec's wife Enite, come to harm. Wolfram's habit of mentioning major characters from the literature of his time probably served a double purpose: it kept the audience's interest going, and it established himself as a master in the art, in his own right.

18. Curneval educated Tristan in Gottfried von Strassburg's *Tristan*. Parzival has not yet been educated. There may be an ironic attack here, since even the educated Parzival never uses his education for adulterous love, as Tristan does. Gottfried may be the better stylist, as he claimed to be, but Wolfram can at least claim for himself that he exalts true loyalty, as a true knight should.

19. By Ither. He had ridden into Artus's court and seized his goblet, a symbolic gesture emphasizing his claim to Artus's kingdom. Some of the wine in the goblet was spilt on Ginover.

20. A little later on in the story. These short proleptic sentences are a favorite reciter's trick, a kind of "sneak preview" to keep the audience intrigued and, therefore, interested.

21. It was the custom that whoever swore an oath before a judge would touch the judge's staff of office while doing so.

22. The traditional image of Keie in Arthurian literature. Wolfram takes issue with it later on.

23. Ither has not been killed with the "right" weapon, i.e., not with a weapon knights would normally use in combat. He has therefore died in disgrace.

24. The choice of words here is a comment on Parzival's eating habits.

25. Tables consisted of boards put down on trestles. When the meal was over, both the boards and the trestles were carried away. Tables could therefore literally be "lifted," if we visualize the boards being lifted from the trestles.

26. Who beg for their bread in front of the windows of houses. Wolfram seems to suggest that poor knights, of whom there were quite a few, have a harder time of it than mere beggars since the code of chivalry makes it harder for them to beg openly.

Book Four

1. Parzival becomes aware of the genetic inheritance his father has left him: he becomes interested in love and ladies.

2. He does not ride along any known road, since roads were often marked by means of crosses and hedges.

3. As the children on the swings were in theirs. One of Wolfram's more "daring" or, depending on your appreciation of his style, "obscure" comparisons. His opponents would probably have considered it a borderline case, whereas they would have condemned other comparisons of his as downright "uncouth."

4. This was considered impolite in the Middle Ages, as it still is today. People were supposed to wipe the grease off their lips before drinking from goblets, not least because two or more people frequently shared the same goblet. Since hunger reigns within the castle, there is little danger of any of its inhabitants eating anything greasy, and therefore little danger of any of them forgetting to wipe the grease off their mouths and getting it into the wine.

5. Very little fat; much fat would normally drip on the coals if animals were roasted over a coal fire.

6. Fortunately, Wolfram not infrequently directs his irony against himself, often reinforcing the image of the poor knight who happens to be rather good at composing verse, but who is not one to get his subject matter from books, as others (Hartmann, Gottfried) are wont to do. Whether Wolfram actually was a poor knight or not cannot really be proved or disproved, nor does it matter at all.

7. Their body is now pledged to death: they are destined to die of hunger.

8. Parzival seems to have been awakened to the existence of ladies and the possibility of love by Liaze. He does not really love her; she merely acted as a catalyst in the process of his discovery of love.

9. The host is Gurnemanz, of course. Condwiramurs's non sequitur sounds much less odd if it is recited by a reciter briefly impersonating her in front of an audience.

10. They had had very slim pickings indeed in the course of their "hunt" for food.

11. Because he sees that there are no other beds in the room: the knights therefore cannot have come to sleep around his bed.

12. Their wooing appears to be conducted in the language of combat.

13. Condwiramurs's behavior is far less virginal in Wolfram's source, *Li Contes del Graal,* by Chrestien de Troyes. Once more, Wolfram plays on the audience's "horizon of expectation." Those listeners who have perked up their ears in anticipation of a "juicy" passage are in for a surprise, not just because Wolfram, like Gahmuret, displays a sense of "elfin" mischief, but also because he wants to establish that Condwiramurs, destined to become queen of the grail, belongs on a higher level than the normal Arthurian heroine who is not above the occasional dalliance in the dark.

14. The part of the army that "backs up" the vanguard, which is most exposed to attacks from the city.

15. Obviously whichever lady had aggravated Wolfram had done a very good job. It is not hard to see who must have stood model for his not infrequent descriptions of wicked women.

16. Parzival wears Ither's red armor to combat.

17. Married women wore headdresses; virgins did not.

18. They strike such heavy blows with their swords on each other's helmets that sparks of fire can be seen flying from the metal. It is hard to decide whether Wolfram pokes gentle fun at stock in trade descriptions of combat in works by others, or whether he admires the combatants' skill like the trained knight he was.

19. Parzival and Clamide had agreed to a truce: no soldiers from either army would be allowed to intervene while the heroes fought in single combat. Parzival's blows are now battering the tired Clamide so thick and fast that the latter thinks Parzival's army has broken the truce and that Parzival's soldiers are aiming stones at him with their slingshots.

20. Parzival replies somewhat ironically that the stones Clamide complains about exist only in his imagination; what he feels are the very real blows of Parzival's sword.

21. Suddenly Wolfram speaks in his own voice. A slip of the tongue or a quiet assertion of his status among other masters?

22. Spessart, a famous forest region in Germany.

23. Again a somewhat graphically down-to-earth image: the young ladies urge their knights on against their opponents. The keepsakes they give their knights to wear, and their support are thought to propel the knights into combat like arrows shot from a bow.

24. Keie is trying to justify his beating of the lady Cunneware, not very convincingly. He is also trying to forestall Clamide's possible avenging of Cunneware by speaking of himself in the third person, as if he were not "really there."

25. The biblical Pilate.

26. A somewhat-unsavory character taken from Hartmann's *Erec*. Wolfram continues his policy of introducing characters from other writers' works into his own.

27. The fear that one of his former enemies might try to harm him while he is a prisoner at Artus's court.

28. One of the sentences that have earned Wolfram the reputation of being "obscure." The syntax is even more convoluted in the original. In fact, it has been "regularized" here to no small extent, if to relatively small avail.

Book Five

1. Dramatic irony: the fisherman is Anfortas, as would be known to those in the audience familiar with the adventure. They would also know that Parzival does not thank Anfortas well.

2. By any other castle in the world. In other words: this castle has at least as many walls as any other.

3. They did not care at all. The fisherman in book 3 uses the same expression to tell Parzival he is not welcome in his house.

4. Where a castle stood, close to one of the places Wolfram may have been connected with. It used to be customary for commentators to try to piece and puzzle Wolfram's geography together. I feel little is to be gained from this, since the places are either well-known, such as Baghdad, or not known at all, in which case a footnote

saying something to the effect: "a village/castle somewhere in Germany" will not exactly hit the reader with all the power of revelation.

5. Their sorrow is not (yet) caused by Parzival. They are sad because they know of the king's condition and because they know it is hopeless, unless Parzival asks him what ails him.

6. It was the custom to offer clothes to esteemed guests. The "yet" in the chamberlain's speech reflects the fact that his mistress fully expects Parzival to ask the question and to stay on as king of the grail. There will be ample time to have clothes cut for him then.

7. Everybody in the castle lives under the pall of Anfortas's illness. Since they cannot openly request Parzival to ask his question, they openly show their sorrow to get him to inquire whether anything is wrong.

8. A fair amount of ink has been spilt over the fact that Wolfram calls the grail somewhat irreverently "a thing." The most appealing theory—to me at least—holds that Wolfram was somewhat embarrassed by the fairy elements within the adventure and that he tried to play them down, or explain them in a more rational manner, as he attempts to do in book 9.

9. Balsam was primarily used for lighting rooms in the Middle Ages.

10. This is probably the closest Anfortas can come to make Parzival ask his question without rendering that question invalid. Anfortas can be cured only if a man especially called to the castle asks of his own accord what is wrong with him. If the question is not asked spontaneously it will have no curative power whatsoever.

11. Wolfram delivers an "apology" for his own style, which was criticized by his opponents for relying too heavily on digressions. As was to be expected, the apology is not exactly without obscurity. Most people, Wolfram says, tend to like straight stories, i.e., stories with a linear development and without digressions. But sometimes pulling the string of a straight story, so that it is pulled back and no longer straight, gives that story more power and succeeds in holding the audience's interest to a greater extent. Still, all this art is lost on those who quite simply do not like it: they will not listen to it in the first place.

12. Wolfram's constant interventions in the story were also not appreciated by those in the opposite camp. They were considered a cheap trick to keep the audience interested, or at least awake.

13. He therefore assumes they are not supposed to sleep in the same chamber, just as he did in Pelrapeire.

14. Parzival remains true to his marriage vows. Wolfram gives extramarital love short shrift. It may be good for dalliance, as described in the lyrical poetry of his time, but it should not be allowed to interfere in serious matters, such as loyalty and dynastic considerations. Yet Wolfram also slyly suggests that being married to the most beautiful woman in the world makes fidelity a little easier to achieve.

15. Since Parzival has not asked the question that would have meant their deliverance, the people who live in the castle have no further interest in, or use for him. It is therefore made quite obvious to him that he is no longer welcome.

16. An elaborate pun. Wolfram uses the dice, and throwing the dice as a metaphor for fate (as at the end of the Gurnemanz episode). When he says here "the dice had been thrown," he uses the dice metaphorically. He then proceeds to treat the

metaphor in a more literal way: there are no "real" dice there, and no hand throwing them. The "eyes" of the nonexistent dice are then equated with Parzival's own eyes.

17. Wolfram uses *adventure* as a verb in the original, and even as a reflective verb. A literal translation would read something like: "It adventures itself now." The suggestion that he has no power to shape the adventure himself can be interpreted both as an "homage" to Chrestien, his source, and as a defense against those who accused him of tampering with his source. If the adventure is sovereign, what is a poor poet to do?

18. Signune again, and again she is described with the by-now-familiar mixture of awe and the grotesque, especially since she is forced to lean the balsamed body of her lover against a tree.

19. Or rather, his contriving to do so on the basis of knowledge he has acquired; if he has not been "called to the grail" all that knowledge will not be of any help to him.

20. A derivation from either the Latin *mons salvationis* (the mountain of salvation) or the Latin *mons silvaticus* (the wooded mountain) or the Old French *mont salvage* (the savage, wild, rough mountain). All three of these mountains would obviously be situated beyond any geography, reconstructed by scholars or not.

21. *Terre* was—and is—French for "land."

22. Not as strange as it seems if we remember that Parzival's visor must still be down.

23. Wolfram's heroines are not as fickle as Hartmann's: Lunete is a character in Hartmann von Aue's *Iwein*. She advises her mistress Laudine to marry Iwein, even though he has killed her husband. The new husband will be compensation for the one she lost. Even though this appears somewhat crude to the modern sensibility, it was essentially how things went: many a noble woman became the wife of the man who had killed her former husband. The only alternatives were the convent or the course obviously chosen by Signune: total withdrawal from the world.

24. That Anfortas (the man of many sorrows) would no longer be subjected to this slow living death.

25. The sword is used as an "example" for Parzival's future peregrinations. By not asking the question Parzival has "fallen to pieces." He will become whole again when he finally asks the question in book 16. He will know what question to ask, and why, after he has enlisted Trevrizent's help in book 9.

26. By asking it.

27. The marriage relationship was also modeled on the feudal relationship, with the husband as lord and the wife as vassal. Jeschute stands in the tradition of the stoically suffering guiltless woman who manages to win back her husband's love in the end. Its prototype is the long suffering Griseldis, who was treated by her husband as a serving woman for a quarter of a century, and then told that her husband had merely wanted to test her loyalty.

28. Parzival has to speak the word that will mean life or death to Orilus. His hand is the "messenger" of that word: it will carry out whatever "sentence" the word embodies.

29. Keie gave to Cunneware de Lalant.

30. A little box containing the relics of a saint: usually a bone, a strand of hair, or some object that had belonged to him or her in life.

31. Normally the oath would have been administered by someone else, and Parzival would have repeated the other person's words.

32. The order of chivalry.

33. Life on earth and the afterlife.

34. Parzival reiterates once again that he is prepared to face the full consequences of his oath.

35. A character who appears in both Hartmann von Aue's *Erec* and *Iwein*. Otherwise the spear is probably a "loose end," since it does not assume any relevance anywhere else in the poem.

36. Orilus's coat of arms. It would also have figured in some way or other in the coat of arms of his brother Lehelin—just as it figures on the banner that flies above Cunneware's tent—which is why Cunneware is not quite sure who he is exactly when she first sets eyes on him.

37. A "great" example of Wolfram's cavalier attitude toward the identification of characters in the story. The first he is Kingrune, the second Keie.

Book Six

1. Artus does so because the army is not far from where Munsalvaesche is reputed to be, and he knows the territory is guarded by Knights Templar of the grail, who are fierce warriors and give no mercy.

2. Wolfgang defiantly points out another variation of his on a traditional Arthurian theme. His Arthur is not connected with May, as tradition would have it.

3. Meaning either from a source altogether different (i.e. Kyot's adventure, not Chrestien's, as will be explained later), or from different sources, i. e., Chrestien, Kyot, and others. In the latter case Wolfram appears to be saying that he has based his story on various other stories.

4. That they would not engage in any jousts.

5. Hardly a shining example of "good measure." Segramors is therefore described as a fairly grotesque figure.

6. To Artus's tent, which would be the central tent in the middle of a circle of tents pitched around it. Wherever Artus is, there, too, is the court.

7. He is so happy "he could have died." Wolfram makes sure the audience does not take this expression literally.

8. A comparison based on the falcon hunt. Bells were tied to the falcon's legs so that it could easily be found again. The sentence seems to mean that Segramors and his horse make the same noise as a falcon on the hunt. Since a falcon is thrown into the thornbushes to hunt down pheasants, Segramors might as well be thrown into the thornbushes too.

9. The fact that Parzival has ridden so close to Artus's camp, fully armed, is construed as a challenge to Artus and must be answered. The irony is, of course, that Parzival does not even know where he is.

10. He is supposed to negotiate with Segramors, or even to kill him, but he is not interested in the least.

11. Wolfram speaks about the so-called *Ovidian* concept of love, which had been introduced into Medieval German and Dutch literature by Henric van Veldeke, in his epic poem *Eneide*. That kind of love is totally irrational and totally subject to the senses. No wonder Wolfram, who set such great store by loyalty, could never really think of it as "true" love.

12. Wolfram obviously has not, hence he is less than impressed with Lady Love.

13. In other words, Veldeke seems to have cut his lesson short, omitting the most important element.

14. Does Wolfram claim to speak for all men (and women) in love?

15. Once more Wolfgang "proudly" deviates from his source. His characterization of Keie is not the traditional one. Wolfram's Keie is a much more positive character than the traditional Arthurian Keie, so much so, in fact, that Wolfram obviously feels called upon to defend his own positive characterization of an archetype essentially considered negative.

16. This also suggests that Wolfram thinks his predecessors have not realized why Keie's reputation is so bad. Since they have not, their knowledge of human nature may be said to be somewhat deficient. On the other hand, Keie's beating of Cunneware de Lalant is not easy to reconcile with Wolfram's positive characterization of him, unless Keie, too, is allowed his one (or two) "flaws," which would, after all, only put him in the same league as Anfortas and Gahmuret.

17. The modern German Thuringia. The burgrave was one of Wolfram's patrons.

18. Walther von der Vogelweide, the lyrical poet. Both Wolfram and Walther resided at Hermann of Thuringia's court, the Warburg, for a number of years. They knew each other there. Wolfram suggests that Hermann is generous to a fault, that his generosity attracts good and bad alike, and that he fails to discriminate between the members of his household.

19. Meaning as much as: "That I could approach this in a different manner," and thus amounting to a veiled threat, somewhat in the vein of: "Since you seem to want to do combat with me, I am very willing and able to do combat with you. However, I suggest we talk a little first."

20. These are obviously allusions to other adventures featuring Gawan, which have not come down to us.

21. Orilus's brother.

22. Another one of Wolfram's precarious ventures into the realms of syntactic equilibrium.

23. Meaning: "I actually stayed in my saddle; nobody has ever unhorsed me."

24. Like love relationships, the relationship between man and God is also described in feudal terms, i.e., in terms of the most basic type of relationship dominating the Middle Ages.

25. Gawan has to enlighten Parzival, who no longer remembers that he actually unhorsed Keie a short time ago.

26. Not the best mount to have: horses and mules had their nostrils slit when they could not breathe well, and they were branded when they had sores, or wounds.

27. Arabic, the language of the heathens that Western Europe had discovered during the Crusades.

28. Wolfram apologizes for having to describe Cundrie in this way. He has never described any other lady in similar terms.

29. Irony.

30. It was relatively commonplace in medieval jurisprudence that those who had committed a crime involving the use of a certain limb had that limb amputated: thieves, e.g., often had their hands cut off. Cundrie here suggests that Parzival should lose his tongue since he did not use it as he should have.

31. Parzival's behavior is all the more galling since he is so handsome. It will be remembered that physical beauty was thought to be indicative of a noble soul. Since this is obviously (at least to Cundrie's mind) not the case with Parzival, and since Parzival is the epitome of manly beauty, the discrepancy between his appearance and his actions can be construed as a kind of betrayal.

32. Later, in book 16, Parzival tells Feirefiz that they must now both be equally rich.

33. Since Parzival has taken Condwiramurs away from Clamide, he is supposed to help Clamide woo and win Cunneware de Lalant.

34. Cunneware is obviously not consulted, which was normal practice in the Middle Ages.

35. Remained in the saddle.

36. Parzival is beginning to lose what Wolfram might have termed his *arrogance:* he is no longer supremely self-confident. This is the beginning of a long process of conversion that culminates in the meeting with the hermit Trevrizent in book 9.

37. Neither Parzival nor the modern reader understands the medieval God too well. The modern reader would concur wholeheartedly with Parzival in asking why he is punished for sins he did not knowingly commit. The answer is as shocking as it is absolute: since man is inevitably trapped in sin anyway, as a result of Adam and Eve's original sin, it does not really matter whether he is "really" guilty of this or that "particular" sin or not. Only when man admits his own sinfulness before God or, in Parzival's case, before God's representative, the hermit Trevrizent, will he be saved. Even though Parzival is no longer absolutely sure of himself, he turns away from God at this stage, not toward Him. Parzival's real conversion occurs in book 9.

38. This is exactly what happens during the combat between Parzival and Feirefiz in book 15. Significantly, though, Feirefiz calls on his wife first. Parzival, who has had his thoughts turned to God by Trevrizent, only does so later, when he is in danger of losing. This is just one instance among many of the "echoes" and internal allusions Wolfram has built into his work. It should also be remembered that the medieval mind was relatively well trained in looking for these "echoes": theologians spent a great deal of their time looking for "foreshadowings" in the Old Testament of events and statements belonging to the New Testament.

39. It will become obvious that Anfortas is Parzival's uncle.

40. Wolfram has also lamented the existence of a "sorry band" in the household of Hermann of Thuringia, his patron.

41. Wolfram is able to speak better of women in general in his epic poetry than of one woman in particular in the—presumably blistering—lost lyrical poem addressed to the mysterious lady who must most definitely have "aggravated" him.

42. This is the end of the sixth book of *Parzival*, and what amounts to the "provisional end" of the first version of the whole work. It is widely believed that books 1–6 were circulated as a unit, recited, read, and criticized. Wolfram reacted to the criticism by means of later interpolations in the first six books, and by means of asides in the following ten books. Wolfram wants to give the impression that Parzival has been composed in the service of a female patron; we have no independent evidence of this.

Book 7

1. A plea to prospective patrons not to give assistance to poets of that ilk.

2. Most probably the poets Wolfram approves of, but who do not always succeed in finding a patron, or even lose him or her because they stick to the "old" style.

3. An even stronger "warning" to patrons.

4. Ironically probably the only reference—by implication—to women who do not belong to the nobility in all of *Parzival*. Women of the lower classes were indeed "hunted" as a rule by knights in search of a little dalliance.

5. Anger is another emotion (sin) that threatens the social fabric: it lures people away from loyalty to the social code and turns them into destructive powers. The story told in this book is mainly that of the needless death of many people caused by a young man's anger and a young woman's arrogance. Arrogance, too, is destructive, since it puts loyalty to the self above loyalty to God, the guarantor of the social code.

6. It is obvious that the young king wants his reward too early, and equally obvious that Obie thinks a trifle too highly of herself.

7. Gahmuret's brother. The allusion is full of irony: Annore lived on to a ripe old age and died of natural causes. She "chose death" indeed, but by no means soon after Galoes's death. It is hard to escape altogether the impression that Wolfram enjoys poking fun at the tradition of courtly love. Obie is certainly not an example of true womanly virtue in Wolfram's sense, and Obilot, who could be, is still too young. Gawan's later encounter with Queen Antikonie veers toward the grotesque and his last—and final—love, Orgeluse, is the most hateful female character in the whole work, until she is redeemed by her marriage to Gawan, in which she discovers "true," as opposed to mere "courtly" love. By using the analogy of Galoes and Annore Wolfram also casts some doubt on the real depth of Obie's feelings.

8. The young king ventures on very treacherous ground here: by threatening to revoke the bond of loyalty that exists between lord and vassal he threatens to cut into the very heart of feudal society. He is therefore taught a lesson in this book.

9. True arrogance: it does not recognize the constraints of the social fabric, except where they can be made to serve its goals.

10. As soon as the king threatens action against one vassal, all vassals close ranks.

11. It is not insignificant for Wolfram's rather conservative leanings that the noble Lippaut, a representative of the old aristocracy, is the true hero of this story, whereas the young king is the villain, until he sees the light, i.e., until he recognizes that the values Lippaut himself has taught him are the real values that rule society. In reality the nobility was beginning to feel threatened by the incipient policy of kings to conclude pacts with the new cities and their burghers against both the church and the aristocracy.

12. The generation gap: the young king creates more nobles who will do his bidding, especially if they are offered the prospect of replacing the old noblemen who now act as a check on the young king's power.

13. Knights did not approve of merchants, who were quietly creating the kind of ecomomy that would eventually ruin the feudal system.

14. Arrogance prevents those who suffer from it from acknowledging reality.

15. In Wolfram's ideal feudal world the burghers are eminently loyal to their lord; in the real world they would have probably sided with the young king against their lord.

16. As my captive.

17. The victorious Poydiconjunz is perfectly justified in making his captives fight for him.

18. Gawan's possessions, and/or the sale thereof, will be enough to equip seven knights for battle.

19. She had come to his defense against her sister's aspersions.

20. It is remarkable indeed that Obilot's love for Gawan is much more mature than Obie's love for the young king. One plausible explanation might be that all of this is still abstract to Obilot: she tries out on Gawan what other women have taught her about love. Gawan plays up to her, and since Obilot has to wait five years to give love, chances are that she will not discover the discrepancy between the abstract and the concrete just yet.

21. Knights used to ride into battle with their ladies' keepsakes attached to their spears or shields, as Gawan does here.

22. When the two young ladies are of the right age for love, knights will waste many a forest on their account; or rather, the wood of many a forest that will have been used to produce the lances that knights will break for the two young ladies.

23. The castle is obviously situated on a hill inside the city.

24. King Philip of Swabia, the son of Emperor Frederick Barbarossa, was besieged in Erfurt (to use the modern spelling of the name) by Wolfram's patron, the Landgrave Hermann of Thuringia, in 1203. The allusion allows us to date Wolfram's *Parzival* with some accuracy. It also represents another instance of the very process described in this book: the struggle between king and nobility.

25. Who had come to help the beleaguered city.

26. Descriptions of battle scenes such as the one translated here were very popular with Wolfram's knightly audience; it would not be too much of an exaggeration to say that they also served a somewhat didactic purpose: you could learn from literature how to behave in your next combat. Since these descriptions tend to be somewhat

tedious to the modern readers' taste—simply because so much of what is said means so little to them, through no fault of their own—I have cut most of them in what I hope will be seen to be a judicious manner.

27. As a battle cry.

28. Knights despised archers who could kill from afar, without exposing themselves to "honest" combat, face to face. The church also took a dim view of the use of archers in battle.

29. Gawan, who has overcome him in battle, and who therefore has the right to keep him captive.

30. He has to call his daughter "My Lady" since she will become his queen.

Book Eight

1. Wolfram keeps addressing the audience, trying to draw his listeners into the story.

2. Another reference to Henric van Veldeke's *Eneide*. Dido and Aeneas, as portrayed in this work, were to become the prototypes of "Ovidian" love in German and Dutch literature of the Middle Ages.

3. Gawan is sure to fall under the king's sister's spell. He will therefore wish the king would stay away as long as possible, and even longer.

4. Probably another instance of Wolfram's impatience with the "dominant" style of the day. He may well have felt that too many dscriptions would, in the end, detract from the serious purpose behind the story he was telling. Hence probably the distance he maintains between himself and his material throughout.

5. Elizabeth, sister of Ludwig I of Wittelsbach. She died in 1204, and had been a widow for some time. A somewhat tenacious tradition insists on linking her romantically with Wolfram. She may—or may not—have been the lady for whom *Parzival* was composed.

6. This sentence and the following one provide the basis for the tradition romantically linking Wolfram with his presumed patron. How else could Wolfram have known? the—to my mind somewhat-naive—reasoning goes.

7. A general, moralistic aside. Wolfram sprinkles them throughout his work. They have been taken as evidence for the theory that he set out to write *Parzival* with obvious didactic intentions. It should be remembered in that context that much of medieval literature was what we would now call didactic in one way or another, that a didactic component was not unusual in literature and that it was therefore not necessary for Wolfram to decide to be "overtly" didactic, since the literary tradition expected it of him to some extent.

8. Probably a half-ironic "homage" to the composer of the *Eneide*. In all likelihood Wolfram does not doubt that Veldeke is better at descriptions of this kind, but it is not impossible that Wolfram has his doubts as to the—moral—value of those descriptions.

9. The queen of France whose wooing of Gahmuret has been described in book 2.

10. Antikonie should not be afraid of any kind of mésalliance: she would be bestowing her favors on a man who is her peer. It is hard to judge Gawan's behavior

in this episode; it might therefore be better not to try to do so, and to take the whole episode as one more parody of courtly love: Gawan observes all the rituals of formal wooing, as does Antikonie, but in the end sex is foremost in his mind—and hers. The words of courtly love, Wolfram seems to suggest, only serve to embellish the same old reality.

11. Just as ladies would have been sleeping in the queen's chamber at night, just so would they be working, reading, singing in her chamber by day. They can take a hint, though.

12. A stock situation taken from the courtly love lyric that nearly always contrasts the lovers on the one hand with the jealous people who wish them ill on the other.

13. And, by doing so, dishonoring not only the woman—a very doubtful proposition in this case—but also her whole family. The knight most likely has the king's honor in mind, not the queen's well being.

14. Irony: she is so in fact, but not in intention. Conversely, the "white" knight "sees" the fact of rape, which is not at all Gawan's intention.

15. This is not as grotesque as it may sound to the modern ear: medieval chess pieces were big and heavy indeed, and could be used as projectiles in time of need.

16. The women of the village of Tolenstein probably engaged in a mock tournament during carnival.

17. Maybe the simile to end all similes connected with the discourse of courtly love. No doubt another indication of the distance Wolfram keeps between himself and his material. And, of course, also a way to emphasize how slim and slender Antikonie is.

18. This is no tournament: his opponents want Gawan dead, they are not interested in ransom of any kind.

19. If I were a man, and a knight, I would fight much better than you ever did.

20. If a knight implores the protection of a lady, other knights should leave him alone out of respect for the lady. Vergulath has failed to do so, and brought dishonor on himself as a result.

21. The constant threat to the medieval world order: if kings do not behave well, or if princes are not loyal, there will be conflict between the crown and the princes. Sooner or later the repercussions of that conflict will be felt throughout society as a whole, causing the social fabric to unravel altogether in the end. Wolfram and his contemporaries had lived through a fairly protracted period of such strife after the sudden death of the emperor Frederick Barbarossa.

22. Wolfram looks on kinship as the natural guarantee of loyalty, but he is not unaware of the fact that this guarantee does not always work in practice. Either kinsmen are not loyal to each other, after all, or disloyal people claim kinship with the powerful to further their own ends.

23. Wolfram introduces his "real" source. Since part of his audience objected to the liberties he took with Chrestien's *Li contes del Graal*, Wolfram countered by suggesting that Chrestien himself had taken many liberties with the "original" version of the story, as told by Kyot, a "singer" (reciter) from Provence. The fact that Kyot translated the source from the "heathen" language known as Arabic has the strategic advantage of making the "true" original almost inaccessible for reading and

comparison. At the same time Wolfram offers "Kyot" as a convenient sop to those among his audience who need to be reassured as to the authenticity of the story. For their benefit Wolfram keeps insisting that he has not "invented" the story out of thin air. He studiously neglects to inform them that he has invented the "original" storyteller.

24. The argument between Liddamus and Kingrimursel reflects many an argument between royal councillors. Kingrimursel is the rather blunt warrior who lives by the code of knighthood and is prepared to die for it, without much reflection and without much consideration for realpolitik. Liddamus is the opposite type: he is no hero in battle, but he is able to detect and predict the ramifications of people's actions, whether undertaken in the name of the knightly code or not. Wolfram's sympathies seem to lie with Kingrimursel, but it would be unrealistic to think that the Liddamus type lost many an argument. In fact, Liddamus represents the future: the knight turned politician, who is therefore able to survive at court. The knight who was, and remained merely able to fight gradually lost his status at court and was more often than not forced to become the leader, or a member of a group of mercenaries.

25. Or: "that you were always in the forefront of the flight." In other words: at those fateful moments when knights and foot soldiers waver between fighting on and running away, Liddamus was always the first to run away, thereby helping to decide the fate of the battle against his own side.

26. A true cliff-hanger sentence, designed to entice the audience back for another session.

Book Nine

1. Maybe Wolfram introduces a personification of the "adventure" because this is the pivotal book in the whole work, the one that will save Parzival from despair and set him on the course that will eventually take him to the grail.

2. God's intervention is emphasized. It is the only way to salvation. Parzival's own thoughts or actions cannot save him by themselves.

3. Schianatulander is buried in the hermit's dwelling. Sigune prays over his grave. She uses it as a kind of altar.

4. Wolfram probably makes another ironic comment on the excesses of courtly love; on the other hand, Sigune could be seen as the embodiment of true loyalty, but maybe she goes too far even in that.

5. It should be remembered that life expectancy was much lower in the Middle Ages and that "serial marriages" terminated by death, not divorce, were the rule rather than the exception. Men often made their intentions (wanting to be considered a possible "next in line") known to women, "just in case." It has, in fact, been suggested that this might well be the material basis of courtly love poetry. If that is so, the terms *service* and *reward* tend to make more sense: a knight "invests" his service in a lady, in the hope of reward, which may still be sexual in nature, of course, but also implies higher rank, more status, and more possessions.

Wolfram merely wants to say that true loyalty between man and woman ends with death, and that woman—it is not without significance that he does not say anything about man—should not break that bond. The fact that he says so at this precise place in the work probably denotes a certain disapproval of Sigune, who appears to be taking loyalty to extremes.

6. It was considered impolite for knights to wear their swords in the company of ladies, and also to remain seated on their horses.

7. Signune cannot "invite Parzival in" because there is no door to the dwelling: she has had herself immured together with the body of her lover. This becomes clear in book 16, when Parzival wants to see her again and his men have, literally, to "break in," only to find her dead.

8. Signune here sounds the theme of the *felix culpa*, or "happy guilt." If man recognizes that he is entangled with sin, even through no fault of his own, divine redemption is extended to him. Parzival has not reached this stage yet, but Signune already intimates that he is a better man—paradoxically—*because* he has sinned.

9. It is remarkable that the two knights tend to talk about God as they would talk about any other knight: the gray knight first tries to establish God's kinship, to make sure they are talking about the same person. Another instance of the utter pervasiveness of the feudal model in all medieval discourse.

10. One of the "sententious" sentences often referred to as a hallmark of Wolfram's style. They may sound more trite to the modern ear than they did to the ears of Wolfram's audience. This kind of sentence tends to sum up what went before and, at the same time, to invite the audience to react, even if only with a nod of the head, a sigh, some verbal equivalent of "you can say that again," or a combination of the three.

It is also not altogether unlikely that a fair number of Wolfram's sententious or, to use another term often bandied about in Wolfram criticism, *gnomic* utterances may have been made because they represent the thirtieth in a section of thirty lines, the compositional unit of the work as a whole.

11. Parzival no longer trusts in himself, and he is now prepared to let God take over. God sees to it that he meets his uncle, the hermit Trevrizent, who helps him further along the path of salvation.

12. This is probably the clearest distinction Wolfram makes between the *adventure*, which might be roughly defined as "the material," the whole accretion of motifs and plot lines loosely connected with Parzival, and the story, the structure the composer imposes on the adventure for his own purposes. (One is struck by the obvious resemblance with Russian Formalist thinking about narrative: *adventure* would correspond to "fabula" in Formalist terminology, whereas *story* would correspond to *skaz*.) Wolfram is not entirely satisfied with the story Chrestien has made out of the adventure, so he makes up a story of his own, which deviates from Chrestien's. The constraints of authorship were such in his time that Wolfram had to invent another story, supposedly translated by Kyot from the Arabic, to justify his own restructuring of the adventure.

13. The library of Toledo was justly famous in the Middle Ages. It was originally founded by the caliphs of El Andalus, or Moorish Spain. After the city had been conquered by Alfonso VI, the library was maintained and avidly used by scholars from all over Europe. In the thirteenth century the famous "Toledo School of Translators" was pivotal in the spread of Moorish and classical knowledge throughout Europe. It is therefore not illogical that "Kyot" would find an Arabic manuscript in the Toledo library and translate it, probably with the help of a speaker of Arabic. The School of Translators also afforded an example of Christian/Moorish cooperation that must have appealed to Wolfram.

14. One of the theological paradoxes of the Middle Ages: it did not take the Crusaders very long to see and acknowledge that the civilization of Islam was farther advanced than that of Christian Europe. If that was the case, why were the heathens not Christians? Presumably because God intended Christian Europe to play the main part in human history after all. If He did, and there was no reason to doubt this, the backward Christians could justifiably feel superior to the heathens, while availing themselves of the knowledge those heathens had accumulated in various fields.

15. This is the story Wolfram distills out of the adventure of the grail. It is not insignificant that he calls it "a thing" (also in Middle High German). He may well have intended it as a central symbol for his dream of a world ruled by knighthood regenerated. Wolfram must also have realized that, like most central symbols, the grail would function best if it was left relatively "empty," undefined, so that it could mean many things to many people who could all identify with it in some way. This is probably also the reason why Wolfram eschews any mention of the popular rival interpretation of the grail as the chalice in which Christ's blood was collected as he died on the cross.

16. Another important concept in Wolfram's thinking: true knighthood does not really need the Church as it then existed. That is why Parzival is helped by Trevrizent, an ex-knight turned hermit, and by Sigune, and most emphatically not by some priest or bishop obviously associated with the "official" church. Wolfram holds that it is possible for a man to be at the same time a knight and, as such, very involved with the world and all its ways of fighting and high living, *and* a true believer in the Christian faith. This ideal had, to some extent, been tested during the Crusades and found sadly wanting. Yet Wolfram obviously pins his hopes on the semireligious orders of knights, such as the Templars and the Knights of Malta that arose during the Crusades. It is no coincidence that the grail is guarded by "Templars," who have only the name in common with their historical model.

17. The simple core of Wolfram's creed.

18. As it stands, the Latin phrase makes little or no sense. Needless to say, thousands of guesses have been hazarded as to what it might mean. It seems relatively pointless to add the one-thousand-first guess here. It is, in my opinion, more important to point out that Wolfram's grail is a stone, and that it bears no resemblance at all to the chalice of the rival tradition.

19. The Trinity, God. Wolfram is referring to the angels that remained neutral in the conflict between Lucifer and the Lord. It later turns out that this information is false. Trevrizent explicitly recants it in book 16. There is no middle road: man (or angel) is either for God or against Him.

20. A kind of wood, aromatic.

21. It was believed that people had to wipe their hands after eating fish; touching the eyes with unwiped hands was considered harmful. No such harm will come to Parzival and his uncle, however, since the food they are eating does most definitely not include fish.

22. If he were a bird he would get so little food from them that he would be eager to hunt, if only to supplement his food intake.

23. That is the essence of Parzival's sin: he does not see that he is cut off from salvation. Of course he has committed particular sins, mostly through no "actual"

fault of his own, but those are not all that important. If he undergoes a mind change now, he will not sin again.

24. Also, the king's very name denotes chastity, which makes consummation of the marriage rather unlikely.

25. Perhaps a touch of irony directed at the official church. This is the only passage in *Parzival* where priests are mentioned, and in a rather perfunctory manner. Their status is also somewhat pointedly equated with that of women.

26. Christ's death on the cross that has redeemed mankind.

27. Parzival's change of heart has occurred. Good things will happen to him from now on, even if he does not always recognize them immediately as such.

28. Wolfram cheats his audience of one of the stock scenes of Arthurian romance: the elaborate leave-taking. The scene is utterly unimportant to him. Rather, his concern is with Parzival's conversion. Omitting the scene, and in this manner, is his way of directing his audience's attention to the really important aspects of his work.

It is also a way of directing those in the audience who are eager for this kind of scene toward "the adventure" in general, or toward other "stories" distilled from it by others. Wolfram implies that he does not really care all that much for that kind of listener.

Book Ten

1. Gawan thinks of ways to equalize combat against a woman. He envisages a situation in which he fights on foot while she stays on her horse.

2. Protracted wrestling may well take on sexual overtones. The lady's sexual attraction would then bring Gawan "down," and he might have intercourse with her, which she could either interpret as rape or as an expression of affection, and react to accordingly.

3. The spear has gone through the shield and left a hole in it.

4. Another "sententious" utterance, whose "gnomic" quality may well owe a good deal more to the demands of meter and rhyme than to any obvious "gnomic/ sententious" intention on Wolfram's part.

5. Probably a description of internal bleeding.

6. In other words: "Why he fought you."

7. That would propel the heart in love.

8. This is the first of Orgeluse's many put-downs. Like Orilus's, her name is also derived from the Old—and Modern—French word for "proud, arrogant." Her arrogance, once again, is seen to bring distress to many people. If Jeschute stands in the tradition of Griseldis, Orgeluse belongs to that of the *belle dame sans merci*, (the beautiful lady who has no mercy).

9. Gawan has not—yet—served Orgeluse in any way. Again, Wolfram exaggerates a stock situation connected with courtly love: the lady who asks her knight to perform tasks for her in exchange for her love. Orgeluse's demands are outrageous, and so is her behavior.

10. Love, it is suggested, also depends on the luck of the throw. The eyes of the knight match the eyes of a die. Both sometimes come up with a "winning number."

11. Irony, of course. Gawan uses it to parry Orgeluse's venom.

12. Before he receives his reward, but also afterwards. Gawan makes it clear that he is no fly-by-(k)night lover who is likely to abandon the lady once he has received her reward.

13. The ribbons used to hide most of the face. Orgeluse performs the Lady's equivalent of lifting her visor.

14. Irony: Wolfram uses the traditional preparatory formula preceding statements of courtly love, but the statement itself does not match the formula in any way. Wolfram relies on the effect produced by this clash.

15. If he did not he would indeed be "lost" from her sight.

16. He does indeed allow Gawan to be unhorsed in what follows, and in a most ironic manner.

17. Physicians made their own medicines and offered them for sale in jars. Orgeluse taunts Gawan: if he is a physician he cannot be a knight. If he is not a knight he cannot aspire to her love.

18. French for "misshapen creature."

19. Irony again.

20. By the river Ganges in India.

21. He was unhorsed by Orgeluse's knight.

22. Since he is in love with her—and he is in love with her because she is who she is—Gawan accepts that he will have to keep "losing" her, when she turns on him, and "finding" her, when she turns toward him.

23. Wolfram's own not altogether favorable description of Ovidian love. He proceeds to reiterate the contrast between Ovidian love and true love, and leaves no doubt as to where his own loyalties lie. His immediate master is Veldeke, in this respect, and then Veldeke's followers.

24. Torches, also associated with Cupid and love that goes on at night.

25. Gawan has obviously been smitten with love of the Ovidian variety, which explains why he puts up with Orgeluse. Later on their relationship changes and becomes rooted in true loyalty.

26. Orgeluse summons the ferryman who takes her across the river to the castle.

27. A hostage to combat. Orgeluse fully expects Gawan to be defeated by the knight who approaches, and who has defeated all other knights who have come to her.

28. Wolfram's ironic aside aimed at the traditional descriptions of combat, in which horses do nothing if not fly.

29. The money the ferryman will get as ransom for a knight will be much more than what he would get if he merely sold a horse.

30. The ferryman is portrayed more sympathetically than the fisherman Parzival encounters in book 3. The reason may be that he mainly indulges in the only form of

barter, or trade that knights were also allowed to indulge in, and which could turn out to be very profitable, as it now does, much to the ferryman's delighted surprise: the collection of ransom.

31. It will be remembered that "losing" and "finding" have both been desribed as being "parts" of Orgeluse.

32. As is also obvious from the beginning of the next book. The ferryman would be very pleased indeed if his daughter was either to marry Gawan, or become his mistress. Courtly love, it would appear, is not practiced all that much among the lower classes; in contrast Bene, the ferryman's daughter, turns out to be very loyal to Gawan, even though she is never given his love.

The ferryman's behavior would not have been condemned (much) by Wolfram's audience: if a man has daughters, the reasoning would have gone, he might as well invest them in a potentially profitable (ad)venture.

Book Eleven

1. Wolfram mentions the glass explicitly because it was still rare and expensive in his time.

2. Lower-class common sense in sharp contrast with courtly love. The ferryman obviously thinks of love mainly in terms of upward mobility.

3. This is of course the castle where all the ladies are sitting— all four hundred of them. Cundrie has alluded to it and to them before. Four hundred ladies in one castle smacks a little of overkill, and the *Schastel marveile* episode has, accordingly, often been interpreted as a parody of the "true" Arthurian tales.

4. The question is, of course, to what extent the ferryman's loyalty is dependent on a more mercenary motivation.

5. It is not insignificant that the ferryman feels he has to introduce the knight to the ways of merchants.

6. A corruption of "Muminim." It is indicative of the state of Wolfram's actual knowledge about Islam that the name of the people becomes the name of an imaginary king, or sultan.

7. The ladies' behavior appears strange at first sight: not one of them is on hand to welcome Gawan. It becomes clear later on that the ladies are all afraid of the power of Clinschor the magician who keeps them captive in the castle.

8. This is probably the book most obviously tributary to fairy tale material, which may also explain why it is the shortest book in the work as a whole. Since Wolfram has to follow Chrestien he has little choice. One gets the impression, though, that he tries to do what he has to do as expeditiously as possible.

9. He is addressing the bed.

10. It is obvious that Gawan has to contend with weapons not deemed fit for a knight.

11. Gawan seems to react with embarrassment, rather than fear: he may have to fight somebody who is his social inferior and who uses weapons no knight would fight with.

12. Paradoxically, the blood that is slippery in itself makes it easier for Gawan to find and keep his footing on the slippery floor of the hall.

13. Gawan drives the sword into the lion's chest, until his hand touches that chest: the sword has completely disappeared "into" the lion.

14. If the wounds do not take Gawan's life away from him, he shall live a happy life, since he has overcome the hardships of the Castle of Wonders. If he lives a happy life, the ladies shall be happy with him.

15. Messengers who brought good news were rewarded with food.

16. In Celtic fairy tale material roots often display magic powers and healing powers.

Book Twelve

1. The pangs of love seem to have a somewhat homeopathic effect on the physical pain Gawan feels after his combat.

2. Another reference to Ovidian love.

3. Another reference to some part of the Gawan adventure that has remained unknown to us.

4. As opposed to Gawan, who does not sing of love but is oppressed by it. This may be an ironic dart aimed at the—mainly lyrical—poets of courtly love. Many of them, Wolfram may have felt, did not really know what they were singing about: they simply repeated formulas and ran variations on stock themes.

5. Maybe Wolfram should be silent too, now. Not because he does not "know" about love but possibly because he has never achieved happiness in love, at least if we are to believe the pronouncements he makes when he speaks as his public persona.

6. Gawan.

7. The pillar appears to be an enormous crystal ball, as would befit a magician's castle. Later on we learn that the pillar must have originally belonged to Queen Secundille, wife to Feirefiz. It has definitely not been put together in Western Europe, but in the Orient. The belief in the technical superiority of the Orient was so widespread that the audience would have wholeheartedly concurred with Wolfram in assuming that the pillar was "imported" from the East.

8. Gawan will not dishonor himself by kissing people whose status is inferior to his, even though they are not immediately known to him.

9. If Gawan had not been so in love with Orgeluse, he might have been tempted by one of the ladies. To the medieval mind it probably would not have mattered much that one of the three ladies, Sangive, was the mother of the other two, since marriages among noble lineages were often arranged entirely for political reasons, with no consideration of age at all: old ladies married boys, and young girls married old men.

10. Another one of Wolfram's similes that may not wholly agree with the modern reader's sensibilities. It should be remembered, of course, that the discourse of love has changed considerably in the interval. It should also be remembered that Wolfram did not view courtly love with an altogether unjaundiced eye.

11. With the wealth he has earned with his spear. The knight in question may have

vanquished some, or a fair number of rich colleagues, and negotiated terms for their release that must have been very advantageous to him.

12. Gawan interprets the presence of a fully armored knight so near his castle as a challenge to his authority. It will be remembered that Parzival's unwitting presence close to Artus's encampment was immediately interpreted in the same way.

13. Orgeluse at her best/worst. She chases Gawan back to the castle and also belittles his wounds: he has to ride back to the ladies because they will fall over each other to set his broken or bruised finger—for that is what Gawan's wounds amount to in Orgeluse's eyes.

14. The knight, of course; no lady would have dreamed of taking care of the ferryman who, it is strongly hinted, is more than able to take care of his own financial well-being.

15. Gawan is referring to the grief that comes to him from the fact that Orgeluse has not given him her favor yet.
Paradoxically, in the world of love—true or courtly—this kind of playing on the pity/guilt of the beloved may well result in her granting her favors to the knight after all, which is why Gawan resorts to this tactic.

16. And therefore obviously an enchanted forest, another not altogether novel and unexpected topos related to the world of the fairy tale.

17. Wolfram suggests that Gawan should have pushed Orgeluse off her horse and raped her on the grass, the kind of behavior that is definitely not expected of a knight devoted to courtly love. Wolfram sees courtly love much more in terms of a—relatively pointless—game of cat and mouse in which the lady is at liberty to tease the knight, mercilessly and ad infinitum. He may be suggesting here that ladies might behave differently if knights called an abrupt end to the game in the manner hinted at above. It should be clear that courtly love has nothing whatsoever to do with Wolfram's ideal of true love. Yet Orgeluse is capable of both, when she finds the right knight.

18. This, too, would not have been out of the ordinary in the Middle Ages. Kings and princes often only saw the portrait of the woman they were about to marry before the actual wedding took place, and sometimes not even a portrait. Instead, they would marry sight unseen. Paradoxically, Ovidian love, the utter antithesis of marriages arranged for political reasons, also tells in favor of the possibility of two people falling deeply in love with each other without ever having seen each other.

19. It was the custom that he who lost the combat was under the obligation to reveal his identity. The victor was under no obligation to do so. Since there is neither victor nor vanquished in this situation, Gawan seizes the initiative. Gramovlanz obliges, but warns Gawan not to "reckon [that] as his shame." There is probably also an inside joke here between Wolfram and those of his listeners familiar with Chrestien's *Li contes del Graal:* they may have recognized the character before Wolfram names him.

20. This is the first time the word *loyal* is used in connection with Orgeluse. She is now ready for true love.

21. A heavily ironic understatement, especially the "once." The reader/listener will remember that Orgeluse has hardly ever spoken to Gawan without abusing him. But true love—as opposed to courtly love—forgives everything.

22. The unicorn is a nonexistent, mythical animal. Cidegast's loyalty must therefore literally have been "out of this world."

23. Wolfram "proves" that Orgeluse has been capable of true love before. Only when she is blinded by hatred and the desire for revenge does she play the game of courtly love. Wolfram "forgets" to mention that many ladies had no other choice in the Middle Ages: they had to manipulate men if they wanted to achieve their goals, and what better opportunity for manipulation than that offered by the rites of courtly love?

24. The unicorn.

25. In fact Gawan demands sex, on the spot, as the long-delayed "reward" for his long-suffering "service." Wolfram seems to reiterate that the high-flown discourse of courtly love does, in the end, always amount to just one thing.

26. To purchase its contents.

27. Again, Orgeluse is cynically playing the game of courtly "love."

28. Wales.

Book Thirteen

1. A host who was poor would not have been able to afford this kind of castle, let alone the carpets in it.

2. Should not be thought of as a chair, but rather a "place for sitting," "constructed" with cushions and "dismantled" afterwards.

3. It is a little strange that Gawan should not know Itonje who is, after all, his own sister, but not altogether unlikely: sons of noblemen were, as a rule, sent to castles of other noblemen to train for knighthood. They therefore grew up apart from their families. It is not illogical to assume that this happened to Gawan. If we also keep in mind that Itonje, her mother, and her sister have been held captive in the castle for a long time, Gawan's ignorance should strike us as less farfetched. It remains true, though, that he also does not recognize his own mother.

4. A probably unconscious *mise en abyme:* this is exactly the way young ladies did learn about love, whether they listened to those stories, or in the relatively unlikely event that they were able to read them for themselves. It should not be forgotten that many of the medieval epics doubled as how-to guides, at least to some extent. Hence the extensive descriptions of battle, clothes, banquets, and other relatively common occurrences of daily living.

5. Itonje may be said to view love on the same abstract level as Obilot did. They both have had little alternative, of course: their "love" is precisely the love they have heard of in the stories they have heard or read.

6. People have not forgotten Judas's kiss.

7. The stars act as squires or servants for their "lady": Night. They have to find lodging for her before the day fades altogether.

8. Once again, Wolfram skips a set piece: the description of a banquet. He does so with the flimsiest of excuses, and he probably does so because the end is in sight for him: this is the thirteenth book of *Parzival* as we know it, and therefore the last book of Chrestien's Wolfram has to follow. He will be free to spin his own tale entirely once this book is finished. He may well be chafing at the bit a little.

9. From the court of Wolfram's patron, the landgrave Hermann, which was then the center of literary and artistic pursuits. Wolfram uses gentle irony to emphasize the difference between Hermann's court and other courts—such as Gawan's—which are less advanced in the world of fashion.

10. Once again, the host's "night drink" signals the end of the festivities. The same custom is described at the end of Gahmuret's first visit to Belakane in book 1.

11. Again, the description of the beds will have to be skipped, for the same reasons the description of the banquet has been skipped above. These descriptions were definitely not without importance; they represented an eagerly anticipated part of the tale. Especially at a time when the German nobility wanted to imitate its French counterparts, these descriptions assumed a position more or less comparable to that of the "(Noble) *Ladies' Home Journal.*"

12. We might even be not altogether unjustified in mentally adding something like: "And these are my own."

13. A gentle and fairly obvious hint: Orgeluse need not be afraid of displaying all her talents.

14. Another sentence that drives translators to despair. The magicians mentioned are not mentioned again anywhere, ever.

15. Keie is jealous of Gawan because Gawan goes on so many adventures.

16. It should probably be located on Sicily. It should be remembered that Sicily was at the time a more or less unique amalgam of Arab, Norman, Italian, and German cultural and social influences. It must have seemed more than a little exotic to the "average German at home." That average German would therefore not have been surprised that magicians were connected with it in some way.

It is not inconceivable, moreover, that Sicily, which had fairly recently come under the domination of the Hohenstaufen dynasty, and which had come to them with a system of strong central authority and cultural tolerance bequeathed to them by its former Norman rulers, functioned in Wolfram's thinking as a model for the Holy Roman Empire of the German nation itself.

17. A medieval translation of the Roman poet Virgil. Since Virgil's Fourth Eclogue was interpreted by early Christian commentators as predicting the imminent birth of Christ—in fact it predicted the birth of a son to Augustus, but Livia, his wife, miscarried—Virgil was seen as a "proto-Christian" in the Middle Ages. In addition to this, Virgil's late "pagan" commentators had begun to point out the many instances of both useful information and wisdom contained in his writings. Hence his growing reputation as both a "wise man," and a "magician."

18. If noblewomen are not active in public life they may well fall prey to effete lovers in their castles, a not altogether uncommon occurrence in the Middle Ages, also because noble women hardly ever married for love. They would therefore look for love elsewhere. It is not impossible that the cult of courtly love developed among other things to help those caught in this type of situation sublimate it more or less successfully, which may also explain why the Church did not altogether disapprove of it, even though it technically represented more or less open invitations to adultery of the mind, if not of the body. It is probably because Wolfram did not believe that this distinction could be maintained that he could not bring himself to take courtly love very seriously.

19. Which is again somewhat puzzling to the modern reader, used to think more in terms of realpolitik: since Artus's and Oregluse's armies have the same enemy now, they are objectively allies. But Gawan's medieval mind does not function quite that way: here is an opportunity for knights to show off their skills in many a joust, and such opportunities should be taken wherever and whenever they present themselves.

20. The battle is obviously seen as a barter of blows.

21. Again, it strains the imagination somewhat that Artus does not recognize his own mother.

22. Irony: not only has Artus been "widowed" of part of his army; it is also extremely unlikely that he derived any "profit" at all from the battle.

23. The expression also denotes that the "looking" is done with martial intent.

24. This kind of combat does not take place in fields or meadows, but in bed rooms. The duchess is of course referring to Gawan as her "attacker."

25. Keie shows more of his jealousy by contrasting Gawan's behavior unfavorably with his father's.

26. An obvious didactic touch.

27. A diplomatic move: Gawan wants to ensure the continuing loyalty of his former rivals.

Book Fourteen

1. Which would make it technologically superior.

2. Knights were not supposed to fight against their own kin. It will be remembered that Gawan's combat against King Vergulath had been annulled for the same reason. Here Gawan is unwittingly attacking his kinsman Parzival. The combat of kin against kin is a breach of loyalty (as is the "adultery of the mind" propagated by courtly love) and therefore abhorred by Wolfram, who describes it here more or less "in jest," precisely to highlight its potentially disruptive consequences.

3. If it did not look as if a clear winner was about to emerge fairly soon, the combat was stopped by experienced knights acting as "umpires," much in the way Parzival's combat against Gramovlanz is stopped later in this book.

4. Itonje has indeed left Clinschor's castle where she was held for many years.

5. Technically Gramovlanz will indeed not be fighting Gawan to "snatch" Itonje from his "evil clutches" in any way. Yet his prowess in combat is sure to strengthen her love for him, as she looks on.

6. Bene is repeating what Itonje told her to tell Gramovlanz. Since this is Itonje's first attempt at an approximation of the abstract love she has grown up on to the real love that may soon be hers in flesh and blood, the message she sends is likely to be sound somewhat naive, or childlike to the more experienced Gramovlanz.

7. Parzival is so used to unhappiness that he treats it more or less as his coat of arms: the feature that identifies a knight to the outside world.

8. Gawan has lost his honor in this combat because he was about to be overcome by Parzival. He wants to find his honor again.

9. Crooked stupidity is imperfect because all things crooked are imperfect. If crooked stupidity becomes straight it becomes perfect. Perfect stupidity.

10. Parzival's heart does, of course. Gawan may be trying to shift the blame for his unsuccessful combat to fate, or away from himself, at any rate.

11. We would more readily say something like: "What have I done wrong?" (that revenge should be taken on me?).

12. Metaphorically, of course: by Cundrie at the Plimizoel.

13. Parzival appears to be afraid that the knights and ladies of Artus's household still believe Cundrie's aspersions.

14. Gawan points out that he is not old enough yet to allow others to fight his battles for him.

15. The posts that demarcate the lists where combat is to be done. King Gramovlanz had ordered them put up at his own expense, as he should have, since he is the challenger.

16. Normally Itonje's existence would bring pleasure to Parzival, in the sense that he would enjoy having her as a member of the family.

17. Itonje obviously still sees Orgeluse, the duchess, as the evil scheming force behind all this.

18. In the same way Parzival should be able to enjoy Itonje: both Parzival and Gawan would be happy if Itonje turned out to be a happy member of their family.

19. Itonje obviously does not plan to outlive Gramovflanz.

20. The princes and rulers of his realm, who have experience in these matters and can advise him, all the more so since they, collectively, represent the very code of chivalry.

21. Itonje, at last.

22. If I could learn the language of loving/longing looks I could tell you what they said.

23. This is said in jest, of course. Artus wants to talk to Brandelidelin in private.

24. Again, the modern reader may be mildly surprised at the ease with which noble ladies are disposed of. Much becomes understandable if we keep in mind that noble ladies tended to act as a drain on the resources of whoever was responsible for their keep. Fathers, brothers, and guardians were relatively easily persuaded to let the ladies entrusted to their care go to another man.

25. The disappointment that inevitably comes with courtly love: once the adored lady really makes a choice, she cannot help but disappoint all others who have entered her service.

26. Condwiramurs, his wife.

Book 15

1. If I am telling the story as a good artist should.

2. But Wolfram does not change the story, which is why his art is not spoiled.

This is all the more significant because Wolfram is no longer following Chrestien here.

3. They moved the combat from one venue to another.

4. Because both are the epitome of loyalty.

5. It is remarkable that the heathen observes more or less exactly the same code of chivalry as Parzival does. He behaves like a Christian, and could be one, if only he were baptized.

6. They are both Gahmuret's son, of course.

7. It was widely believed that diamonds had curative powers.

8. The power of her love is so great that it sustains Parzival in the hour of his need, even though he is far away.

9. After he had killed Ither in a manner not fit for a knight, in book 3.

10. The heathen knight has never been vanquished in combat before. He therefore has been able to "keep his honor" all this time.

11. Since Parzival has not lost in combat, he should not be the one to reveal his name, especially since he was not afraid of combat in the first place.

12. Parzival sees Feirefiz as a contender to his name and possessions. That is obviously not Feirefiz's intention, even though Parzival suspects him of having invaded Anschouwe, as is obvious from the next line.

13. Without his armor and other weapons, except for his sword.

14. Wolfram recognizes that Feirefiz is a potential Christian and prepares the audience for his eventual conversion.

15. Feirefiz is described first, because of the color of his skin.

16. An almost didactic aside: this, Wolfram seems to point out, is how the French hold their banquets. His listeners would do well to emulate them. His listeners were probably grateful for the information.

17. The didactic suggestion seems to be that it does not hurt to ask: the lady can always decide to say yes or no. It may also be that it would be nice to ask, since the behavior of various knights in *Parzival* also suggests that they take without asking.

18. They know the art of conversation, which was considered very important at the dinner table.

19. If the woman he loved did not reward Feirefiz, her servants would be entitled to hate her.

20. She has taught him the social graces a king should have.

21. This praise of Secundille in Feirefiz's mouth stands in shrill contrast to his behavior in the final book of *Parzival*. There he drops Secundille without batting an eyelid so that he can be baptized and marry Repanse de Schoye. Maybe they were perfectly matched within the confines of heathendom, but once Feirefiz has seen the light of baptism Secundille pales by comparison? A somewhat flimsy explanation. One gets the impression that Wolfram, too, does not really know how to handle this kind of situation, and that he therefore takes the easy way out: he has Secundille die.

22. Probably the most obvious instance of the distance with which Wolfram treats his material.

23. A contradiction. The knights seem to have observed the social hierarchy in their procession, but the ladies, who had no official place in it, were left to fend for themselves. Wolfram probably enjoys contrasting this "custom," painfully rooted in reality, with the more abstract customs of courtly love.

24. Jousts ridden by groups of knights.

25. Cundrie has come to retract the accusations she has hurled against Parzival in the past. She can only do so after Parzival himself has made his peace with God.

26. Which would give it a blue/violet color.

27. Even now Parzival is already peerless. How much more so later.

28. Since the heathen Flegetanis was the first to discover the grail among the stars, it seems fitting that Cundrie should list the planets here, and that she should do so in an attempt at Arabic.

29. Parzival acknowledges that God works in wondrous ways, but without any bitterness: he now simply accepts that fact.

30. Without giving them any presents. A king's generosity was one of the marks of his true greatness. Feirefiz does not want to be found wanting.

31. A slightly tongue-in-cheek rationalization of the main fairy tale motif in the poem.

Book Sixteen

1. Anfortas wants to be given death in a way that is fitting for a knight.

2. The helmet and the shield.

3. His past feats of armor do not benefit him now, nor, by extension, his people.

4. As we have been told, Parzival left Munsalvaesche the first time without asking Anfortas any question. Anfortas now says that not only he, Anfortas, suffered from this, but Parzival as well. He also points out that Parzival has suffered from this because he believes in the code of loyalty that is the foundation of knightly behavior. If he did not, he would not have suffered. In fact, a case might be made for the proposition that Parzival would then have behaved in the manner of the typical Arthurian knight, but not in the more exalted manner of one called to the grail.

5. It is rather remarkable that Anfortas should ask Parzival for death, while everybody in the castle knows that Parzival's question will bring him deliverance. Anfortas may well be doing this for heightened dramatic effect.

6. Wolfram refers to two miracles. The first reference is to the legend of Saint Silvester. The saint and a Jew fight over the faith before the emperor Constantine. The Jew whispers the name of his God in the ear of a bull. The bull promptly drops dead. Saint Silvester then whispers the name of his God into the ear of the bull and the bull comes back to life, gets up, and walks away. The second reference is to Jesus' raising of Lazarus from the dead. Lazarus's sisters had asked Jesus to come to their brother on his deathbed, to cure him. Jesus came too late to save Lazarus from death, but he raised him from the dead instead.

7. This sheds new light not only on the story Trevrizent told before, but also on his previous behavior. It is obvious that Trevrizent did not tell Parzival the whole truth. This may be construed as a "final test" Parzival has to pass before God will finally take pity on him. It should be remembered that it is God's privilege to act in ways beyond human understanding, and that His plans are not immediately obvious to man. Trevrizent's revised story also establishes that there is no middle way between good and evil: the so-called neutral angels who appeared in his first story turn out not to be neutral after all. Or rather, they may have tried to remain neutral, but God would not allow them to do so. God's creatures—angels or men—must choose between good and evil. Neutrality is out of the question.

8. Kyot, Wolfram's imaginary source, not to be confused with the duke of the same name.

9. Wolfram reassures the audience that he does not have any tricks up his sleeve this time. The audience now expects an ending that gives all characters their due and forestalls any questions any listener might still have.

10. Irony, of course.

11. Condwiramurs is too tired to be kissed, either by the characters in the poem, or by Wolfram himself, who is human enough, after all, to want to kiss—in book 16—the epitome of feminine perfection he has been mentioning at least once in most of the preceding books.

12. The evening of Parzival's first visit to Munsalvaesche, which ended in total disaster.

13. A kind of wood, much prized for the aromatic scent it produced.

14. A piece of precious cloth, usually emerald green in color.

15. A literal rendering of Wolfram's syntactic construction. Most of these have been silently "regularized" in this translation, in order to increase its readability. It should be obvious, though, that the sentence makes much less immediate sense as printed than when it is read aloud. Since Wolfram's was an essentially oral art, it is not unsafe to assume that this kind of syntactic construction, decried as "obscure" by critics ever since Gottfried von Strassburg, Wolfram's younger contemporary and colleague, did not confuse the audience nearly as much as critics who judge works composed for oral recitation by the standards of the written work are likely to assume.

16. The reference would have been immediately obvious to the contemporary audience, just as it is immediately lost on the modern reader. Wolfram then proceeds to elaborate on the "five kinds," no doubt to the delight of the knights in the audience, and probably also to remind that audience of the fact that he is also a knight, albeit one who knows how to compose epic poetry.

17. The "heathen" does, of course, show little loyalty to his "heathen" wife. He could count on the audience's sympathy in this, since the marriage of a Christian to a heathen, or of two heathens, was considered invalid under Church law anyway. If anything, Feirefiz would be congratulated on forsaking his heathen "paramour," no matter if his reasons for doing so could, at best, be said to be rather dubious. Love easily carries a lot more weight than religion, especially if it is able to use religion as an excuse.

18. The formula recurs a number of times in Wolfram, since it is a stock formula in medieval theology. Wolfram probably also makes use of it because it is a "safe"

formula. If he had tried to use a formulation of his own he might have been accused of heresy sooner or later by some overzealous priest or monk.

19. The redemption of man (Parzival, Anfortas) is again emphasized by means of one of the endless medieval variations on one of the most popular medieval theological paradoxes: the incarnation of Christ, the fact that omnipotent God who has created man and guided his destiny finally becomes man himself.

20. The real hierarchy in Feirefiz's thinking is probably the inverse. But then again, Repanse de Schoye can be seen as the (unwitting?) instrument by means of which God converts Feirefiz to the true faith. Wolfram takes great pains not to resolve the ambiguity. Like most of the women in *Parzival*, Repanse de Schoye is little more than "an instrument." The only independent women appear to be widows—as long as they do not marry again—like Arnive and Herzeloyde, hermits like Sigune, who withdraw from society altogether, and—preferably—beautiful women of independent means, like Orgeluse, but even she has to manipulate men to achieve what she wants to achieve. The depiction of women here corresponds rather well with the reality women had to cope with in Wolfram's time. It should also be remembered that the women mentioned are invariably "ladies," i.e. noble women. Other women are definitely not taken into account, except as occasional game for a "noble" man.

21. Again, the difference in age—Repanse de Schoye is literally old enough to be Feirefiz's mother—does not matter at all.

22. Because of Secundille's "providential" death. It is interesting to note that Wolfram seems to hint that female solidarity appears to be stronger than the teachings of religion. Alternatively, Repanse de Schoye's relief may be inspired mainly, or only by the fact that the death of Secundille means that there will be no legal complications once she assumes the throne of India as its queen: there is nobody left to challenge her.

23. An important, if shadowy figure in the worldview of the Christian West. Legend had it that there was a Christian kingdom somewhere "on the other side" of the Islamic world. Such a kingdom did indeed exist, in Ethiopia. Yet its real existence seems to have accounted for less than its mythical potential: here was an ally against the infidels and, moreover, one very strategically located. If only the Christian West could make contact with the legendary Prester John, Islam would find itself surrounded. Since Wolfram does not set great store by war against Islam, his Prester John is introduced mainly for genealogical and etiological reasons: Wolfram's audience knows now why there are Christians in India. Ethiopia is not mentioned since it is not linked in any way with any of the main characters in the story.

24. At the end of his work Wolfram masterfully pulls the different strands together. It turns out that the many and variegated adventures can all be traced back to one family, or dynasty, if you will, which has been kept together by the mutual loyalty of its individual members, and which has loyally accepted and carried out the mission given to it by God, even if some of its members, such as Parzival, did not always understand that mission too clearly, and even if some of its members, such as Anfortas, failed miserably. The real strength of the individual lies in the (extended) family; man's real strength lies in God. The concept that links members of a family together is the same concept that links man to God: loyalty, *triuwe*, the basis of emotional, social, and religious life.

25. A little encore, also because the audience often did want to know what "really" happened to the offspring of the heroes and heroines whose exploits it had witnessed.

26. The kingship of the grail would seem to far outweigh the position of duke of Brabant, even though Brabant was, in Wolfram's time, one of the most prosperous and powerful regions contained in the Holy Roman Empire of the German nation. Loherangrin probably also wants to reassure the nobles of Brabant that he is no mere bounty hunter.

27. Legend has it that Loherangrin was brought to Antwerp by a swan. He is fetched back by a swan also, but this time the swan has a small ship in tow, as may be more fitting for a man who has proved himself, after all.

28. A final dig at Hartmann von Aue. Erec, the hero of Hartmann's eponymous poem, forbids his wife to speak to him, threatening her with dire punishment if she does. She invariably does, and invariably to save his life. He never actually punishes her; he just keeps threatening her with more punishment. Wolfram's hero, on the other hand, is a man of his word, loyal to his calling, even if that loyalty causes him personal hardship.

29. A final attempt to establish Kyot as the "real" source of the work.

30. A statement richly laced with irony: because he invented Kyot, Wolfram was able to tell much more (books 1, 2, 14, 15, and 16) than Chrestien ever told. The use of the word *master* here is a very judicious one indeed: Wolfram is his own master, who changes the work of previous masters like Chrestien, and uses nonexistent masters, like Kyot, as a mask and a sop to a segment of the audience. Since he is his own master, Wolfram is entitled to keep the company of other masters.

31. Notice the "I" here: Master Wolfram speaks in his own voice at last.

32. A final allusion to the lady who may or may not have commissioned *Parzival*. She also may or may not have given Wolfram his "reward." We shall probably never know and, after all, it is none of our business.

THE GERMAN LIBRARY
in 100 Volumes

Wolfram von Eschenbach
Parzival
Edited by André Lefevere

Gottfried von Strassburg
Tristan and Isolde
Edited and Revised by Francis G. Gentry
Foreword by C. Stephen Jaeger

German Medieval Tales
Edited by Francis G. Gentry
Foreword by Thomas Berger

German Humanism and Reformation
Edited by Reinhard P. Becker
Foreword by Roland Bainton

Immanuel Kant
Philosophical Writings
Edited by Ernst Behler
Foreword by René Wellek

Friederich Schiller
Plays: Intrigue and Love and Don Carlos
Edited by Walter Hinderer
Foreword by Gordon Craig

Johann Wolfgang von Goethe
The Sufferings of Young Werther
and *Elective Affinities*
Edited by Victor Lange
Forewords by Thomas Mann

German Romantic Criticism
Edited by A. Leslie Willson
Foreword by Ernst Behler

Friedrich Hölderlin
Hyperion and Selected Poems
Edited by Eric L. Santner

Philosophy of German Idealism
Edited by Ernst Behler

G. W. F. Hegel
*Encyclopedia of the Philosophical Sciences in Outline and
Critical Writings*
Edited by Ernst Behler

Heinrich von Kleist
Plays
Edited by Walter Hinderer
Foreword by E. L. Doctorow

E. T. A. Hoffmann
Tales
Edited by Victor Lange

Georg Büchner
Complete Works and Letters
Edited by Walter Hinderer and Henry J. Schmidt

German Fairy Tales
Edited by Helmut Brackert and Volkmar Sander
Foreword by Bruno Bettelheim

German Literary Fairy Tales
Edited by Frank G. Ryder and Robert M. Browning
Introduction by Gordon Birrell
Foreword by John Gardner

F. Grillparzer, J. H. Nestroy, F. Hebbel
Nineteenth Century German Plays
Edited by Egon Schwarz in collaboration with
Hannelore M. Spence

Heinrich Heine
Poetry and Prose
Edited by Jost Hermand and Robert C. Holub
Foreword by Alfred Kazin

Heinrich Heine
The Romantic School and other Essays
Edited by Jost Hermand and Robert C. Holub

Heinrich von Kleist and Jean Paul
German Romantic Novellas
Edited by Frank G. Ryder and Robert M. Browning
Foreword by John Simon

German Romantic Stories
Edited by Frank Ryder
Introduction by Gordon Birrell

German Poetry from 1750 to 1900
Edited by Robert M. Browning
Foreword by Michael Hamburger

Karl Marx, Friedrich Engels, August Bebel, and Others
German Essays on Socialism in the Nineteenth Century
Edited by Frank Mecklenburg and Manfred Stassen

Gottfried Keller
Stories
Edited by Frank G. Ryder
Foreword by Max Frisch

Wilhelm Raabe
Novels
Edited by Volkmar Sander
Foreword by Joel Agee

Theodor Fontane
Short Novels and Other Writings
Edited by Peter Demetz
Foreword by Peter Gay

Theodor Fontane
Delusions, Confusions and The Poggenpuhl Family
Edited by Peter Demetz
Foreword by J. P. Stern
Introduction by William L. Zwiebel

Wilhelm Busch and Others
German Satirical Writings
Edited by Dieter P. Lotze and Volkmar Sander
Foreword by John Simon

Writings of German Composers
Edited by Jost Hermand and James Steakley

German Lieder
Edited by Philip Lieson Miller
Foreword by Hermann Hesse

Arthur Schnitzler
Plays and Stories
Edited by Egon Schwarz
Foreword by Stanley Elkin

Rainer Maria Rilke
Prose and Poetry
Edited by Egon Schwarz
Foreword by Howard Nemerov

Robert Musil
Selected Writings
Edited by Burton Pike
Foreword by Joel Agee

Essays on German Theater
Edited by Margaret Herzfeld-Sander
Foreword by Martin Esslin

German Novellas of Realism I and II
Edited by Jeffrey L. Sammons

Friedrich Dürrenmatt
Plays and Essays
Edited by Volkmar Sander
Foreword by Martin Esslin

Max Frisch
Novels, Plays, Essays
Edited by Rolf Kieser
Foreword by Peter Demetz

Gottfried Benn
Prose, Essays, Poems
Edited by Volkmar Sander
Foreword by E. B. Ashton
Introduction by Reinhard Paul Becker

German Essays on Art History
Edited by Gert Schiff

German Radio Plays
Edited by Everett Frost and Margaret Herzfeld-Sander

Hans Magnus Enzensberger
Critical Essays
Edited by Reinhold Grimm and Bruce Armstrong
Foreword by John Simon

All volumes available in hardcover and paperback editions at your bookstore or from the publisher. For more information on The German Library write to: The Continuum Publishing Company, 370 Lexington Avenue, New York, NY 10017.